INSPIRE / PLAN / DISCOVER / EXPERIENCE

PROVENCE
AND THE CÔTE D'AZUR

PROVENCE
AND THE CÔTE D'AZUR

CONTENTS

DISCOVER 6

EXPERIENCE 58

NEED TO KNOW 204

Left: Weathered painted shopfront in Marseille
Previous page: Sunset over Gordes
Front cover: The verdant Parc Naturel Régional des
Préalpes d'Azur, Alpes Maritimes

DISCOVER

Pont St-Bénézet over the Rhône, Avignon

WELCOME TO PROVENCE

Fragrant fields of lavender and relics of ancient realms. Restaurants that rank among the world's finest and glamorous Riviera nightspots. Lush vineyards, snow-capped peaks and sun-soaked beaches: this region has it all. Whatever your dream trip to Provence entails, this DK Eyewitness travel guide is the perfect companion.

1 Les Arènes, Nîmes.

2 Basket filled with freshly picked Provençal lavender.

3 Yacht docked in the harbour at Monte Carlo.

4 Sunflower field in Vaucluse at sunset.

Provence might just be France's most alluring region. Its cities have something to seduce every visitor, from the vibrant streetlife of Marseille and Nice to the sun, sand and bling of Riviera resorts such as St-Tropez and Cannes. Roman amphitheatres, papal palaces and medieval abbeys hark back to the power and glory of vanished empires, and fabulous galleries celebrate the work of some of the greatest artists of modern times.

Stretching from the sunny shores of the Mediterranean to the snow-capped peaks of the French Alps, Provence's amazing diversity of terrain and terroir make it a paradise for foodies. Vineyards produce luscious reds and extraordinary bone-dry rosés. From mountain pastures and fishing harbours come culinary treasures like truffles, saffron and a cornucopia of seafood. Lovers of the great outdoors are spoiled for choice, too: hikers can watch the sun rise from the summit of Mont Ventoux, kayakers can tackle the rapids of the Gorges du Verdon, and wildlife watchers can spot flamingos on the lagoons of the Camargue.

With so many different things to discover, Provence can seem overwhelming. We've broken the region down into easily navigable chapters, with detailed itineraries, expert local knowledge and colourful, comprehensive maps to help you plan the perfect visit. Whether you're staying for a weekend, a week, or longer, this DK Eyewitness travel guide will ensure that you see the very best the region has to offer. Enjoy the book, and enjoy Provence.

REASONS TO LOVE
PROVENCE

Magnificent Roman architecture, picturesque vineyards, excellent cuisine and fine modern art: there are so many reasons to love Provence and the Côte d'Azur. Here, we pick some of our favourites.

1 PALAIS DES PAPES

Within the white limestone walls of Avignon's Palais des Papes, echoing vaulted chambers and serene courtyards evoke the power and the glory of a succession of pious yet cunning medieval pontiffs (p158).

SUN, SEA AND SAND 2

Whether you are looking to be pampered at a private beach club or splash around with the kids, Provence's beaches have something for everyone (p32).

3 DIVINE WINES

From the Châteauneuf-du-Pape vineyards in the Rhône valley, the hinterland of Côtes de Provence and the sandy coasts of Camargue come complex red wines, flinty rosés and luscious vins doux (p40).

4 CELEBRITY SPOTTING

Ever since the 1950s, the beaches of St-Tropez, Antibes, Juan-les-Pins and Monaco have been bywords for celebrity glamour. If you're hoping to photograph the stars, Cannes is the place to be when the world's greatest film festival is in full swing (p70).

ABBAYE DE SÉNANQUE 5

Vast sunflower prairies and purple lavender fields surround the serene Abbaye de Sénanque (p170), where blossoms create a bee-buzzing haze of colour, scent and sound around the cool medieval cloisters.

ROMAN ARENAS 6

At Roman arenas like those at Arles (p134) and Orange (p168) it's easy to imagine audiences roaring as gladiators battled to the death. These days, events range from concerts to operas.

WILD WETLANDS 7
Flocks of flamingos, storks and other waterfowl patrol the shallow lagoons and reedbeds of the Camargue delta, where sturdy half-wild white horses and black cattle roam *(p138)*.

RIVER CRUISING 8
The mighty river Rhône has shaped Provence's culture for millennia. Cruising down its waters while sampling fine cuisine is an experience to remember forever *(p23)*.

9 LIVE MUSIC
Nice hosted the world's first great international jazz festival in 1948 and the tradition continues with a year-round calendar of events held at stunning venues, from medieval chapels to Roman theatres *(p48)*.

10 PARC NATIONAL DU MERCANTOUR

Raptors soar above alpine peaks in the Parc National du Mercantour *(p80)*, where adventurous visitors can ride whitewater rapids and abseil down rugged limestone crags.

FINE SEAFOOD 11

Colourful fishing boats still pootle out to sea from Provence's pretty village harbours, returning with squid, anchovies, grouper and many other fruits of the sea for you to savour at the best quayside restaurants *(p38)*.

GREAT ARTISTS 12

The landscapes and colours of Provence inspired artists like Picasso, Matisse and Cézanne, and turned harbours like Cassis and St-Tropez into havens for creative adventurers *(p36)*.

EXPLORE
PROVENCE

This guide divides Provence into five colour-coded sightseeing areas, as shown on the map below. Find out more about each area on the following pages.

FRANCE

Lalley

Aspremont

Valréas

Verclause

Pont St-Esprit   Bollène

Vaison-la-Romaine

Bagnols-sur-Cèze   Orange

Sault-de-Vaucluse

Uzès   Carpentras

VAUCLUSE
p154

Lurs

Forcalquier

Avignon

Nîmes   Cavaillon   Apt

BOUCHES-DU-RHÔNE AND NÎMES
p124

Parc National Régional du Luberon

Arles   Pertuis

Salon-de-Provence

Parc Naturel Régional de Camargue   Miramas   Coudoux   Venelles

Aix-en-Provence   St Maximin

Saintes-Maries-de-la-Mer   Martigues   Marignane   Auriol

La Couronne   Marseille

Aubagne

Bandol

Mediterranean Sea

0 kilometres   25
0 miles   25

N

GETTING TO KNOW
PROVENCE

When you think of Provence, sun-kissed Riviera beaches and splendid medieval palaces and abbeys may come to mind. But the most varied of France's regions offers much more, from bustling big-city streets and galleries dedicated to great modern artists to the wide-open wetlands of the Camargue and the gorges and peaks of the Alpine hinterland.

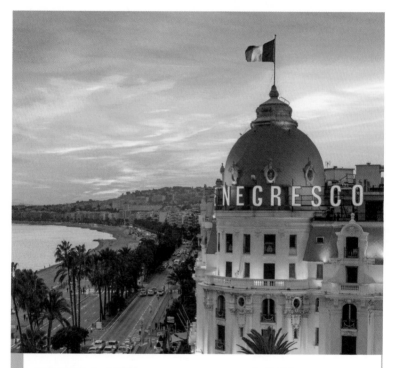

PAGE 60

RIVIERA AND ALPES-MARITIMES

Superyachts in upmarket marinas testify that this is still the world's most glamorous coastline, and the favoured retreat of plutocrats and movie stars. Finding space on the beaches of Cannes, Antibes or Juan-les-Pins in summer can be a challenge. Escape a short distance inland and you'll find breathtakingly pretty villages perched above steep gorges. Plunge deeper into the hinterland and you can explore canyons with soaring eagles and year-round alpine resorts.

Best for
Celebrity-spotting, sunbathing, hiking, skiing

Home to
Nice, Cannes, Monaco

Experience
Hiking through the Vallée des Merveilles in the Parc National du Mercantour

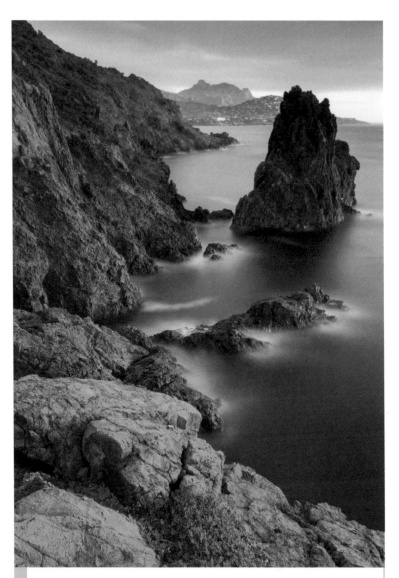

VAR AND ÎLES D'HYÈRES

The Var encapsulates all that Provence has to offer in one handy package. Midway along a rugged coastline interspersed with sandy beaches, St-Tropez is the ultimate resort, with smart cafés around its bustling old harbour. Offshore, the Îles d'Hyères offer underwater adventure. Toulon, further west, is Var's big port city, with a lively artists' quarter. Just inland are the thickly wooded slopes of the Massif des Maures, while grand abbeys and vineyards nestle in the foothills of the Haut-Var.

Best for
Market shopping, swimming and snorkelling, wine-tasting

Home to
St-Tropez, Îles d'Hyères, Toulon

Experience
Diving and snorkelling around the island of Port Cros

→

PAGE 124

BOUCHES-DU-RHÔNE AND NÎMES

The Bouches-du-Rhône is full of contrasts. Flamingos wade and black cattle roam in the wild Camargue wetlands not far from the throbbing streets of Marseille, France's biggest seaport. Reminders of the heyday of the Roman Empire can be seen in Nîmes and at the Pont du Gard nearby. The towns of Arles, Aix-en-Provence, Tarascon and St-Rémy-de-Provence, and the serene Silvacane and Montmajour abbeys, have a rich medieval heritage.

Best for
Sightseeing, beachcombing, city life

Home to
Nîmes, Aix-en-Provence, Marseille, Arles, Camargue

Experience
Seeing flamingos, half-wild white horses and black cattle on a four-wheel tour of the Camargue wetland

PAGE 154

VAUCLUSE

The lonely summit of Mont Ventoux, inspiration for painters and poets for centuries, looms over the Vaucluse as a challenge to cyclists and hikers. Scattered below its slopes and along the Rhône and Durance rivers are Roman and medieval relics, such as Orange's Théâtre Antique and the Palais des Papes in Avignon. The hilltop ruins of Châteauneuf-du-Pape castle overlook vineyards, while the Abbaye de Sénanque is surrounded by swathes of purple lavender. There are pretty walks in the Dentelles mountains or through orange and crimson canyons in the Luberon.

Best for
Roman and medieval heritage, wine-tasting, shopping for antiques

Home to
Avignon, Villeneuve-lès-Avignon, Théâtre Antique d'Orange, Mont Ventoux

Experience
Sampling fine food and wine on a Rhône river cruise

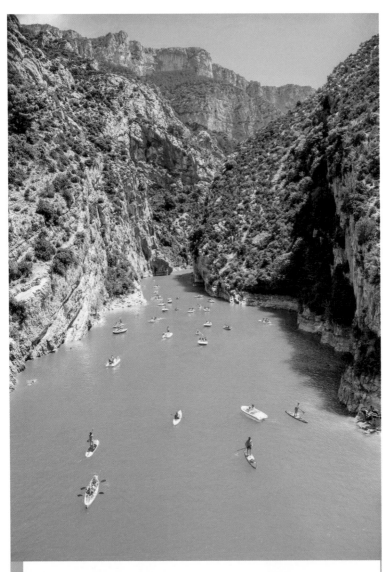

ALPES-DE HAUTE-PROVENCE

The most peaceful part of Provence is a region of rugged alpine foothills where the upper Durance and the Verdon rivers have carved dramatic deep canyons beneath limestone cliffs, forming an area of exceptional natural beauty. The gentler lowlands around the town of Valensole make up France's biggest lavender-growing area. Mighty fortresses built to guard Provence's eastern frontier loom over strategic mountain passes, and the air is said to be the clearest in all of France.

Best for
Getting away from it all, dramatic scenery, whitewater sports

Home to
Gorges du Verdon

Experience
A day trip on the Train des Pignes from Entrevaux to Digne-les-Bains

←

1 La Maison Carrée.

2 The covered market Les Halles bustling with visitors.

3 Jardins de la Fontaine.

4 Raising a glass of rosé at Le Cheval Blanc.

Provence is a treasure trove of things to see and do, and its relatively small size means that you can navigate the region easily. These itineraries will inspire you to make the most of your visit.

1 DAY

In Nîmes

Morning

Start the day with a self-guided tour of Les Arènes *(p128)*. Built almost 2,000 years ago, the well-preserved tiers of seats within this ring of arched walls are still used for concerts and other spectacles. Afterwards, stroll up boulevard Victor Hugo to place de la Maison Carrée to discover the Maison Carrée *(p129)*, said to be the world's best-preserved Roman temple, and watch a fascinating multimedia presentation, *Nemausus: the birth of Nîmes*, which focuses on the story of the Roman Empire in Provence. Pause for a coffee on place de la Maison Carrée, then cross the square to the gleaming Carré d'Art *(p129)* to glimpse challenging 20th- and 21st-century works of art. .

Afternoon

For lunch, head for Nîmes's covered market, Les Halles, where Aux Plaisirs des Halles *(4 rue Littré)* offers a fusion menu that combines nouvelle cuisine with traditional favourites like brandade. Then walk through the serenely beautiful Jardins de la Fontaine *(p129)*. The main highlight of this tranquil space is the ruined 2nd-century Temple of Diana. Its white marble columns stand among lawns, greenery and pools and splashing fountains fed by underground springs. The temple was built on a site that was likely a place of worship for Celtic people long before the Roman conquest.

Finish the afternoon by making your way up wooded slopes to the summit of Mont Cavalier. At 114 m (374 ft) high, it's less a mountain, more a low hill, and not a particularly challenging ascent. At the top, the 32-m (105-ft) Tour Magne, the most impressive of a ring of Roman towers that once guarded Nîmes, adds enough altitude for a spectacular sunset view. On the way back, pause for a photograph at the Castellum, an impressive vestige of an ancient world. Despite its name, this tower built into the Roman ramparts was not a castle; it was the reservoir for water which flowed to Roman Nîmes over the Pont du Gard aqueduct *(p145)*.

Evening

Dine at Le Cheval Blanc *(1 place des Arènes)*, where the menu features traditional cuisine and an excellent selection of wines. After dinner, join Nîmois locals at the lively Bar 421 *(37 rue Fresque)* to round off your day in Nîmes with a nightcap and some live music.

←

 Palais des Papes, Avignon.

2 River cruise on the Rhône.

3 Painting in the Musée du Petit Palais.

4 Meal at Restaurant Sevin.

2 DAYS

In Avignon and Villeneuve-lès-Avignon

Day 1

Morning Grab coffee and croissants at one of the cafés on the place du Palais, then head to the Palais des Papes *(p158)* as soon as it opens to avoid the crowds. Take a self-guided audio tour of the serene halls and courtyards, then stroll to the end of the famously curtailed Pont St-Bénézet *(p160)* for a mid-river photo opportunity. Next, walk through the historic centre to the bustling Les Halles *(p159)*. Sip a pre-prandial glass of rosé on place Pie, then take your pick of amazingly fresh seafood at La Cabane d'Oléron *(p160)*, tucked away in a corner of the market hall.

Afternoon Admire masterpieces of early medieval art in the Musée du Petit Palais *(p159)*, then visit the grandiose Cathédrale Notre-Dame des Doms *(p160)* before walking through the flower-filled hillside gardens of the Rocher des Doms *(p163)* for a sunset view of Avignon and the mighty river.

Evening Take a dinner cruise on the Rhône to enjoy the sight of the floodlit palace and bridge while savouring traditional dishes and vintages from Châteauneuf-du-Pape *(www.bateaux deprovence.fr)*.

Day 2

Morning Rent a Vélopop' bike *(p211)* to ride across Pont Daladier to Villeneuve-lès-Avignon *(p164)*. After no more than 20 minutes of pedalling, your first stop is the Tour Philippe-le-Bel *(p165)*, a formidable landmark that once marked the boundary between the French realm and the Papal territory of Avignon. Climb the 176 steps to the viewing terrace at the top of the tower for an unbeatable panorama. Next, ride through Villeneuve to walk through the lavender-fragrant gardens of the Abbaye de St-André, within the impressive medieval ramparts of Fort St-André *(p164)*.

Afternoon Take a leisurely lunch break in the sunny courtyard at Les Jardins d'Été. Afterwards, visit the Chartreuse du Val de Bénédiction *(p164)*. The cool, echoing cloisters and gardens, shaded and scented by cypress trees, are a pleasant place to linger on a hot afternoon before cycling back to Avignon.

Evening Back in town, treat yourselves to dinner at the highly regarded Restaurant Sevin *(p160)*. Located in a 12th-century villa overlooking the Palais des Papes, this restaurant serves exquisite tasting menus.

2 WEEKS

A Grand Tour of Provence

▐ *Day 1*

Arrive on an early flight to Nice and pick up a hire car to make the two-and-a-half-hour drive to Avignon. On your way, stop at the famous Châteauneuf-du-Pape vineyards to stretch your legs with a walk to the ruined papal château, which offers great views of the surrounding countryside.

Make a second stop at Villeneuve-lès-Avignon *(p164)*, grabbing an alfresco lunch at one of the lively cafés on place Jean-Jaurès. Wander through the Chartreuse du Val de Bénédiction, a vast Carthusian monastery, before taking a short walk to the Tour Philippe-le-Bel. Ascend this majestic medieval tower before crossing the Rhône to your final stop in Avignon.

Treat yourself to a refined meal at Restaurant Sevin *(p160)*, located inside a medieval house.

▐ *Day 2*

Explore Avignon – follow the first day of the Avignon itinerary *(p23)*.

▐ *Day 3*

It's a short 40-km (25-mile) morning drive to Arles from Avignon, so stop off en route in Tarascon *(p146)* for coffee and a peek at the gleaming white ramparts of King René's 15th-century Château Royal de Tarascon *(p146)*. Once in Arles, your first stop must be Les Arènes *(p134)*, the 20,000-seat Roman theatre that is still used for concerts and other spectacles. Then go back to the future at the Luma cultural centre *(p136)*, an amazing slice of futuristic 21st-century architecture.

In the afternoon, take a guided tour of the Cryptoportiques *(p134)*, an underground labyrinth carved 20 m (60 ft) beneath the limestone bedrock some 2,000 years ago. Afterwards, wander through Les Alyscamps *(p137)*, a vast necropolis that Romans believed was haunted.

To see Arles after dark as Vincent van Gogh saw it, visit the place du Forum and the Restaurant-Café Van Gogh *(p137)*, still painted just as it was when it inspired his *Café Terrace at Night* (1888).

5

⑴ The scenic Rhône river valley.

⑵ Tour Philippe-le-Bel, Villeneuve-lès-Avignon.

⑶ Camargue flamingos.

⑷ Café in Aix-en-Provence.

⑸ Ombrière, Marseille.

Day 4

Set off early to drive down the Rhône on the D35, passing through the seemingly endless reedbeds, lagoons and rice fields of the Camargue fringes. Make time to stop and see stunning flocks of flamingos and other fowl at Étang du Fangassier *(p140)*.

Stop in Aix-en-Provence *(p130)* for lunch. Stroll through the historic centre, with its elegant 17th- and 18th-century townhouses, to visit L'Atelier de Cézanne *(p131)*, preserved exactly as it was when artist Paul Cézanne *(p36)* died in 1906. Enjoy the view of Montagne Ste-Victoire, the imposing summit on the northern horizon that was one of Cézanne's favourite subjects. Afterwards, carry on to Marseille, a 40-km (25-mile) drive that should take no more than 45 minutes on the A51/A55 autoroute, the fastest way through Marseille's vast urban sprawl.

Aim to arrive in Marseille *(p132)* before sunset, then stroll along La Canebière to pick a café where you can sip a glass of pastis, the city's signature apéritif, before dinner.

Day 5

Begin at the Museé des Civilisations de l'Europe et de la Méditerranée *(p132)* to discover works of art from all the shores of the Mediterranean, then head for the Vieux Port for lunch beside Norman Foster's dazzling mirrored steel canopy, the Ombrière.

Hop on a boat to Château d'If for a fun voyage across the bay to an island prison replete with legends and true histories.

For dinner, sample bouillabaisse, richly flavoured with saffron and garlic, Marseille's ultimate signature dish, at the excellent L'Épuisette *(p38)*.

Day 6

Drive along Les Calanques *(p153)* to Cassis *(p152)*, where you can stop for a morning coffee. Arrive in Toulon for lunch at harbourside Le St Gabriel *(p110)*.

Stroll through the rejuvenated rue des Arts quarter *(p110)*, then hop on the cable car to the summit of Mont Faron *(p111)*.

Dine on old-school favourites like *magret de canard* (duck breast) at Le Bistrot du Boucan *(p110)*.

→

Day 7

Catch a morning ferry to the island of Porquerolles *(p112)* to discover a labyrinthine world of contemporary art at Fondation Carmagnac.

Hire a bike in the afternoon to explore the island's hinterland of pine-scented woods and dunes, and take a dip in the sea before catching the return ferry.

Back on the mainland, Le Lavandou *(p120)*, with its lively club and bar scene, is a great place to unwind in the evening.

Day 8

Begin your day by driving round the picturesque D559 coast road towards St-Tropez, a 40-km (25-mile) drive which takes around an hour. Divert through Ramatuelle *(p121)* to the bay of Pampelonne, then tear yourself away from the beach to arrive in St-Tropez for lunch on the place des Lices *(p103)*.

Walk to the Musée de l'Annonciade *(p102)* to admire works by Signac and other 20th-century greats, then ascend to the ramparts of the Citadelle de St-Tropez *(p103)* to admire the spectacular view.

Glam up for a night at one of St-Tropez's legendary nightspots, such as Les Caves du Roy or the Bar du Port *(p102)*.

Day 9

Follow the coast road that loops round the shore of the Gulf of St-Tropez then head east to Fréjus, a journey of 38 km (23 miles) that takes around an hour. Wander through the old town's quiet streets and visit the Arènes de Fréjus.

In the afternoon, relax in the sun at Fréjus Plage, just outside the old town, where you'll find plenty of café-bars with loungers and parasols on the beach.

Take a sunset stroll round the marina before dinner at a waterside restaurant such as L'Amandier *(19 rue Desaugiers; www.restaurant-lamandier-frejus.com)*.

Day 10

Rise early to drive to Cannes *(p70)* through the wooded slopes of the Massif de l'Estérel, along a road that follows the line of the ancient Roman Aurelian Way. The journey takes around 90 minutes.

1 Sailboat at Porquerolles.
2 Musée de l'Annonciade.
3 Street food in St-Tropez.
4 Nice's Cathédrale Ste-Réparate.
5 Port Grimaud.
6 Casino de Monte Carlo.

Explore Les Allées de la Liberté for the colourful flower market (p70), then treat yourself to a luxurious lunch on a lounger at a private beach club on La Croisette, such as the Grand Hotel's Hyde Beach (p71).

Finish the day with a nightcap at the Carlton Beach Club (p71).

Day 11

Take the 50-minute A8 autoroute from Cannes, bypassing Antibes, to Nice (p64) and stroll through Nice's Italianate Old Town on arrival. Don't miss the Cathédrale Ste-Réparate with its art-filled chapel.

Stroll along the promenade des Anglais and consider lunch and a swim at a casual beach club along the sea front.

Make your way to the summit of the Colline du Château for the best sunset view over the Baie des Anges.

Day 12

Start your second day in Nice by exploring the grand Baroque Palais Lascaris (p69), with its collection of antique musical instruments.

Head for the Cimiez district to discover works by two great artists who lived and worked in Nice at the Musée Matisse (p66) and Musée National Marc Chagall (p64).

Enjoy dinner on the cours Saleya, then spoil yourselves with a nightcap in the bar of the iconic Negresco hotel (p65).

Day 13

Carry on from Nice to Monaco (p72) along the A8 autoroute. Visit the Palais Princier, and watch for the ceremonious changing of the royal guard at 11:55am.

Lunch at a seaside restaurant such as Quai des Artistes (p74), then explore the Jardin Exotique's desert plants.

Dine at Café de Paris (p74), before spending the evening at the belle époque Casino de Monte Carlo (p73).

Day 14

Drive back to Nice along the impressive coast road that runs through Èze (p93), stopping for lunch and one last swim in the sea at Villefranche-sur-Mer (p92) before heading back to Nice airport.

Moustiers-Ste-Marie

Perched on the edge of a deep ravine overlooking the azure expanse of the Lac de Sainte-Croix, the pretty village of Moustiers-Ste-Marie *(p202)* is famous for its distinctive tin-glazed ceramics. Fine examples can be seen in the Musée de la Faïence, and many shops sell perfect reproductions of delicately coloured 17th- and 18th-century works.

 ←

Scenic view over the rooftops of Moustiers-Ste-Marie, a village famous for its ceramics

PROVENCE'S
PICTURESQUE VILLAGES

Each of Provence's glorious villages has its own character and unique history. Settings are distinctive, too, from the rugged crags that turned hilltop villages into strongholds in turbulent times to the fjord-like inlets of Les Calanques.

Les Baux-de-Provence

Located on the fringes of the Camargue and crowned by a ruined 10th-century citadel atop a limestone spur, Les Baux-de-Provence *(p148)* is the most spectacular fortress site in the region, with red-roofed stone houses that descend in tiers beneath the hilltop castle. From its battlements, the Seigneurs de Baux could be lords of all they surveyed, from the rugged Alpilles to the reedy flatlands of the Camargue.

↓ The citadel at Les Baux-de-Provence

St-Paul-de-Vence

It's easy to see why great artists like Picasso and Matisse fell in love with St-Paul-de-Vence *(p76)*. Ringed by ramparts that gaze out over the foothills of the Alpes-Maritimes and the Mediterranean coast, this former farming community is an artistic hotbed, and its narrow streets are lined with upmarket galleries and ateliers.

Galleries lining one of the narrow medieval streets in arty St-Paul-de-Vence

Bormes-les-Mimosas

Clusters of yellow blossom make Bormes-les-Mimosas *(p120)* dazzlingly colourful in spring. There are splendid panoramic views from the village's medieval château, below which steep alleyways and centuries-old stone houses appear to tumble down the hillside. Almost 100 different species of mimosas can be found here.

←
Blossom-framed view from the castle at Bormes-les-Mimosas

Cassis

With its clear light, vivid blue water and steep limestone cliffs, this delightful fishing port *(p152)* attracted painters such as Dufy, Derain, Matisse and Peploe, as well as amateurs such as Winston Churchill (who taught himself to paint here). The unspoiled rocky coves of Les Calanques *(p153)* are within walking distance, and beaches include the sweeping sandy crescent of Plage de la Grande Mer. The local delicacy is sea urchins, harvested from the rocky shallows around Cassis, and best served with a glass of the village's famous full-bodied white wine.

The pretty port of Cassis, overlooked by a 9th-century château

Mont Ventoux

Known as the "Giant of Provence", this lonely 1,912-m (6,242-ft) peak dominates the Provençal countryside for miles around (p174). In winter it is often snow-capped, while on a clear summer's day the treeless limestone summit remains a dazzling white against the deep blue sky.

→

Hikers taking in the view at the summit of Mont Ventoux.

PROVENCE'S
NATURAL WONDERS

Beyond Provence's sun-kissed Mediterranean shores, a dazzling array of landscapes wait to be discovered. Rugged summits loom above limestone canyons, fast-flowing rivers carve their way to the sea, and the Rhône delta creates a watery world unlike any other part of France.

Gorges du Verdon

France's answer to the Grand Canyon cuts a swathe through limestone cliffs that in some places are up to 700 m (2,300 ft) deep, making it a favourite destination for climbers. The thunderous rapids of the Verdon, which flow for some 25 km (16 miles) through the gorge, are also a big draw for watersports enthusiasts (p192).

→

Panoramic view over the vast Gorges du Verdon

Camargue Lagoons

A unique expanse of wetlands between the channels of the Petit Rhône to the west and the Grand Rhône to the east, the Camargue *(p138)* is home to a dazzling array of wildlife. Flocks of greater flamingos, European beavers, wild boars and migrating and resident birds roam its numerous marshes and reed-beds, while modern-day cowboys (called *gardians*) herd its distinctive half-wild white horses and bulls.

Horses and flamingos in the the Camargue

Îles d'Hyères

Underwater exploration is the big attraction at Port-Cros, one of three tiny but adventure-packed isles just off the Var coast, where rich marine life throngs the rocky seabed of France's first marine national park. On land, the natural forested habitat of Port-Cros and its neighbour Porquerolles is also protected as a national park *(p112)*.

← Tranquil sea view from one of the beaches on Port-Cros

↑ The snow-capped peaks of the Parc National du Mercantour

Parc National du Mercantour

Vultures and eagles soar above the bare summits and wooded lower slopes of the Parc National du Mercantour *(p80)*, where chamois, ibex and mouflon roam. Some peaks rise to heights of more than 2,000 m (6,500 ft). Beech, maple and sweet chestnut trees cloak the lower valleys, and tall conifers grow at higher altitudes.

Les Calanques, Bouches-du-Rhône

Nestled between Marseille and Cassis, Les Calanques *(p153)* are narrow inlets of turquoise water sheltered by chalk-white cliffs. Often only accessible via boat or on foot, these bijou bays are nonetheless highly popular in Provence. The craggy cliffs are also favoured with climbers, who can often be seen clambering up the rocks.

$\leftarrow$

Visitors relax on the picturesque Calanque d'en Vau, near Cassis

PROVENCE FOR
BEACH LOVERS

Those who like the feeling of sand between their toes are spoiled for choice in Provence. You'll pay a hefty premium to be pampered in the private beach clubs around Cannes, St-Tropez or Antibes, but you don't have to look far to find stunning coves and bays where there's no entry charge.

Îles d'Hyères, Var

Island beaches always feel special, and those on the Îles d'Hyères *(p112)* are no exception. With its pure white sand and azure sea, Plage Notre-Dame on Porquerolles would not look out of place on Caribbean shores.

$\rightarrow$

Steps leading to Plage Notre-Dame on the island of Porquerolles

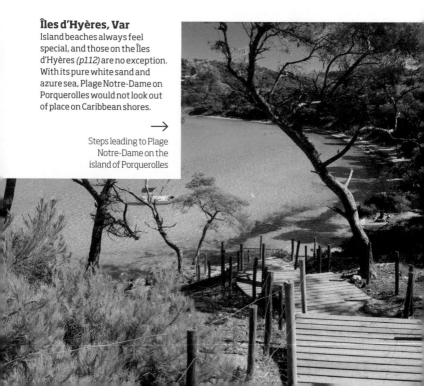

Lac de Sainte-Croix, Alpes-de-Haute-Provence

Not all of Provence's best stretches of sand are on the Mediterranean seafront. The human-made Lac de Sainte-Croix (p193) has a plethora of family-friendly freshwater beaches that are pleasantly free of marine pests such as jellyfish, and offer an array of activities from kayaking to water-skiing.

→

Golden sandy beaches lining the human-made Lac de Sainte-Croix

Baie de Pampelonne, Var

The beach clubs scattered along Pampelonne, a 5-km (3-mile) crescent of perfect, powdery white sand south of St-Tropez (p103), have been by words for glitz and glamour for more than half a century.

←

One of the many luxury beach clubs located on the Baie de Pampelonne

 PICTURE PERFECT
Deserted Beach

Walk east from Stes-Maries-de-la-Mer and keep going for the perfect sunset shot of one of the last deserted beaches in Provence, Plage Est.

Camargue, Bouches-du-Rhône

Rainbow-coloured kites swoop over the seemingly endless miles of white sand that stretch eastward from the family-friendly resort of Stes-Maries-de-la-Mer to Plage de Beauduc (p138). This, the emptiest part of coastline in Provence, is adored by beachcombers and naturists. For stunningly beautiful sand dunes, head further along the strip to Plage Piémanson.

Sand dune in Stes-Maries-de-la-Mer, Camargue's capital ↑

Pont du Gard

This triumph of Roman engineering *(p145)*, with its triple tier of arches made of unmortared limestone blocks, was the tallest aqueduct in the whole of the Roman Empire and carried 20 million litres (5 million gallons) of water every single day from Fontaine d'Eure, just outside Uzès, to Nîmes. Wonderfully preserved, it was added to UNESCO's list of World Heritage Sites in 1985.

→

The colossal 1st-century AD Pont du Gard, with its three tiers of arches

PROVENCE FOR
ROMAN
ARCHITECTURE

Provence's portfolio of Roman relics almost outdoes Rome itself. In vast, echoing amphitheatres you can imagine gladiators locked in mortal combat and cheered on by crowds of thousands. Triumphal arches celebrate the Roman Empire's power and glory, and aqueducts, bridges and civic buildings are testament to the genius of Rome's great engineers.

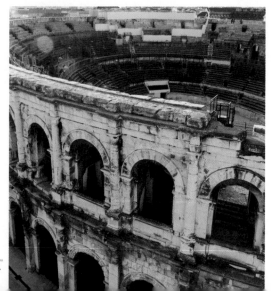

Les Arènes, Nîmes

With its ring of tall, multi-arched walls, the Roman amphitheatre in Nîmes *(p128)* is one of France's most spectacular and best-preserved Roman relics. Built in the 1st century AD, it was used for gladiatorial combat until the collapse of the Roman Empire. Today, it hosts dramatic spectacles such as the Festival of Nîmes.

←

The exterior of the impressive Roman amphitheatre in Nîmes, seen from above

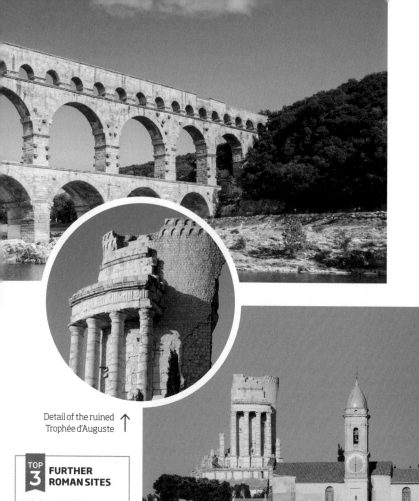

Detail of the ruined → Trophée d'Auguste

TOP 3 **FURTHER ROMAN SITES**

Théatre Antique, Orange
The semi-circular multi-tiered Théatre Antique *(p168)* once seated 7,000 people.

Maison Carrée, Nîmes
Built in the 2nd century, this is arguably the world's best preserved Roman temple *(p129)*.

Site Archéologique de Glanum
A triumphal arch dating from 10 BC to celebrate Julius Caesar's victories is the high point of the Roman site at Glanum, where a series of dramatic memorials line the roadside *(p147)*.

La Trophée d'Auguste

The white columns of the Trophée d'Auguste *(p94)* can be seen from miles around, marking the ancient border between Italy and Roman Gaul. Built in the 6th century BC the 50-m (164-ft) rotunda was partially destroyed after Rome's fall.

↑ La Trophée d'Auguste, looming over the town of La Turbie

Yves Klein

Blue is the colour that defines the work of Yves Klein (1928–62). For most of his career, Nice-born Klein concentrated on "monochrome art" using a unique blue pigment of his own invention, now recognized in the art world as International Klein Blue.

Yves Klein's
striking *Le Buffle*
(1960–61) ↑

Paul Cézanne

Cézanne (1839–1906) spent most of his life in his native Aix-en-Provence. The surrounding landscapes inspired many of his most famous works, which would prove hugely influential for 20th-century art.

→

Cézanne's *Still Life with Apples and a Pot of Primroses* (1890)

PROVENCE FOR
AMAZING ART

Provence's sun-soaked, colour-saturated landscapes and warm climate inspired masters of the avant-garde from Bonnard, Pissaro, Signac and Cézanne in the 19th century to 20th-century titans like Picasso, Chagall, Matisse and Klein.

Paul Signac

Signac (1863–1935) discovered St-Tropez long before the jet set. Along with a group of other artists, many of whom stayed with him in St-Tropez, he developed a unique painting technique that would come to be known as Pointillism.

→

Signac's Pointillist masterpiece *Place des Lices, St-Tropez* (1893)

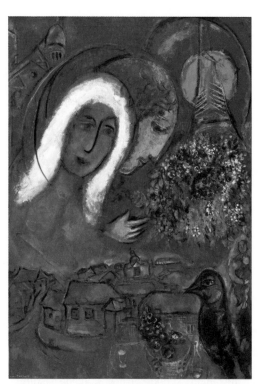

Marc Chagall

Provence's dazzling colours provided new inspiration for Chagall (1887–1985), who settled in St-Paul-de-Vence in 1949. His work draws on his Russian-Jewish heritage.

Chagall's *Field of Mars* (1954), painted in the artist's studio in St-Paul-de-Vence

TOP 3 WORKS OF ART IN PROVENCE

Nu Blue IV, Matisse
Created in 1952, the most instantly recognizable of Matisse's famous "cut-outs" can be seen in the Musée Matisse in Nice *(p66)*.

La Joie De Vivre, Picasso
Pablo Picasso (1881–1973) portrays himself as a flute-playing centaur in this 1946 painting in the Musée Picasso, Antibes *(p88)*.

L'Été, Bonnard
This glowing oil painting of a landscape by Pierre Bonnard (1867–1947) is a jewel in the crown of the Fondation Maeght in St-Paul-de-Vence *(p78)*.

Vincent Van Gogh

The exotic culture and landscapes of Provence drove the Dutch genius Vincent van Gogh (1853–90) to create his greatest works during the time he spent in Arles and St-Rémy-de-Provence between 1888 and 1889.

Van Gogh's evocative *Wheat Field with Cypresses* (1889)

Taste of the Sea

Bouillabaisse, Provence's famous fish stew, tops the menu at the region's seafood restaurants. Other items include shellfish such as mussels and *violets* (sea figs), fish such as *loup* (sea bass), and grilled sea bream. Top seafood restaurants where you can try these delicacies include: L'Épuisette *(156 rue du Vallon des Auffes, Marseille)* and L'Oustau de la Mar *(20 quai des Baux, Cassis)*.

Fresh oysters for sale in a restaurant in Cannes

PROVENCE FOR
FOODIES

From fine-dining establishments in glamorous resorts to authentic family-run village bistros, Provence's chefs produce mouth-watering menus using fresh produce sourced from the region's sun-kissed plains, Alpine pastures, Camargue rice fields and Mediterranean fisheries.

Dine Like a Local

Locals favour the family-run Provençal bistro for lunch or dinner. You'll find one on any village square or marketplace. The menu is usually simple, with dishes such as steak and moules-frites, and local wines often served by the glass or *pichet* (small carafe). Big cities also have small bistros. Try: Bistro du Cours *(13 cours Julien, Marseille)* and Le Bistrot d'Antoine *(27 rue de la Préfecture, Nice)*.

TOP 5 TRADITIONAL DISHES

Bouillabaisse
Fish stew containing a dozen types of fish and seafood, always including *rascasse* (scorpion fish).

Boeuf à la Gardiane
Bull's meat stew from Camargue, served with lashings of nutty red Camargue rice.

Brandade de Morue
This purée of salt cod, cream, potatoes and olive oil is a real Nîmes speciality.

Pissaladière
Nice's take on the pizza is very heavy on the anchovies.

Saucisson d'Arles
Salami-style sausage, traditionally made from donkey meat but now usually from pork.

↑ Chef Mauro Colagreco at the Michelin-starred restaurant Le Mirazur in Menton

Fine Dining

A hushed, reverent atmosphere prevails in Provence's finest temples of gastronomy. The region features a galaxy of fine-dining restaurants in plutocratic playgrounds such as Cannes, Antibes and Monaco, and in the Provençal hinterland. Restaurant Sevin *(p160)* and Christophe Bacquié *(Hôtel du Castellet, Le Castellet)* rank among the best spots.

Market Restaurants

Lunch with the locals at a covered produce market such as Les Halles in Avignon *(p159)* is a real treat. The food comes from stalls piled high with local produce, and you'll find restaurants specializing in fresh seasonal ingredients. Among the best market restaurants are Jon Chiri *(Cuisine Centr'Halles, Avignon)* and Les Tapas de la Major *(Les Halles de la Major, Marseille)*.

↑ Fresh Provençal tomatoes on display at a market stall in Avignon

← Locals dining alfresco at a bistro restaurant in Forcalquier

Did You Know?

The Green Wall on Les Halles's façade in Avignon was created by botanist Patrick Blanc.

Châteauneuf-du-Pape

Medieval pontiffs founded the Côtes du Rhône vineyards that still produce Provence's best-known red wine. Today, the region's dry, rocky and sun-soaked soils produce 110,000 hectolitres (2.5 million gallons) of the renowned Châteauneuf-du-Pape each year, which is more wine than the entire North Rhône region produces. This heady, intense wine goes best with robust meat dishes (particularly red meat), but can also complement spicier dishes, depending on the blend.

$\rightarrow$

Châteauneuf-du-Pape, bottled sunshine from Côtes du Rhône

PROVENCE'S
DIVINE WINES

Stone-dry rosé, best served chilled on a hot day, is the signature wine of the Provençal summer. But Provence's multifarious microclimates also nurture vines that yield muscular reds, delicious dessert wines, and unique vintages from sandy soils.

Beaumes de Venise

The hot sun and arid soils beneath the Dentelles de Montmirail nurture sugar-rich muscat grapes that are fermented into *vins doux naturels* (naturally sweet wines). They can be drunk chilled as an apéritif, or enjoyed as a dessert wine.

$\leftarrow$

Vineyard at sunset in the village of Crestet in the Dentelles de Montmirail

↑ Sommelier pouring Gris de Gris wine from the Camargue

Vins de Sables

Unique to Provence, the Grenache vines that grow on the sandy fringes of the Camargue produce wines such as Gris de Gris that are prized for their steely-pink glint and a bouquet that perfectly complements local seafood.

←
A Vin de Sable wine from the Camargue

GRAPE VARIETIES OF PROVENCE

Grapes such as Cabernet-Sauvignon, Syrah, Grenache and Cinsault are all integral to the divine wines of Provence. But alongside these stalwarts of the winemaker's trade are several less well-known varieties like Rolle (perhaps better known as Vermentino) and Tibouren, which imparts an intense, distinctive, almost herbal aroma to the rosé wines of Côtes de Provence.

Côtes de Provence

The vineyards of Côtes de Provence stretch from the rocky, wooded slopes of the Haut Var all the way to the Mediterranean coast. Dry rosé wines made from Grenache and Cinsault grapes predominate.

↑ Juicy Grenache grapes hanging from vines in Provence

Les Halles, Avignon

The façade of Avignon's covered market *(p159)* is an artificial cliff covered with greenery. Within this paradise for foodies, more than 40 stalls display fine fresh produce, cheeses, sausages and shimmering seafood. There are cooking demonstrations by local chefs on Saturdays, and many casual wine bars offer a place to sit and savour the refreshing wines.

→

Vertical Garden by Patrick Blanc, on the exterior of Avignon's covered market Les Halles

PROVENCE FOR
MAGICAL
MARKETS

A rainbow of colours and a plethora of aromas greet shoppers at markets which – especially on Saturdays – are the social hub of local communities. Stalls are piled high with fresh garden produce, cheese and charcuterie.

Place des Lices, St Tropez

This market square, immortalized by Charles Camoin in his 1925 painting *Place des Lices*, still has some of the atmosphere that the artist captured in his work. Locals shop here on Tuesdays and Saturdays for pastries and fresh fruit and vegetables. Visitors can browse for vintage clothes, accessories, artisan-made pottery and other handmade arts and crafts.

→

Stalls selling vintage items and crafts on place des Lices

L'Île-sur-la-Sorgue

Every Sunday, the riverside streets of Provence's antiques capital *(p181)* become one huge market, with items spilling onto the road. Dozens of dealers display collectables ranging from prints, paintings and stamps to jewellery, furniture and vintage weaponry. The international antiques fairs, in particular, attract huge numbers of connoisseurs every Easter and in mid-August.

→

Vintage film cameras for sale at the market in L'Île-sur-la-Sorgue

Marché Forville, Cannes

Canny residents of Cannes shop here from Tuesday to Saturday for the freshest regional produce. Visitors can pick up a range of Provençal treats to take home, such as *anchoïade* (anchovy paste) and lavender-tinged honey. On Mondays, the market sells an eclectic range of antiques and bric-a-brac.

←

Bric-a-brac and antique items for sale at Marché Forville

Cours Saleya, Nice

The most photogenic market in Provence, Nice's Cours Saleya flower market explodes with colour and floral scents every morning except on Mondays, when the square is given over to antique and bric-a-brac stalls. Nice has a strong history of flower markets and was the first city to open a wholesale cut flower market back in 1897. Food produce from local farms is also sold at Cours Saleya, but the spectacular flowers steal the limelight.

→

Fragrant peonies on sale at a flower stall in Cours Saleya

Meet Denizens of the Deep at Musée Océanographique

The mission of this museum in Monaco *(p72)* is to raise awareness of the plight of the oceans. The life-size model of a giant squid is bound to impress, and there are charming smaller marine monsters like leafy sea-dragons in the aquarium *(www.oceano.mc)*.

💬 INSIDER TIP
Mini-Trains

Almost every town in Provence has a hop-on, hop-off "mini-train" that slowly weaves around all the key sites. These are a great way to explore without tiring little legs. Some offer audio tours as well. Cheap tickets can usually be purchased at a stall near the train stop or from the tourist office.

PROVENCE FOR
FAMILIES

Families with children of all ages, from toddlers to teens, are spoiled for choice in Provence. Activities range from rollercoasters to sailing, and for those rare rainy days there are plenty of all-weather attractions, too.

Riding Rollercoasters at Parc Spirou

Loveable cartoon bellboy Spirou stars at this theme park at Monteux, near Avignon *(p158)*, where children can ride thrilling rollercoasters, drop towers and swing carousels, or meet other characters like laid-back cowboy Lucky Luke and bouncy fictional creature Marsupilami in person. The immersive comic book-inspired park opened in June 2018 and quickly became a favourite for families visiting the area *(www.parc-spirou.com)*.

→

Thrill-seekers enjoying the Spirou Racing rollercoaster in Parc Spirou

Visitors admiring the aquarium in Musée Oceanographique

Ride a Carousel in Avignon

The pretty painted ponies of the traditional carousel in Avignon's historic square, place de l'Horloge *(p158)*, will delight small children. The square marks the lively heart of the city and is also home to a wide range of open-air eateries.

←

Traditionally painted carousel horses in place de l'Horloge

Learn to Sail and Canoe at Lac de Sainte-Croix

The lifeguards and sheltered blue waters at Lac de Sainte-Croix's beaches make this inland sea *(p193)* the perfect place for younger family members to learn to sail, pedalo or canoe. Older children can also try their hand at windsurfing.

Families learning to ↑ pedalo on the waters of Lac de Sainte-Croix

Ride Rapids in the Gorges du Verdon

The old city of Castellane is the gateway to Provence's grand canyon *(p192)*, where adventurers can ride inflatable rafts, canoes and kayaks along miles of thrilling turbulent white water in the deepest gorge in France. While travelling through the Gorges du Verdon, look out for the vultures, eagles and other birds of prey that inhabit the area.

→

Kayaks and rafts on
the Gorges du Verdon

PROVENCE FOR
ADVENTURERS

Provence's rushing rivers, rugged cliffs, and even its clear blue skies offer thrill-seekers a supremely varied choice of adventures all year round. A plethora of specialist agencies based all over the region provide exciting experiences for novices and experts alike.

Climb the Via Ferrata in the Alpes-Maritimes

Metal ladders bolted to sheer cliffs near St-Martin-Vesubie *(p80)* allow novices with a good head for heights to safely ascend precipices that otherwise only expert rock climbers dare to scale. The famous climbing area offers a range of graded routes to suit all abilities. The views from the rocky walls and the swinging bridges are spectacular, with meadows and beautiful lakes to be discovered at the summits.

←

A climber walking across a
bridge above the Gorge du
Guil at Château Queyras

TOP 4 AERIAL SPORTS IN PROVENCE

Hot-Air Balloons
🌐 france-balloons.com
Float over Luberon's lavender fields from Forcalquier *(p199)*.

Skydiving
🌐 skydivecenter.fr
Take off from Gap-Tallard in Alpes-de-Haute-Provence.

Hang-Gliding and Paragliding
🌐 aerogliss.com
Soar above the Lac de Castillon from St-André-les-Alpes *(p203)*.

Microlighting
📞 06 62 20 96 82
Take a microlight ride at St-Maximin-la-Ste-Baume *(p106)*.

Slide and Scramble in the Parc National du Mercantour

The craggy Parc National du Mercantour *(p80)* is one of the birthplaces of the exhilarating sport of canyoning, which involves abseiling and jumping down rocky watercourses. The vertical cliffs here offer challenging rock-climbing routes.

→

Hikers on an alpine trail in the Parc National du Mercantour

Jump Over the Gorges du Verdon

A bungee jump from the Pont de l'Artuby, said to be the highest bridge in Europe, is guaranteed to set your pulse racing. Only the brave dare to leap 182 m (600 ft) over the plunging Gorges du Verdon *(p192)*.

→

The imposing Pont de l'Artuby, a popular bungee-jumping site over the Gorges du Verdon

Chorégies d'Orange

Lovers of opera and classical music flock to Orange each summer for this world-famous celebration of opera and classical music. Big screens display images of performers to complement the amazing acoustics provided by Orange's 2,000-year-old Théâtre Antique *(p168)*. Dating from 1869, this is France's oldest music festival, and it has gained an international following.

→

Opera performance of
Lucia di Lammermoor at
the Chorégies d'Orange

PROVENCE FOR
MUSIC
FESTIVALS

Gypsy guitars and violins, hot jazz and cool blues, opera performances and classical music: you'll find all this and more at Provence's many music festivals. All year round, venues from Roman theatres to intimate bars and clubs host performances to cater for all tastes.

Fêtes Latino-Mexicaines

The alpine slopes around Barcelonnette *(p196)* are alive with the sound of mariachi music for one week in August. It's an odd setting for a foot-stamping fiesta, but the region's links with Mexico go back to the 19th century, when locals who migrated to South America brought home a love of Latin-American rhythms.

←

Dancing to the sound of mariachi music at the Fêtes Latino-Mexicaines

Le Pèlerinage des Gitans

Flamenco guitars and Hungarian accordion music provide the soundtrack for this unique gathering of thousands of pilgrims from the Gitan, Rom and Manouche communities in Stes-Maries-de-la-Mer in May *(p138)*.

→

Guitarist performing at Le Pèlerinage des Gitans in Stes-Maries-de-la-Mer

Jazz in Arles

For free gigs and street performances, plus big-ticket events starring some of jazz's biggest names, head to Arles *(p134)* for this ten-day event which takes place in mid-May. The 17th-century Chapelle du Méjan is the event's main hub, but there are smaller gigs performed throughout the city.

Street performance during Arles's annual jazz festival in May

Nice Jazz Festival

There's something for everyone at the world's longest-established jazz festival in Nice in July *(p65)*, which was first headlined by Louis Armstrong and His All Stars in 1948. Jazz purists head for the open-air Théâtre de Verdure, while the stage on place Masséna hosts acts spanning rock, pop, soul, funk and world music. During the festival and all year round you can catch an excellent range of gigs and some superb late-night jam sessions at ever-popular local jazz bars like Shapko *(5 rue Rossetti)* and La Cave Romagnan *(22 rue d'Angleterre)*.

→

Jon Batiste performing in the Théâtre de Verdure at the Nice Jazz Festival

Lavender and Sunflower Fields

Make for Vaucluse *(p154)* from June to August for shots of sunflower and lavender fields. Sunflowers face the sun, so aim to photograph them in early morning light. Sault and Valréas are some of the best spots to snap lavender fields.

←

Rows of luminous lavender photographed at Plateau de Valensole

PROVENCE FOR
PHOTOGRAPHERS

Purple lavender fields, golden sunflower prairies and rugged limestone crags make Provence's hinterland a magnet for photographers, while village markets are rich environments for snappers looking for shots of local life. In smaller coastal towns and villages, the focus is on colourful fishing boats in picturesque harbours, while the region's medieval abbeys and châteaux make imposing subjects for shots that sum up Provence's rich history.

WILDLIFE PHOTOGRAPHY

Keen birders looking for perfect shots of Camargue bird life can set up their tripods in hides connected by walkways among the lagoons of the Parc Ornithologique du Pont de Gau *(p138)*. Storks nest on the roof of the park headquarters, and stilts, avocets and a dozen other species wade with flamingos in the shallows. Spring and autumn, when flocks of migrant waterfowl pass through, are the best times to visit.

Luberon's Ochre Quarries

Friends back home will think you've been to Mars when you show them your snaps of Le Colorado Provençal *(p176)*. Visit in late afternoon, when the sun brings out the red and orange glow of these weird human-made canyons around Roussillon and Rustrel most vividly.

→

Vivid colours of the ochre quarry in Roussillon

Picturesque Harbours

Looking for a postcard-pretty shot of brightly painted fishing boats? Steer clear of bigger commercial harbours and marinas filled with gleaming yachts, and instead seek out bijou villages like Cassis *(p152)*, Stes-Maries-de-La-Mer *(p138)* and Port-Cros *(p112)*, where traditional pastel-coloured quayside houses make an attractive backdrop to images of tiny fishing vessels bobbing up and down in turquoise water.

←

The rustic harbour in the small town of Martigues

Avignon Icons

For an uncluttered silhouette of Avignon's historic skyline and the Palais des Papes, take your longest lens across the Rhône to Ile Barthelasse and the riverside promenade du Chemin de Halage. From here, you can capture great shots of the palace, the famed Pont St Bénézet and the gold Madonna atop the cathedral *(p160)*.

→

The famously truncated Pont St Bénézet in the historic city of Avignon

↑ Citrus fruits for sale at Les Halles in Avignon

Open-Air Markets

Rise and shine on Saturday or Sunday mornings for the evocative images that late-rising visitors miss. Market traders set up their stalls at daybreak as if to tempt photographers to focus on pristine pyramids of scarlet tomatoes and piles of glossy purple aubergines. Crowds of hungry local buyers soon descend, and by midday most of the stalls are empty.

A YEAR IN
PROVENCE

JANUARY

△ **Rallye Monte-Carlo** *(late Jan)*. Monaco's high-performance cars hurtle through its streets.

Truffle Festival *(last Sun in Jan or first or second Sun in Feb)*. Provence's prized "black gold" is auctioned and tasted at the Les Halles market.

FEBRUARY

△ **Fête du Citron** *(last fortnight in Feb)*. Floats spectacularly decorated with heaps of Menton's favourite citrus fruits are celebrated and marched around town.

Corso Fleuri *(second Sun in Feb)*. Village perché Bormes-les-Mimosas celebrates the region's signature spring blossoms.

MAY

Fête des Gardians *(1 May)*. Colourfully costumed Camarguais cowboys *(gardians)* prance through the streets of Arles.

△ **Festival de Cannes** *(two weeks in May)*. Cannes is packed with paparazzi, stars, producers and directors for the movie business's most prestigious festival.

JUNE

△ **Fêtes de la Tarasque** *(last weekend in Jun)*. An effigy of a legendary monster is paraded through Tarascon.

Festival Estival de Musique *(Jun–Jul)*. Classical musicians perform at various open-air venues around Toulon.

SEPTEMBER

△ **Fête du Vent** *(mid-Sep)*. Rainbow-coloured kites perform breathtaking aerobatics in the skies above the Plages du Prado in Marseille.

Jazz dans les Vignes *(Sep–Dec)*. Jazz musicians perform in vineyards and villages around Sérignan every weekend from mid-September until December.

OCTOBER

△ **Fête de Sainte Marie Salomé** *(Sun nearest 22 Oct)*. In Stes-Maries-de-la-Mer, Romani people gather to pay their respects to Saints Mary Salome and Mary Jacobe. A procession ends in the ritual blessing of the sea.

MARCH

△ **Paris to Nice "Race to the Sun"** (eight days in early Mar). The final leg of the year's first major international cycling race.

APRIL

△ **Feria de Pâques** (Easter). Arletans in traditional costume dance the farandole to the accompaniment of tambourin drum and galoubet flute.

Plantes Rares et Jardin Naturel (weekend in mid-Apr). A delight for gardeners and flower lovers, Sérignan hosts dozens of stalls, guided walks through local gardens and nurseries, exhibitions and workshop sessions.

JULY

△ **Chorégies d'Orange** (all month). Long-established season of opera, classical and choral music in Orange's acoustically perfect Roman theatre.

Festival d'Avignon (mid–late Jul). Avignon hosts France's largest arts festival, with performances in historic venues like the courtyard of the Palais des Papes.

AUGUST

△ **Fête de la Véraison** (early Aug). Actors in medieval costume bring the past to life with a weekend of music, dancing, jousting and wine in Châteauneuf-du-Pape.

Fête du Jasmin (first weekend in Aug). Floral floats, music and dancing in Grasse.

NOVEMBER

Millévin (mid-Nov). The fabulous vintages of Côtes du Rhône are celebrated in and around Avignon.

△ **Festival de Danse** (biennial, late Nov or early Dec). International stars of classical ballet and contemporary dance perform in Cannes.

DECEMBER

△ **Foire aux Santons** (all month). The colourful clay figurines that are an integral part of Christmas in Provence are celebrated and sold in the region's largest pre-Christmas festival in Marseille.

A BRIEF
HISTORY

The great drama of Provence's past stretches from some of the earliest human settlements in Europe to the glitz and glamour of the swinging Sixties and beyond. Celts, Greeks, Romans, Franks, medieval princes and pontiffs have all left their imprint on the region's cities and countryside.

From Stone Age to the Greeks

Rock carvings, fragments of cave paintings and remains of primitive settlements suggest that Provence was inhabited a million years ago by early hunter-gatherers. Nomadic tribes roamed the land for centuries, notably the Celts from the north and the Ligurians from the east. Not until the arrival of the Greeks did trade flourish in a more structured way.

The Roman Empire

Rome conquered Provence in 118 BC, turning it into a prosperous region with flourishing towns like Arles, Nîmes and Orange, as

1 Map of Provence dating to the 1600s.

2 Early horse painting, Cosquer Cave.

3 Detail from a relief sculpture on a Roman arch, Glanum.

4 Medieval engraving of Charles the Bald.

Timeline of events

60,000 BC
Neanderthal dwellers settle in caves at Verdon.

c.800 BC
Early Celtic settlers arrive.

1,000,000 BC
Earliest human presence shown by bone tools found at the Grotte de l'Observatoire in Monaco.

600 BC
Greek settlement at Marseille.

118 BC
Roman conquest begins.

well as imposing monuments like the Trophée d'Auguste (*p94*) and the Pont du Gard (*p145*). Christ's followers are reputed to have brought Christianity to the region when they landed at Stes-Maries-de-la-Mer in AD 40.

Medieval Provence

With the fall of the Roman Empire, stability and relative prosperity began to disappear. Although Provence became part of the Holy Roman Empire, local counts retained autonomy and towns became fiercely independent. People withdrew to the hilltops to protect themselves from a series of invaders, most notably the Saracens, who were finally expelled in AD 974.

Papal Avignon

When the papacy temporarily abandoned war-torn Italy, Avignon became the centre of the Roman Catholic world. From 1309 until 1377 seven French popes ruled unchallenged. When a new Italian pope, Urban VI, was elected, the French cardinals rebelled. In 1378, they chose a rival pope, Clement VII, thus causing a major schism that lasted until 1403.

↑ Second seal (or emblem) of Raymond VII (1197–1249) who was known as the Count of Toulouse, Duke of Narbonne and Marquis of Provence, from 1222 until his death

AD 476
Final collapse of the Roman Empire.

536
Provence ceded to the Franks by King Theodahad.

974
Saracens driven from Provence by William I.

1032
Provence becomes part of the Holy Roman Empire.

1309
Pope Clement V moves Papacy to Avignon.

1

2

War and Peace

Provence became fully part of France with the death of its last count, René the Good, in 1480. It was thus drawn into 16th-century wars between France and the Hapsburg Empire, and into the Wars of Religion between "heretic" Protestants and Catholics, which resulted in a wave of massacres and the wholesale destruction of churches and their contents. For ordinary Provençal men and women, the next two centuries were relatively peaceful, interrupted by brief skirmishes with England and Savoy.

Revolution, Republic and Empire

Provençal peasants pillaged châteaux and monasteries during the Revolution of 1789. British forces were driven from Toulon in 1793 by the young artillery officer Napoléon Bonaparte, who was to visit Provence again in 1815 at the beginning of his last desperate bid to recover his empire. In the less turbulent 19th century, the warm winter climate of the Riviera began to attract foreign visitors and artists. The first railways from Paris opened in the 1850s, and grand hotels and villas started to be built.

↑ 1920s advertisement poster of the Côte d'Azur Pullman-Express.

Timeline of events

1480

Provence becomes fully part of France with death of Count René the Good.

1562

Wars of Religion begin, lasting until 1598.

1720

Plague kills half the population of Marseille.

1789

Provençal peasants pillage châteaux during the French Revolution.

1860

Savoy cedes Nice to France.

The Glamorous 1920s

Provence was far from the front lines of World War I, and when peace came the Riviera boomed, attracting bright young things and literary stars like F Scott Fitzgerald and Noel Coward. The party ended with World War II (except for those who collaborated with the occupiers, like the designer Coco Chanel). From 1942 Provence was occupied by the Germans. Liberation began when US and Free French troops landed near St-Tropez in June 1944.

Into the Present

After the war, holidaymakers drawn by Provence's summer sun arrived in droves. The first Cannes Film Festival was held in 1946, and film stars and musicians made the Riviera one of the most glamorous places in the world. Expanded airports and high-speed train lines have made Provence even more accessible to sun-worshippers in the 21st century, and the superyachts of billionaires and film stars continue to dock in its marinas. However, the region's environment has suffered from over-development, and new challenges, including racial and political tension, must be faced.

1 René d'Anjou, King of Naples. ↑

2 Painting of the Battle of Toulon.

3 The walk down La Croisette in Cannes.

4 Yacht at the Monaco Yacht Show, 2015.

Did You Know?

Marseille volunteers supported the Republic in Paris in 1792. Their song, *La Marseillaise*, is the national anthem.

1946
First Cannes Film Festival held.

2001
TGV Méditerranée link with Paris launched.

1942–44
Germans occupy southern France.

2019
Nice's second Tramway route opens between port and airport.

2021
Nice proclaimed a World Heritage Site by UNESCO.

EXPERIENCE

Aerial view of a beach on the Riviera

RIVIERA AND ALPES-MARITIMES

The French Riviera is, without doubt, the most celebrated seaside in Europe. Just about everybody who has been anybody for the past 100 years has succumbed to its glittering allure. This is the holiday playground of kings and courtesans, movie stars and millionaires, where the seriously rich never stand out in the crowd.

But the Riviera is not just a millionaire's watering hole: a diversity of talent has visited, seeking patrons and taking advantage of the luminous Mediterranean light. This coast is irrevocably linked with the life and works of Matisse, Picasso, Chagall, Cocteau and Renoir. It lent them the scenery of its shores and the rich environment of hill villages like St-Paul-de-Vence. This village has echoed to the voices of such luminaries as Bonnard and Modigliani, F Scott Fitzgerald and Greta Garbo. Today, its galleries still spill canvases on to its medieval lanes.

The Alpes-Maritimes, which incorporates the principality of Monaco, is renowned for its temperate winter climate. The abundance of flowers here attracted the perfume industry and the English – who created some of the finest gardens on the coast. Inland, the mountainous areas of Provence offer a range of skiing activities in superb mountain scenery, and a chance to try traditional Alpine food.

RIVIERA AND ALPES-MARITIMES

Must Sees

↑ Nice's promenade des Anglais, stretching along the coast

❶

NICE

🚉 Nice, 7km (4 miles) SW 🚌 Ave Thiers
ℹ 5 promenade des Anglais; www.nicetourisme.com

With the blue curve of the Baie des Anges in front and the white summits of the Alpes-Maritimes as a backdrop, Nice has enchanted visitors since the 19th century, when British, German and Russian aristocrats wintered here, revelling in its mellow climate. Painters, enchanted by Nice's vibrant light, endowed the city with a rich artistic legacy. But Nice is much more than a resort. It's a bustling city with its own distinct dialect and culture.

① 🔯 ⓜ 🏛

Villa Masséna

🏛 65 rue de France 📞 04 93 91 19 10 🕙 11am–6pm Wed–Mon (May–Oct: from 10am)

The golden age of aristocratic tourism in Nice is brought to life in this museum within a 19th-century Italianate villa. Religious works, paintings by Niçois "primitive" painters, and white-glazed faïence pottery are among the exhibits. The villa was built for Prince Victor D'Essling, grandson of Nice-born André Masséna, one of Napoleon's greatest marshals, whose bust has pride of place in the Empire-style main hall.

② 🔯 ⓜ 🏛

Musée d'Arts Modernes et d'Art Contemporain (MAMAC)

🏛 Place Yves Klein 🕙 11am–6pm Tue–Sun (May–Oct: from 10am) 🌐 mamac-nice.org

The enfants terribles of Pop Art, New Realism and the modernists of the École de Nice are found in this complex of marble-faced towers and transparent walkways. Andy Warhol and Yves Klein are among the stars of a collection that celebrates the avant-garde from the 1960s to the 21st century.

③ 🔯 ⓜ 🏛

Musée National Marc Chagall

🏛 36 ave du Dr Ménard 🕙 10am–5pm Wed–Mon (May–Oct: to 6pm) 🌐 en. musees-nationaux-alpesmaritimes.fr

Paintings from Marc Chagall's Biblical Message series – including five versions of The Song of Songs – form the core of this museum, home to the world's largest portfolio of the painter's work. Three stained-glass windows depict the Creation of the World, and a shallow pool reflects a dazzling mosaic of the prophet Elijah.

→

The Loch Ness Monster by Niki de Saint Phalle at MAMAC

Le Negresco

📍 37 promenade des Anglais 🕐 24 hrs daily 🌐 hotel-negresco-nice.com

Built in 1912 by Romanian hotelier Henri Negresco, this landmark hotel is even more lavish today than in its heyday. Louis XIII grandeur meets modern amenities in the decadent rooms, and a 16,000-stone Baccarat chandelier hangs in the *salon royal*.

⑤ 🎨 🗺 🏛

Musée des Beaux-Arts

📍 33 ave des Baumettes 🕐 11am-6pm Tue-Sun (May-Oct: from 10am) 🌐 musee-beaux-arts-nice.org

Oil paintings and ceramics by Raoul Dufy steal the show in this 19th-century villa, which was once home to a Ukranian princess. Other highlights include sculptures by Rodin (including a copy of his once-shocking *The Kiss*) and works by Bonnard, Vuillard, Van Dongen and 16th- and 17th-century Flemish masters. There's also a collection of 18th-century art from China and Japan.

⑥ 🗺 🏛

Musée des Arts Asiatiques

📍 405 promenade des Anglais 🕐 10am-5pm Wed-Mon (Jul-Aug: to 6pm) 🌐 arts-asiatiques.com

Surrounded by the exotic gardens of the Parc Phoenix, the Musée des Arts Asiatiques is a work of art in its own right. Inside Kenzo Tange's dazzling white marble, steel and glass building is an outstanding collection of ancient and modern art from China, Japan, India and Southeast Asia. Cultural activities such as formal Japanese tea ceremonies and Qi Gong exercise sessions are among the highlights here.

NICE JAZZ FESTIVAL

Louis Armstrong and his All Stars headlined at the first Nice Jazz Festival in 1948, as the Riviera emerged from the grim years of World War II and post-war poverty. It was the first big international jazz festival, and more than 70 years on it's still a major event.

The Théâtre de Verdure is the main venue and the six-day event kicks off with a lively carnival parade through the city centre.

⑦ 🎨 Ⓜ 🛍

MUSÉE MATISSE

📍 164 ave des Arènes de Cimiez, Nice 🚌 15, 17, 20, 25 🕙 10am–5pm daily
(May–Oct: to 6pm) 🚪 Public hols 🖥 musee-matisse-nice.org

Henri Matisse (1869–1954) first came to Nice in 1917, and lived at
several addresses in the city before settling in Cimiez for the rest of his
life. His devotion to the city and its "clear, crystalline, precise, limpid"
light culminated, just before his death, with a large bequest of his
works to the city.

History of the Museum

Nine years after Matisse's death, the Musée
Matisse opened to the public, with the artist's
bequest forming the main nucleus of the
collection. For decades, the museum shared
space with Nice's archaeological museum in
the Villa des Arènes, a grand 17th-century villa
located next to the Cimiez cemetery, which
holds the artist's simple memorial. Since 1993,
however, the entire villa, complete with its new
extension, has been devoted to celebrating
Matisse's life, work and influence. Today, the
ground and first floors of this gallery display
works from the museum's permanent
collection, from which pieces are sometimes
loaned out to other museums. The subter-
ranean wing is used for exhibitions devoted
to Matisse and his contemporaries.

Works on Paper

Nu Bleu IV (1952) is, for most visitors, the most
immediately recognisable of Matisse's works.
This is one of the artist's famous "cut-outs",
works made from gouache-painted paper that
was cut and pasted into unforgettable collages.

In this piece, the artist has tried several
compositions in charcoal before pasting
down the final lay out.

Paintings and Sculptures

Among the most impressive of Matisse's
sculptural works on show is the bronze *Torse
Debout* (1909), a headless female figure given
to the museum in 1978 by the artist's son, Jean.
The tranquil *Liseuse à la Table Jaune* (1944),
a painting of a woman reading, belies the
troubles that beset Matisse during World
War II, including a major operation that left
him bedridden for a time, and the arrest of

↑ *Jeannette III* (1911), one of
several bronze sculptures
of the subject

←

Matisse's "cut-out" *Nu Bleu IV*
(1952), with its charcoal
composition outlines

Timeline

1917
Matisse relocates to Nice from Paris.

1941
Diagnosed with duodenal cancer, Matisse undergoes surgery that leaves him bedridden.

1944
Matisse's wife Amélie is jailed for her part in the French Resistance.

1945
Matisse's daughter flees to Nice after escaping on her way to a Nazi death camp.

1947–51
Matisse designs and decorates the Chapelle du Rosaire in Vence.

1954
▽ Matisse dies of a heart attack in Cimiez at the age of 84.

his wife and daughter for French Resistance work. *Nature Morte aux Grenades* (1947) features ripe pomegranates in one of Matisse's favourite settings, an interior opening onto a window of blue skies.

Matisse in Person

The museum's collection of photographs offers a unique insight into the man and his work. Hélène Adant's photograph *Matisse in his Studio* shows him drafting the murals for the Chapelle du Rosaire in Vence *(p91)*. A gilded Rococo armchair, the subject of his painting *Fauteuil Rocaille* (1946), is among many of the painter's belongings and painting props on display in the museum.

↑ Exterior of the Villa des Arènes, the setting for the Musée Matisse

↑ Interior of the Musée Matisse, with *Fleurs et Fruits* (1952-3) in the foreground

A SHORT WALK
NICE

Distance 1 km (half a mile) **Nearest tram**
Cathédrale - Vieille Ville **Time** 15 minutes

A dense network of pedestrian alleys, narrow buildings and pastel, Italianate façades make up Vieux Nice (or the Old Town). Its streets contain many fine 17th-century Italianate churches, among them St-François-de-Paule, behind the Opéra, and l'Église du Gèsu in the rue Droite. Most of the seafront, at the quai des États-Unis, is taken up by Les Ponchettes, a double row of low houses with flat roofs, which was a fashionable walk before the promenade des Anglais was built. To the east of this lies the Colline du Château, occupied in the 4th century by Greeks who kept fishing nets on the quay.

Built in 1650 by the Nice architect J-A Guiberto in Baroque style, the **Cathédrale Ste-Réparate** has a fine dome of glazed tiles and an 18th-century tower.

The **Palais de Justice** was inaugurated on 17 October 1892, replacing the smaller quarters used before Nice became part of France.

Did You Know?

The quai des États-Unis took its name in 1917, after America joined World War I.

There's an enticing vegetable and flower market on **cours Saleya**, and it is also a lively area at night.

Built in 1885, the ornate and sumptuous **Opéra de Nice** has its entrance just off the quai des Etats-Unis.

Designed by Guarino Guarini in 1740, the Baroque **Chapelle de la Miséricorde** has a fine Rococo interior.

↑ Tapestries and antique furniture adorning a room in the opulent Palais Lascaris

Sumptuous 18th-century statues of Mars and Venus flank the staircase at **Palais Lascaris**, *and Genoese artists decorate the trompe l'oeil ceiling.*

DE LA LOGE

RUE DROITE

RUE ROSSETTI

RUE ST-JOSEPH

FINISH

RUE BENOÎT-BUNICO

RUE DROITE

RUE DU CHÂTEAU

RUE DU MALONAT

RUE DE L'ANCIEN SÉNAT

E BARILLERIE

RUE JULES-GILLY

PLACE CHARLES FELIX

QUAI DES ÉTATS-UNIS

| 0 metres | | 100 | N |
| 0 yards | | 100 | ↑ |

One of Nice's most unusual architectural features is the row of low white buildings along the seafront, called **Les Ponchettes**. *These were once used by fishermen, and are now a mix of bars and restaurants.*

↑ Striking view over Les Ponchettes and the quai des États-Unis from the stairs of the Montée Lesage

2

CANNES

F5 ✈Nice 28 km (18 miles) 🚉4 place de la Gare 🚌2 place Cornut Gentille 🛈1 blvd de la Croisette; www.cannes-destination.com

There's a sense of faded glory in Cannes. The Cannes Film Festival, first held in 1946, really put the place on the map. Even when the party is over, the glamour remains in the posh stores, on the swanky private beaches, and in the gaming rooms of the casinos.

① La Croisette

The long promenade de la Croisette runs parallel to the city's Plage de la Croisette, a palm-lined crescent of imported sand looking out over the gorgeous Bay of Cannes. Its major landmarks are three luxury hotels, the Carlton, the Majestic and the Martinez, where movie industry hacks hang out at Film Festival time. The rest of the year, the hotels are home to attendees of less glamorous conferences held at the Palais des Festivals et des Congrès, which anchors the western end of the boulevard. Each hotel has its own private beach where, for a hefty fee, visitors can bask in luxury for a while.

② Les Allées de la Liberté

A statue of Lord Brougham, the British Lord Chancellor who initiated the gentrification of Cannes when he built a villa here in 1834, overlooks this green square just inland from the harbour. Locals play boules or sip coffee in cafés beneath the shady plane trees. The square also hosts a colourful flower market (7am–noon Mon–Fri), stalls selling bric-a-brac, antiques and vintage items (7am–5:30pm Sat & Sun), and an array of talented local arts and crafts vendors (8am–1pm Sat & Sun).

③ Rue d'Antibes

Big-name designer boutiques line rue d'Antibes, where the stars shop for shoes, jewellery, handbags and other accessories. Less well-heeled visitors can enjoy window-shopping and may even spot a celebrity.

④ Marché Forville

5-11 rue du Marché Forville ⏰7am-1pm Tue-Sun 🌐marcheforville.com

The air is filled with the smells of coffee, flowers and herbs at this busy open-air market. It's a great place to buy local

> INSIDER TIP
> **Budget beaches**
>
> Rent a lounger, parasol and locker at one of Cannes' public city beaches - like Plage du Midi, Plage de la Bocca or Palm Beach - and bring your own drinks to enjoy the same sun, sea and sand as the glitzy beach clubs but on a tighter budget.

↑ Bright lights of La Croisette glittering in the Baie de Cannes

delicacies, and on Mondays it becomes a flea market.

⑤
Palais des Festivals et des Congrès

📍 1 blvd de la Croisette
🕐 7am-midnight daily
🌐 palaisdesfestivals.com

Built in 1982 and renovated in 2015, this brutally functional modern building dwarfs the Vieux Port, the original heart of Cannes. It comes into its own as the hub of the Cannes Film Festival, when it hosts the presentation of the Palme d'Or, next to the Academy Award as the film industry's most prestigious honour. In front of the Palais, hand-prints set in pavement concrete immortalize screen icons in the Allée des Étoiles.

Musée de la Castre and Tour de la Castre

📍 Château de la Castre
📞 04 93 38 55 26 🕐 10am-1pm & 2-5pm Tue-Sun (Jul-Aug: to 7pm)

It's worth visiting this quirky museum just for the view from its highest point, the 11th-century Tour de la Castre. Built by the monks of Lérins in the 11th and 12th centuries, the former castle now houses an eclectic collection that includes traditional Pacific Island costumes, Asian art-works and African masks. The Cistercian Ste-Anne chapel houses a fine collection of antique musical instruments.

DRINK

Carlton Beach Club
Sip on cocktails while enjoying the 1950s glamour of the French Riviera at this spot.

📍 58 blvd de la Croisette
🌐 carltoncannes-thebeachclub.com

Charly's
This purple-lit, vaulted grotto offers a long list of cocktails and fizz, and has an outdoor terrace for warm summer evenings.

📍 3 rue du Suquet
📞 06 98 92 40 41

Hyde Beach
Sun loungers line the jetty-like boardwalk of the Grand Hotel's beach club. The cocktail list is a mix of classics and inventive innovations.

📍 45 blvd de la Croisette
🌐 grandhotel cannes.com

3

MONACO

🅐 G4 ✈ Nice 15 km (9 miles) SW 🚂 Monaco-Monte Carlo, pl Ste-Dévote 🚌 Place des Moulins 🛈 2A blvd des Moulins; www.visitmonaco.com

The mega-yachts of the world's richest men and women dwarf smaller (but still upmarket) vessels in the Port de Monaco, and world-famous sports stars and their consorts hog the VIP tables in the exclusive nightspots of the world's second smallest country. An ambitious €2 billion project to create a new millionaire's enclave on sand dredged from the seabed began in 2016 and is expected to take 10 years to complete. Meanwhile, Monte Carlo, centrepiece of Monaco's royally belle époque heart, still exerts an undeniable charm.

①

Le Rocher

Set on the Rock, a sheer-sided, flat-topped finger of land extending 792 m (2,600 ft) into the the sea, Le Rocher (also called Monaco-Ville) is the historic quarter of Monaco where one of Europe's oldest dynasties, the Grimaldis, founded their principality in the 13th century. Today, it is a warren of narrow medieval lanes set around the Palais Princier. There are a number of routes up to Le Rocher; the best is via Rampe Major, which starts near the port from place d'Armes.

Timeline

13th–14th century

△ The Genoese Grimaldi family seize Monaco from the Ghibellines, a rival faction.

1633–1815

France and Spain recognise Monaco's independence but the principality is conquered by France; in 1814 it becomes a protectorate of Sardinia.

19th century

France recognises Monégasque sovereignty; the Casino de Monte Carlo opens and is so successful that the principality need no longer collect income tax.

20th century

▽ First Monaco Grand Prix held in 1929; Monaco is occupied by Italy and Germany during World War II; Prince Rainier III marries film star Grace Kelly, who tragically dies in a car crash in 1982.

21st century

Albert II succeeds to throne in 2005; reclamation project launched to expand Monaco's land area by more than 3 per cent.

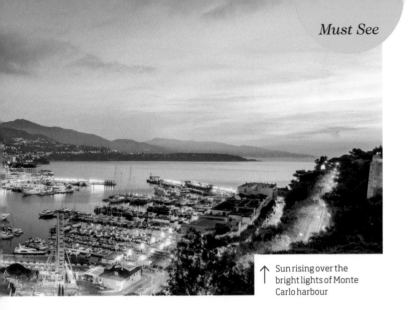

↑ Sun rising over the bright lights of Monte Carlo harbour

②

Palais Princier

🏛 Place du Palais 🕙 Mar-Oct: 10am-6pm daily 🚫 Grand Prix 🌐 palais.mc

Monaco's seat of government, this castle-palace of the Grimaldi dynasty is built on the site of a medieval Genoese fortress and protected by 17th-century cannons donated by Louis XIV of France. The Compagnie du Carabiniers du Prince (equipped with modern weapons, but still in archaic dress uniform) changes its guards with full military pomp every day at 11:55am. Venture inside to discover wonderful frescoes by 16th-century Genoese artists, the opulent throne room, and the stunning blue-and-gold Louis XV Salon. The cour d'Honneur courtyard, outside, is a lovely setting for summer concerts.

③

Casino de Monte Carlo

🏛 Place du Casino 🕙 2pm-4am daily 🌐 casinomonte carlo.com

Monaco owes much of its fame to this spectacular monument to all that was fabulous about the belle époque of the late 19th century, when this tiny principality came to be seen as *the* place to frolic, flirt and play games of chance for high stakes. Built by the architect of the Paris opera house, Charles Garnier, its dazzling interior is decorated with glittering chandeliers, ostentatious frescoes and gilded bas-reliefs. Edward, Prince of Wales (later King Edward VII) was just one of its former royal and aristocratic patrons, drawn by the thrill of roulette, baccarat and chemin de fer. The slot machines now in the Salle des Amériques and Salle Renaissance are an egalitarian innovation, and full evening dress is no longer de rigueur, but the casino still strives to maintain a certain decorum.

EAT

Café de Paris

This classic brasserie serves refined French cooking and local dishes like *stockfish à la monégasque* under white awnings on a flowery terrace opposite the casino.

🏠 **Place du Casino**
🌐 **montecarlosbm.com**

€€€

Quai des Artistes

A classy, contemporary but unpretentious harbourside brasserie that bustles with locals and serves a great selection of seafood and an above-average children's menu.

🏠 **4 Quai Antoine 1er**
🌐 **quaidesartistes.com**

€€€

Jardin Exotique

🏠 **62 blvd du Jardin Exotique**
🕙 **9am–5pm daily (Feb–Apr & Oct: to 6pm; May–Sep: to 7pm)** 🚫 **19 Nov, 25 Dec**
🌐 **jardin-exotique.mc**

Clinging to the steep limestone hillside, this garden is filled with unique tropical and sub-tropical cacti and other plants imported from arid and unpromising native environments in Africa, Asia and the Americas. It has the largest collection of petrophile succulents (plants that grow on bare rock) in the world. But its biggest secret lies beneath the surface. In the Grotte de l'Observatoire, an eerie cavern filled with dripping stalactites, palaeontologists have found evidence of early hominid people from 1,000,000 years BC.

Tropical and sub-tropical plants in the Jardin Exotique, and *(inset)* the Grotte de l'Observatoire lying beneath the gardens ↓

Monaco Top Cars Collection

🏠 **5 Terrasses de Fontvieille**
🕙 **10am–5:30pm daily**
🚫 **25 Dec** 🌐 **mtcc.mc**

This petrolheads' paradise began as the personal collection of Prince Rainier III. It's one of the world's greatest collections of classic cars, from a quaint 1903 De Dion Bouton to sleek thoroughbreds bearing the hood ornaments and badges of Rolls-Royce, Facel Vega, Ferrari, Maserati and Lamborghini. There are also important race and rally contenders from historic Monaco Grand Prix and Monte Carlo Rally events. A specially constructed building displays the cars over five levels.

⑥ Cathédrale

 4 rue Colonel Bellando de Castro 📞0377 99 99 14 00 🕐9am-6pm daily

The 12th-century church of St Nicholas was replaced in the 19th century by this Neo-Romanesque building in white La Turbie stone. The tombs of princes and bishops surround its 16th-century altarpiece, painted by the renowned Niçois artist Louis Bréa. The much-loved Princess Grace is also buried here.

---

⑦ Musée Océanographique

🏛Avenue St-Martin 🕐10am-5pm daily (Apr-Jun & Oct-Dec: to 6pm; Sep: to 7pm); Jul-Aug: 9:30am-8pm 🚫Grand Prix, 25 Dec 🌐oceano.mc

A glass-sided, 6-m- (19-ft-) deep shark tank is the centrepiece of this clifftop museum. Smaller exotic creatures like the charming leafy sea dragons

swim in smaller tanks. The museum was founded by Prince Albert I in 1910, and the legendary undersea explorer Jacques Cousteau was the director from 1958 to 1988. Its ongoing mission is to raise awareness of the plight of the world's oceans and their denizens. The rooftop café also offers superb panoramic views of the coast.

---

⑧   Nouveau Musée National de Monaco

🏛Villa Sauber, 17 ave Princesse Grace; Villa Paloma, 56 blvd du Jardin Exotique 🕐10am-6pm during exhibitions only 🚫1 Jan, 1 May, Grand Prix, 19 Nov, 25 Dec 🌐nmnm.mc

Two spectacular villas house this museum charting the cultural, historical and artistic heritage of the Principality. The Villa Sauber, a fine example of belle époque architecture, hosts a series of entertainment and performing arts exhibits. Villa Paloma, with its lovely Italian garden, displays a fantastic collection of modern and contemporary art, architecture and design.

MONACO GRAND PRIX

The scream of Formula 1 engines resounds throughout Monaco as drivers hurl the world's fastest racers around its streets in the world's most glamorous motorsports event. First run in 1919, the Monaco Grand Prix is a unique urban circuit that loops for 3.367 km (just over 2 miles) through the principality's streets, where drivers must negotiate 78 twists and turns.

⑨ Musée du Vieux Monaco

🏛2 rue Emile de Loth 📞0377 93 50 57 28 🕐Jun-Sep: 11am-4pm Wed & Fri

The paintings, ceramics furniture and costumes on display at this museum aim to preserve national identity and educate visitors about Monégasque traditions.

---

⑩ Théâtre du Fort Antoine

🏛Avenue de la Quarantaine

This ancient fort has been converted into an open-air theatre showing a wide range of productions in summer.

Did You Know?

Residents of Monaco pay no income tax or inheritance tax, and one in three residents is a millionaire.

④

ST-PAUL-DE-VENCE

🗺 F4 ✈ Nice 🚉 Nice, Cagnes sur Mer 🚌 Cagnes sur Mer, Vence, Nice 🛈 2 rue Grande 🌐 saint-pauldevence.com

Set in alpine hinterland with panoramic views of the Riviera coast, the breathtaking location of St-Paul-de-Vence first drew painters in the 1920s. The outstanding art collection of the Fondation Maeght *(p78)* is St-Paul-de-Vence's most powerful magnet, and a stroll through the village's maze of medieval streets is a real delight.

①

Place du Jeu de Boules

Venerable plane trees spread their leaves over the place du Jeu de Boules. Any visit to St-Paul-de-Vence must start on this atmospheric space, where locals still like to meet for a friendly game of *pétanque* when the square is not crammed with visitors.

②

Porte de Vence and Ramparts

A 14th-century tower stands guard over the Porte de Vence, an impressive gateway that leads through St-Paul-de-Vence's formidable ring of 16th-century ramparts into the heart of the village. From here, you can walk around the ramparts – originally built to resist assault from Savoy and Piedmont – for a panoramic view of the vineyards and olive groves that cloak the hilly countryside around the village.

③

Rue Grande

Lined with the studios and workshops of local artists and artisans, the rue Grande is St-Paul's main thoroughfare. Running between the Porte de Vence and Porte de Nice, it resembles an open-air art museum where you can ogle the work of cutting-edge talents in the windows of upscale commercial galleries.

④

Folon Chapel (Chapelle des Pénitents Blancs)

📍 Place de l'Église
📞 04 93 32 41 13
🕐 10:30am–12:30pm & 2–4pm (May–Sep: to 6pm)
🚫 Public hols

Belgian-born artist Jean-Michel Folon (1934–2005) spent much of his life in St-Paul-de-Vence and worked with local artisans to adorn this historic 17th-century chapel with vividly coloured, joyous stained glass windows, graceful sculptures, murals and rich mosaics. The enchanting chapel is immaculately preserved as a celebration of his life and work.

↑ Place de la Grande Fontaine in St-Paul-de-Vence

pilgrimage for admirers, who leave stones in a growing pile as visible tribute to a great artist.

⑥
Église Collégiale Saint Paul

📍 Place de l'Église ⏰ 8:15am-4:15pm Mon-Fri, 10am-6pm Sat, Sun & public hols

This 14th-century church has preserved its Romanesque features. Its Chapelle Saint Clément is the main highlight.

⑦
Chapelle St Charles-St Claude

📍 Chemin Ste-Claire

Perched on a promontory above the ramparts, this chapel was founded in the 17th century. In the early 2010s, Nice artist Paul Conte decorated it with colourful murals depicting scenes from the lives of the saints to whom the church is dedicated.

⑧
Place de la Grande Fontaine

A gushing 17th-century central fountain lends its name to this charming square which was once the village's market-place and communal laundry. The square has long been a favourite subject with artists working in St-Paul-de-Vence.

↑ The medieval village of St-Paul-de-Vence, perched high on a hilltop

⑤
Cimetière

Marc Chagall, who made St-Paul-de-Vence his home, is the most famous resident. His modest grave is a place of

---

TOP 4 ART GALLERIES IN ST-PAUL-DE VENCE

L'Art et le Vin
📍 1 rue de la Pourtoune
This wine bar and gallery is a perfect spot to savour local vintages and work by local artists.

Galerie Gantois
📍 56 rue Grande
Run by the Gantois family since 1963, this gallery features contemporary sculptures and paintings.

Podgorny Robinson
📍 Place de Gaulle
A gallery showcasing bold contemporary works by recognized and emerging artists.

Galerie 337
📍 29 rue Grande
This modern art gallery features exceptional sculptures, prints and paintings by leading contemporary artists.

FONDATION MAEGHT

🏠 623 chemin des Gardettes, St-Paul-de-Vence
🕐 10am–6pm daily (Jul–Aug: to 7pm) 📅 24 & 31 Dec
🌐 fondation-maeght.com

Nestling amid the umbrella pines in the hills above St-Paul-de-Vence, this small foundation houses one of Europe's largest collections of 20th-century art.

The Fondation Maeght was established in 1964 by Cannes art dealers Aimé and Marguerite Maeght, who numbered the likes of Chagall, Matisse and Miró among their clients. Their private collection formed the basis of the foundation, and they enlisted the help of their artist friends when designing the grounds: highlights include a courtyard filled with stick-thin Giacometti sculptures, an elaborate sculpture-filled maze designed by Miró, a bold pool by Braque, and a large mural mosaic by Chagall. The Maeghts intended the foundation not as an art museum, but as a forum to present modern art – a place for artists to gather, exchange ideas and exhibit their work. Today, just a fraction of the vast permanent collection is on display at any one time, with a changing programme of popular temporary exhibitions.

These slender bronze figures by Alberto Giacometti inhabit their own shady courtyard.

Georges Braque designed the Les Poissons mosaic in this pool.

Cowled roofs allow indirect light to filter into the galleries.

↑ Bold exterior of the Fondation Maeght

Alexander Calder's Les Renforts (1963) is what he called a "stabile" – a counterpart to his more familiar mobiles.

Joan Miró's Le Cadran Solaire (1973) is one of many statues in his multi-levelled maze of trees, water and gargoyles.

↑ Temporary Giacometti exhibition inside the Fondation Maeght

Did You Know?

The foundation drew Duke Ellington, Samuel Beckett, André Malraux and a galaxy of artists to its early events.

The Chapelle St-Bernard was built in memory of the Maeghts' son, who died in 1953, aged 11. Above the altarpiece is a stained-glass window by Braque.

← Illustration of the building and grounds of the Fondation Maeght, seen from above

↑ *L'Oiseau Lunaire* (1968), a sculpture in Miró's maze

PARC NATIONAL DU MERCANTOUR

⬛F3 **🏠Alpes-Maritimes** **🚉Tende, Fontan-Saorge** **🚌St-Étienne-de-Tinée, Auron** **ℹ23 rue d'Italie, Nice** **🌐mercantour-parcnational.fr**

This alpine wilderness is a paradise for those who love the great outdoors. Covering 70,000 ha (270 sq miles), the Parc National du Mercantour shelters an abundance of wildlife. Tende, overlooking a mountain pass, and Saorge, set in a natural amphitheatre above the river, are gateways to the park.

Vallée des Merveilles

A hike into this valley, with its breathtakingly clear air and pretty alpine scenery, takes you high into the Mercantour and deep into its vanished past. Etched into the rock of Mont Bégo are some 36,000 engravings, dating from around 2,000 BC. The **Musée des Merveilles** displays original and reproduction petroglyphs from the area and puts them in their Bronze Age context.

Vallée de la Vésubie

Two alpine torrents, the Madone de Fenestre and Boréon, merge to become the Vésubie, which cascades through pine forests and meadows, skirting the fringes of the Parc National du Mercantour, before snaking through the Gorges de la Vésubie to join the Var. St-Martin-Vésubie, where the two sources join, is a popular mountain activity centre. There's a spectacular view of the Gorges de la Vésubie at La Madone d'Utelle, above the fortified village of Utelle.

Forêt de Turini

This lush forest seems a world away from the beautiful but barren upper expanses of the Parc National du Mercantour. A humid microclimate and warm Mediterranean breeze nurture thick swathes of beech, maple, sweet chestnut and pine trees, which soar to great heights. Hike to the 2,082 m (6,830 ft) Pointe des Trois-Communes summit for a superb view of the peaks of the Mercantour.

Breathtaking view over the Gorges de la Vésubie from St-Martin-Vésubie ↑

WILDLIFE OF THE MERCANTOUR

The multifarious environments and microclimates of the Mercantour provide havens for creatures great and small, from wide-winged raptors and shy mountain herbivores to colourful butterflies in the woodland glades and alpine pastures.

① Ibex and mouflon

Some 1,200 ibex roam the remotest mountain slopes of Mercantour. This nimble, exuberantly horned wild goat shares its habitat with the mouflon, a wild sheep introduced to the region from Corsica.

② Marmots

Look out for these cheeky rodents as they pop out of their burrows to nibble the grass and bask in early morning sun on high mountain meadows.

③ Chamois

Listen for the sound of tumbling pebbles as families of chamois scramble across steep scree slopes.

④ Bearded vultures

With its mighty wingspan of up to 2.83 m (9.3 ft), the gypaete (bearded vulture) is one of Europe's most unmistakable raptors. It's also among the rarest.

Saorge

Once a strategic strongpoint on the borders of France, Piedmont and Savoy, Saorge is a typical *village empilé* (stacked village), where slate-roofed houses rise in tiers high above the river Roya. The backdrop of summits is impressive, as is the nearby **Monastère de Saorge**, set amid a wide expanse of terraced gardens. Founded by Franciscan monks in 1633, the monastery is now a cultural centre for writers.

Musée des Merveilles

🕅🏠 🚪Ave du 16 Sept 1947, Tende 🕙10am–5pm Wed–Mon (mid-Jun–mid-Sep: to 6pm) 🔗museedesmerveilles.com

Monastère de Saorge

🕅🕅🏠 🚪Off Derrière le Couvent 🕙10am–12:30pm & 2:30pm–5:30pm daily (Jun–Sep: to 6:30pm) 🚫Nov–Jan 🔗monastere-saorge.fr

Did You Know?

Bearded vultures live almost entirely on bones, which they smash by dropping them in flight.

6 〔⑆〕〔⑊〕〔🍴〕〔🖥〕〔🛍〕

VILLA EPHRUSSI DE ROTHSCHILD

🅰G4 🏠1 ave Ephrussi de Rothschild, St-Jean-Cap-Ferrat 🕐Feb-Jun & Sep-Oct: 10am-6pm daily; Jul-Aug: 10am-7pm daily; Nov-Jan: 2-6pm Mon-Fri (from 10am Sat, Sun & school hols) 🌐villa-ephrussi.com

Béatrice Ephrussi de Rothschild (1864–1934) could have led a life of indolent luxury, but her passions for travel and fine art led to the creation of the most perfect "dream villa" of the Riviera.

Despite interest shown by King Léopold II of Belgium for the land, Béatrice succeeded in purchasing it and later supervised every aspect of the villa's creation. It was completed in 1912 and, although she never used it as a primary residence, Béatrice hosted garden parties and soirees here until 1934. The villa remains a monument to Béatrice's spirit and vision. Its lavish Neo-Classical façade conceals an opulent interior filled with exquisite antique furniture and art, and a covered courtyard hung with magnificent tapestries.

↑ Exterior of the Villa Ephrussi de Rothschild, set in sumptuous gardens

One of the villa's rooms is devoted to a fine collection of working drawings and sketches by Jean-Honoré Fragonard (1732–1806).

Covered Patio

Béatrice's 18th-century writing desk is the star attraction of her Boudoir.

← Opulent decorations in the State Room

BÉATRICE EPHRUSSI DE ROTHSCHILD

Béatrice was born into one of the richest banking dynasties of the 19th century. Aged 19, she married Maurice Ephrussi, a Russian-French banker. Her fortune enabled her to build this opulent villa. She and Maurice filled it with art and antiques, and Béatrice created her own menagerie in the gardens, stocking it with exotic birds and animals.

The lavish State Room features wooden ornamentation from the Crillon in Paris, Savonnerie carpets, and chairs upholstered in 18th-century Savonnerie tapestries.

EXPERIENCE MORE

⑦
St-Jean-Cap-Ferrat

🅰F3 🚉Nice 🚌Beaulieu-sur-Mer 🚌St-Jean-Cap-Ferrat 🛈5 ave Denis Séméria; www.saintjean capferrat-tourisme.fr

The Cap-Ferrat peninsula is a playground for the rich, with exclusive villas, luxury gardens and fabulous yachts in the St-Jean-Cap-Ferrat marina.

King Léopold II of Belgium started a trend for building in the area in the 19th century, when he set his Les Cèdres estate on the west side of the cape, overlooking Villefranche. Further attractive mansions were built nearby for European royalty, industrialists and celebrities. Residents have included the Duke and Duchess of Windsor, British playwright and novelist W Somerset Maugham and singer Edith Piaf. Hedges and gates protect these villas, but one of the finest, the Villa Ephrussi de Rothschild, is open to the public.

There is a superb view from the little garden of the 1837 lighthouse at the end of the cape. A pretty walk leads around the Pointe de St-Hospice, east of the port at St-Jean-Cap-Ferrat, a former fishing village with old houses fronting the harbour.

For a fee, you can enjoy one of the town's two private beaches: **Plage de Passable** or **Plage de Paloma**. Both offer sun loungers, watersports and boat excursions.

Plage de Passable
⊗⊗ 🅰Chemin de Passable 📞04 93 76 06 17 ⏰Easter-Sep: daily

Plage de Paloma
⊗⊗ 🅰1 route de Saint Hospice ⏰Easter-Sep: daily 🅦paloma-beach.com

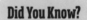

Did You Know?

Europe's first avocados are said to have been grown in St-Jean-Cap-Ferrat.

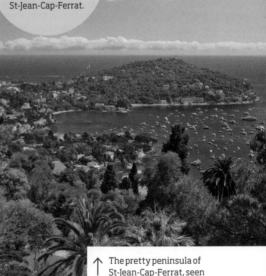

↑ The pretty peninsula of St-Jean-Cap-Ferrat, seen from Villefranche-sur-Mer

The village of Gourdon, perched on a cliff edge above the Gorges du Loup

wooded slopes on its way to the sea, the Loup has carved deep cauldrons in the rock, such as the Saut du Loup. Foaming waterfalls, including the 40-m (130-ft) Cascade de Courmes and Cascades des Demoiselles, plunge from steep cliffs. In places, river spray, rich in lime carbonate dissolved from the surrounding rock, has partly petrified trees and shrubs close to the waterside. For fans of wild river swimming, deep blue pools lie between the Cascade de Courmes and the tiny hamlet of Pont du Loup, at the mouth of the Gorges.

10

Gorges du Cians

⚑F3 🚉Nice 🚌Nice, Touët-sur-Var, Valberg 🛈Pl Charles Ginésy, Valberg; www.valberg.com

Among the finest natural sights in the region, these gorges are a startling combination of deep red slate and vivid mountain greenery. They follow the course of the river Cians, which drops 1,600 m (5,250 ft) in 25 km (15 miles) from Beuil to Touët-sur-Var. At Touët, through a grille in the floor of the church nave, you can see the torrent below.

As you approach from the lower gorges, olives give way to scrubland. At Pra d'Astier, the gorges become steep and narrow: in some places, the rock walls block out the sky.

At the upper end of the gorges, overlooking the Vallée du Cians, is the 1,430-m (4,770-ft) eyrie of Beuil. It was

8

Gourdon

⚑F4 🛈1 place Victoria; www.gourdon06.fr

Built on a hilltop, surrounded by ramparts, Gourdon is a typical *village perché* (perched village), its shops filled with regional produce, perfume and local art. From the square at its precipitous edge, there is a spectacular view of the Loup valley and the sea, with Antibes and Cap Roux in the distance.

There are good views, too, from the gardens of the **Château de Gourdon**, built on the foundations of a Saracen fortress in the 12th century by the seigneurs du Bar, overlords of Gourdon. The terrace gardens – the Jardin à l'Italienne, the Jardin de Rocaille (or Provençal Gardens) and the Jardin de l'Apothicaire – were

laid out by André Le Nôtre when the château was restored in the 17th century. Although the château is privately owned and not open to the public, visitors can take a guided tour of the gardens in groups during the summer months.

Château de Gourdon

🕐⊘ 🚗Off rte de Caussols 🕐May–Aug: by reservation for groups; times vary, check website 🌐chateau-gourdon.com

9

Gorges du Loup

⚑F4

The Gorges du Loup are the most accessible of the dramatic limestone gorges between the hinterland of the Riviera and the coast. Tumbling between thickly

 → Pretty arched doorway in the medieval hilltop town of Mougins

first fortified by the counts of Beuil, members of the aristocratic Grimaldi family (p72). They lived here for two centuries before a conflict with the Duke of Savoy proved fatal to Annibal Grimaldi, the last count of Beuil, who was executed in 1621. The castle was demolished and its stones were used later in the village as window frames and cornerstones.

Mougins

 F5 39 place des Patriotes; www.mougins-tourisme.com

This old hilltop town, huddled inside the remains of its 15th-century ramparts and fortified Saracen Gate, is one of the finest in the region. Mougins is a smart address: royalty and film stars have resided here, while Picasso spent his final years living with his wife in a house opposite the Chapelle de Notre-Dame-de-Vie until his death in 1973. This priory house, sitting at the end of an alley of cypresses, is now privately owned and closed to the public.

Mougins is also one of the top places to eat in Provence. Among its many high-class restaurants is the stylish gastronomic La Place de Mougins, located right on the main square and home of creative chef Denis Fétisson since 2010.

Opened in 2021 in an elegantly restored former presbytery, the **Centre de la Photographie de Mougins** is dedicated to contemporary photography, with a particular focus on female and non-European photographers.

The eclectic collection at the **Musée d'Art Classique de Mougins** includes Roman, Greek and Egyptian art, alongside pieces by Picasso, Cézanne, Andy Warhol and Damien Hirst. There are also displays of jewellery and Greek war helmets and armour.

Centre de la Photographie de Mougins

 43 rue de l'Église Apr–Oct: 10am–7pm Wed–Mon (to 9pm Thu); Nov–Mar: 1–6pm Wed–Sun (to 9pm Thu) Public hols centrephotographiemougins.com

Musée d'Art Classique de Mougins

 32 rue Commandeur Daily 25 Dec mouginsmusee.com

EAT

Resto des Arts
This friendly bistro serves unpretentious Provençal dishes, especially grilled meats and stews, in an arty setting.

 F5 20 rue du Maréchal Foch, Mougins 04 93 75 60 03 Sun & Mon

€€€

Le Rendez-Vous de Mougins
Expect a very Provençal menu, including frogs' legs, snails, fish soup and grilled sardines.

 F5 Place du Commandant Lamy, Mougins rendezvousdemougins.com

€€€

Early distillation methods at the Musée International de la Parfumerie

12
Grasse

 F4 **🚉** **ℹ️ Place de la Buanderie; www.paysde grassetourisme.fr**

Once known for its leather tanning industry, Grasse became a perfume centre in the 16th century. Three major perfume houses are still here. Today, perfume is mainly made from imported flowers, but each year, Grasse holds a jasmine festival (*p53*). The best place to discover the history of perfume is the **Musée International de la Parfumerie**, which has a garden of fragrant plants. It also displays *bergamotes*, decorated scented *papier-mâché* boxes.

Did You Know?

It takes 1 tonne of jasmine flowers to distil 1 litre (2 pts) of jasmine essence.

Artist Jean-Honoré Fragonard (1732–1806) was born in Grasse and the walls of the **Villa-Musée Fragonard** are covered with his murals. The artist's *Washing of the Feet* hangs in the 12th-century Cathédrale Notre-Dame-du-Puy, in the old town. The cathedral also houses three works by Rubens.

Nearby, an excellent collection of 18th- and 19th-century Provençal costumes and jewellery can be seen at the **Musée Provençal du Costume et du Bijou**.

Musée International de la Parfumerie

⊛⊛🅰 **🏠 2 blvd du Jeu de Ballon** **🕐 10am-5:30pm daily** **🔒 1 Jan, 1 May, 25 Dec** **🌐 museesdegrasse.com**

Villa-Musée Fragonard

⊛⊛🅰 **🏠 23 blvd Fragonard** **📞 04 97 05 50 49** **🕐 1-5:15pm daily only during school hols (May-Sep: to 6:45pm)**

Musée Provençal du Costume et du Bijou

⊛ **🏠 2 rue Jean Ossola** **📞 04 93 36 44 65** **🕐 10am-1pm & 2pm-6:30pm Mon-Sat (Mar-Oct & Dec: also Sun)**

13
Îles de Lérins

 F5 **🚢 From Cannes Vieux Port**

The scent of eucalyptus and pine greets you as you disembark on Île Ste-Marguerite or Île St-Honorat, the tiny sister-islands known as the Îles de Lérins. Although just 15 minutes by boat from the bustle of Cannes, the islands reflect a very different history. Tiny chapels dotted around the islands are testament to their Christian heritage, which stretches back to the 4th century, when the Gallo-Roman abbot Honoratus founded an abbey on Île St-Honorat. Some say that Ste-Marguerite was named after his sister, who set up a nunnery there. The 17th-century Fort Ste-Marguerite served as a prison incarcerating the "Man in the Iron Mask" from 1687 to 1698. On the Île St-Honorat, there are some fine coastal views from the 11th-century Monastère Fortifié. Next to it, the Abbaye de Lérins is known for the high-octane Lérina liqueur made by its monks.

PERFUMES OF PROVENCE

Grasse is surrounded by orange and mimosa groves, and fields filled with jasmine, roses and violets. Their rainbow-coloured blossoms are pressed and blended by parfumiers to create the world's most fabulous fragrances.

Grasse did not always smell so sweet. It was originally known for its leather-tanning industry, and it wasn't until the 16th century that local tanners hit on the idea of using floral essences to mask the rank smell of cured skins. When Henri II's queen, Catherine de Medici (1519–89), acquired a pair of perfumed kid gloves made in Grasse they became Europe's must-have accessory. Local entrepreneurs swiftly turned from tanning to perfume-making and the town's fortune was made. Today, there are around 30 parfumeries in Grasse. Artisan parfumiers called "noses" can tell the difference between thousands of basic scents, and it can take them months or even years of experimentation to develop a new perfume. Most guard their secret formulas closely, but a few perfumeries can be visited.

TOP 3 PROVENCE PERFUMERIES

Galimard
🅰 C1 🏠 73 rte de Cannes
🆆 galimard.com
Jean de Galimard, aristocratic parfumier to King Louis X, founded this venerable scent-maker (France's oldest) in Grasse in 1747.

Fragonard
🅰 C1 🏠 20 blvd Fragonard
🆆 fragonard.com
Grasse's most famous perfume house is named in honour of Grasse-born painter Jean-Honoré Fragonard (1732–1806).

Molinard
🅰 C1 🏠 60 blvd Victor Hugo
🆆 molinard.com
Founded in 1849, Maison Molinard achieved fame for its innovative scents and perfume flasks. Visitors are offered the chance to create their own scents.

↑ Grasse perfumes, the product of months of careful blending and experimentation

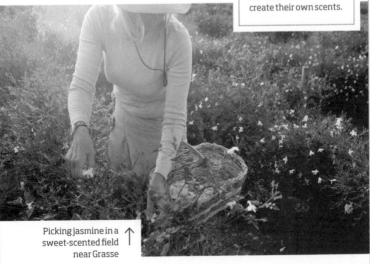

Picking jasmine in a ↑
sweet-scented field
near Grasse

Grotte de St-Cézaire-sur-Siagne

⦿F4 **⌂**1481 rte des Grottes **⦿**Feb–mid-Nov: daily **🌐**grotte-saint cezaire.com

Dramatic stalactites and stalagmites festoon the ceilings and floors of these enchanted caverns, which are tinged a rich rusty red from iron-fortified water that seeps through the living rock. Rock formations have formed shapes reminiscent of flowers, animals and toadstools, and some stalactites chime musically when tapped.

The chambers are connected by a labyrinth of narrow passages that have been given fanciful names: the Fairies' Alcove, the Great Hall, Hall of Draperies and the Organ Chamber (named after its stone tubes, which resemble the pipes of a huge organ). One passage opens rather alarmingly onto the edge of a 40-m (130-ft) abyss.

Above ground, a network of walking trails winds through the picturesque woodlands that surround the grotto.

Juan-les-Pins

⦿F5 **🚆🚌** **ℹ**Palais des Congrès, 60 chemin des Sables; www.antibes juanlespins.com

To the east of Cannes is the hammerhead peninsula of Cap d'Antibes, a promontory of pines and coves where millionaires' mansions can be found. Just next door is one of the finest beaches in the area tucked in the west side of the cape in Golfe-Juan, where Napoleon came ashore from Elba in 1815. This is a 20th-century resort, promoted by American railroad heir Frank Jay Gould, who attracted high society in the 1920s and 1930s when writers F Scott Fitzgerald

and Ernest Hemingway stayed here. Today, in high season, it draws a young and lively crowd. The area at the junctions of boulevards Baudoin and Wilson is filled with bars, while action centres around the Casino Partouche, the Palais des Congrès, and Pinède Gould pine grove, which gives shelter to the international Jazz à Juan festival in July.

Antibes

⦿F5 **🚆🚌🚍** **ℹ**42 ave Robert Soleau; www. antibesjuanlespins.com

Originally the ancient Greek trading post of Antipolis, Antibes became heavily fortified over the centuries, notably by Vauban in the 17th century, who built the main port and Fort Carré, where Napoleon was allegedly temporarily imprisoned.

The old town has a picturesque market-place in cours Masséna. The town's high points include the 12th-century towers of the church and Grimaldi castle on the site of Antipolis. The Cathédrale Notre-Dame, which took over the town's watchtower as a belfry, has a wooden crucifix from 1447, a 16th-century Christ and a fine Louis Bréa altarpiece depicting the Virgin Mary. The Château Grimaldi

nearby houses the **Musée Picasso**, which displays over 50 drawings, paintings and ceramics created by the artist when he used the space as a studio during 1946. The exceptional modern art collection housed here includes works painted by Nicolas de Staël in the last two years of his life, as well as pieces by

DRINK

Helios Plage

A little slice of Bali on the Riviera, this fantastic beach club offers luscious cocktails at tables set on immaculate, groomed white sand.

⦿F5 **⌂**Promenade du Soleil, Juan-les-Pins **🌐**hotelhelios.fr

Le Ruban Bleu

Bask in the shade of palms and parasols at this popular beach club during the day, then sip cocktails at romantic candle-lit tables after sunset.

⦿F5 **⌂**Promenade du Soleil, Juan-les-Pins **🌐**ruban-bleu.com

← Antibes' ancient fortified walls, with views across the Mediterranean

Ernst, Modigliani, Léger and Miró. There are also sculptures on the terrace outside.

Further south, the **Musée d'Archéologie** in the fortified Bastion St-André houses Greek and Etruscan finds, including a 3rd-century BC inscription to the spirit of Septentrion, a boy who danced at the Antipolis theatre.

Marineland leisure park, north of Antibes, includes a shark-filled aquarium and a range of marine animals such as polar bears and whales.

Musée Picasso

🎨🏛️📷 🏠Château Grimaldi, Place Mariejol ☎04 92 90 54 28 🕐Tue–Sun 🚫1 May, 1 Nov

Musée d'Archéologie

🎨🏛️ 🏠Bastion St-André ☎04 93 95 85 98 🕐Feb–Oct: Tue–Sun; Nov–Jan: Tue–Sat 🚫1 May, 1 Nov

Marineland

🎨🏛️📷🏛️ 🏠306 ave Mozart 🕐Feb–Dec: daily 🌐marineland.fr

—————

⓱
Vallauris

🅰F5 🚍 🛈4 ave George Clemenceau & Golfe-Juan Vieux Port; www.vallauris-golfe-juan.fr

In summer, the wares of potters spill on to the avenues of this pottery capital. Picasso revitalized the town's ceramics industry, the history of which is traced in the **Musée de la Céramique**, which houses

ceramics that date from the end of the 19th century to the present day.

In a square just across from the museum, on rue Clément Bel, is Picasso's famous sculpture *L'Homme au Mouton* (1943). His *La Guerre et la Paix* (1952), a striking work of 18 painted wooden panels, is installed around the curved walls and ceiling in the **Musée National Pablo Picasso**, housed in the Romanesque chapel of the Château de Vallauris.

Musée de la Céramique

🎨 🏠Place de la Libération ☎04 93 64 71 83 🕐Wed–Mon (Jul–Aug: daily) 🚫1 Jan, 1 May, 1 & 11 Nov, 25 Dec

Musée National Pablo Picasso

🎨📷 🏠Place de la Libération ☎04 93 64 71 83 🕐Wed–Mon 🚫1 Jan, 1 May, 1 & 11 Nov, 25 Dec

---

CAVES OF PROVENCE

Exploring the underground world of Provence is a fascinating experience. The limestone bedrock of Provence is riddled with caves and grottoes carved over millions of years by underground streams.

GLITTERING CRYSTALS

Some caves, like the Grottes de St-Cézaire-sur-Siagne, are filled with glittering crystals reflected in mirror-calm pools. These are created by the slow drip of mineral-rich water seeping through the ancient rock and drying in elaborate formations.

FOSSILS, BONES AND PAINTINGS

Other Provençal caves reveal signs of humanity's deep past. In the Grotte de l'Observatoire in Monaco *(p72)*, palaeontologists have found fragments of bone tools used by our ancient ancestors around 1,000,000 years ago. Caves in the Gorges du Verdon were used by Neanderthals around 70,000 years ago. From fossil evidence, we also know the same caves were used by giant cave bears, though probably not at the same time! Other caverns, like the Grotte Chauvet, show the remains of cave paintings by the first modern humans around 30,000 years ago.

↑ Alcove filled with crystals in the Grottes de St-Cézaire-sur-Siagne

18

Biot

❹F4 🚌 **ℹ️ 4 Chemin Neuf; www.biot-tourisme.com**

The picturesque village of Biot, which has various themed walks (available at the tourist office), was the main pottery town in the region until Pablo Picasso revived the industry in Vallauris after World War II. Today, Biot is renowned for its bubble-flecked glassware. There are eight glassworks, including **La Verrerie de Biot**, where visitors can marvel at master craftsmen at work.

Biot was once the domain of the Knights Templar, and some fortifications remain, such as the Porte des Migraniers (Gate of Pomegranate Trees), a 1566 stone archway. The church has two fine 16th-century works: *L'Ecce Homo*, attributed to Canavesio, and *La Vierge au Rosaire*, attributed to Louis Bréa.

The **Musée National Fernand Léger** contains many of the artist's vibrant works.

CREATION OF BIOT GLASSWARE

Biot is the capital of glassblowing on the coast. Local soils provide sand for glassmaking, and typical Biot glass is sturdy, with tiny air bubbles (known as *verre bullé*). The opening of Léger's museum led to an increased interest in all local crafts, and to the arrival of the Verrerie de Biot workshop in 1956. This revived old methods of making oil lamps, carafes and narrow-spouted *porrons*, from which a jet of liquid can be poured straight into the mouth.

La Verrerie de Biot

⊕⊕⊕⊕ ❹5 chemin des Combes 🕙10am-1pm & 2-6pm Mon-Sat, 10:30am-1:30pm & 2:30-6pm Sun 🚫1 & 15-27 Jan, 25 Dec 🌐verreriebiot.com

Musée National Fernand Léger

⊕⊕⊕⊕ ❹316 chemin du Val-de-Pôme 🕙10am-5pm Wed-Mon 🚫1 Jan, 1 May, 25 Dec 🌐musees-nationaux-alpesmaritimes.fr/fleger

19

Villeneuve-Loubet

❹F4 🚌 **ℹ️ 16 ave de la Mer; www.villeneuve-tourisme.com**

This old village is dominated by a restored medieval castle built by Romée de Villeneuve. There is also a large church with a square bell tower amid steeply sloping streets leading down to the new town.

It is also where the celebrated chef, Auguste Escoffier (1846–1935), was born. The man who invented the *bombe Néro* and *pêche Melba* was *chef de cuisine* at the Grand Hotel, Monte-Carlo, before he was persuaded to become head chef at the Savoy in London. The **Musée Escoffier de l'Art Culinaire**, in the house of his birth, contains many showpieces in almond paste and icing sugar, and over 1,800 menus dating back to 1820. Each summer, the town celebrates Escoffier with a gastronomic festival.

Musée Escoffier de l'Art Culinaire

⊕⊕ ❹3 rue Auguste Escoffier 🕙Daily 🚫1 May, Nov-Dec, public hols 🌐fondation-escoffier.org

←

Cobbled medieval street with shutters and lanterns in the charming village of Biot

90

The town of Vence, set against the dramatic backdrop of the Alps

20
Vence

F4 ◼ 🛈 8 place du Grand-Jardin; www.vencetourisme.fr

Set on a rocky ridge, Vence is a delightful old cathedral town with a busy central market. Its natural beauty has long attracted artists and writers, including the English novelist and poet D H Lawrence, who died here in 1930.

The old town is entered by the Porte du Peyra (1441), beside the place du Frêne, named after a giant ash tree planted to commemorate the visits of King François I and Pope Paul III. The 16th-century castle of the lords of Villeneuve, seigneurs of Vence, houses the **Musée de Vence – Fondation Émile Hugues**, which displays contemporary art.

The cathedral, one of the smallest in France, stands by the site of the forum of the Roman city of Vintium. Vence was a bishopric from the 4th to the 19th centuries. Its notable prelates included Saint Véran (d AD 492), and Bishop Godeau (1605–72). The 51 oak and pear choir stalls are carved with satirical figures. Marc Chagall designed the mosaic of *Moses in the Bulrushes* in the chapel (1979).

Perhaps the star attraction of Vence is the **Chapelle du Rosaire**, decorated by Henri Matisse (p67) in 1947–51. After undergoing surgery for cancer, the artist was nursed back to health by a Dominican nun, Monique Bourgeois, who later entered a convent in Vence. Matisse bought a house in Vence in 1943 and, to thank Monique for her help, he agreed to help with the design and decoration of a new chapel being built by her convent. The chapel's bright blue roof, stained-glass windows and powerfully simple paintings were all conceived by the artist.

Musée de Vence – Fondation Émile Hugues

🏛 ⊘ 🏠 2 place du Frêne 📞 04 93 24 24 23 🕐 Tue–Sun 🚫 1 Jan, 1 May, mid-Dec–late Jan

Chapelle du Rosaire

⊘ 🏠 466 ave Henri Matisse 🕐 Tue & Thu–Fri, Mon & Wed pm only 🚫 Mid-Nov–mid-Dec, public hols 🌐 chapellematisse.com

EAT

Les Terraillers
Provençal wines accompany lobster bisque, truffles and foie gras at this fine-dining restaurant.

F4 🏠 11 Chemin Neuf, Biot 🌐 lesterraillers.fr

€€€

La Litote
Inventive cooking in a charming setting with tables under lime trees.

F4 🏠 5 rue de l'Évêché, Vence 🚫 Wed & Thu 🌐 lalitote-vence.com

€€€

L'Ambroisie
Chef Bruno Seillery serves refined Provençal cuisine cooked with seasonal produce in this delightfully updated 17th-century chapel.

F4 🏠 37 ave Alphonse Toreille 🚫 Mon lunch, Tue–Wed 🌐 ambroisie-vence.com

€€€

21

Cagnes-sur-Mer

⚠F4 🚆🚌 **ℹ6 blvd Maréchal Juin; www. cagnes-tourisme.com**

Picturesquely perched on its hilltop overlooking the sea, Haut-de-Cagnes is the most appealing part of Cagnes-sur-Mer. It's a pleasing jumble of fine Renaissance houses, narrow lanes, steps and vaulted passages. Members of the Grimaldi royal family are entombed in the church of St-Pierre, and the fortress built by Rainier in 1309 still towers over the town. In 1620, Jean-Henri Grimaldi transformed the fortress into a handsome palace. It survived the ravages of the Revolution and occupation in 1815 by Piedmontese troops, who used its spectacular painted ceiling for target practice.

Within the dramatic battlements of the fortress is the **Château-Musée Grimaldi**, an eclectic complex of museums where two levels

of marble-columned galleries rise around a Renaissance courtyard filled with lush greenery and dappled sunlight.

On the ground floor, the Musée de l'Olivier is devoted to the traditions of olive cultivation that are so central to Provençal history and culture. The Donation Suzy Solidor, on the first floor, includes portraits of the famed 1930s chanteuse by Jean Cocteau and Kisling, along with around 40 other works gifted to the museum by Solidor. A selection of works from the museum's permanent collection of modern Mediterranean art are on the first and second floors.

Below Haut-de-Cagnes, the former fishing village of Cros-de-Cagnes is the town's seaside annexe, with a small beach. There is a market here every Tuesday and Thursday morning, while Cagnes-Ville is the commercial centre.

East of the centre is Les Collettes, where artist Pierre-Auguste Renoir (1841–1919) built a home in 1907, hoping that the climate would relieve his rheumatism. He stayed here for the rest of his life, and his home is now the

Musée Renoir, where visitors can see 14 of his paintings, as well as works by his friends Bonnard and Dufy. Renoir's beloved olive groves are the setting for the bronze *Venus Victrix* (1915–16).

Château-Musée Grimaldi

♿🕑 🏛Place du Château 🚌44 from Haut-de-Cagnes central bus station 🕐Wed-Mon 🌐cagnes-sur-mer.fr/culture/chateau-musee-grimaldi

Musée Renoir

♿🕑 🏛19 Chemin des Collettes 🚌49 from Cagnes-sur-Mer railway station 🕐Wed-Mon 🌐cagnes-sur-mer.fr/culture/musee-renoir

22

Villefranche-sur-Mer

⚠G4 🚆🚌 **ℹJardin François Binon; www.tourisme-villefranche-sur-mer.com**

This unspoiled town overlooks a beautiful natural harbour, deep enough to be a naval port. The buildings here date back to the 17th century,

Did You Know?

The Rolling Stones recorded their album *Exile on Main Street* in a villa in Villefranche-sur-Mer.

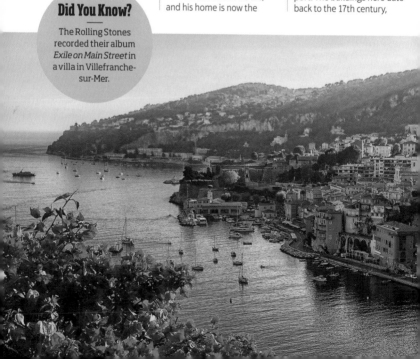

though they now include the oceanographic observatory, the university and a national centre of marine research. The lively waterfront is lined with bars and cafés and the town has a food market every Wednesday and Saturday and a flea market on Sunday.

Chapelle St-Pierre, set on the quay, was once used for storing fishing nets. It was renovated in 1957, when Jean Cocteau added lavish frescoes showing scenes from the life of St Peter, intended as a tribute to the local fishermen. Steep lanes climb up from the quay, turning into tunnels beneath the tightly packed buildings. The vaulted rue Obscure has provided shelter from attack as recently as World War II. The Baroque Église St-Michel contains a 16th-century carving of St Roch and his dog as well as a 1790 organ.

Within the grounds of the 16th-century Citadelle St-Elme are the chapel, open-air theatre and museums.

Chapelle St-Pierre
 🏠 4 quai de l'Amiral Courbet 📞 04 93 76 90 70 🕐 Wed–Mon 🚫 Mid-Nov–mid-Dec, 25 Dec

↑ Interior of the Villa Kérylos in Beaulieu-sur-Mer

23
Beaulieu-sur-Mer

🅰F4 🚉🚌 ℹ Pl Clémenceau; www.beaulieusurmer.fr

Hemmed in and protected by a rock face, this is one of the Riviera's warmest resorts in winter, with two beaches: the Baie des Fourmis and, by the port, Petite Afrique. The casino, formal gardens and belle époque Rotunda, now a conference centre and museum, add to Beaulieu's old-fashioned air. Among its hotels is La Réserve, founded by James Gordon Bennett Jr, the owner of the *New York Herald* from 1866 until his death in 1918.

Beaulieu-sur-Mer is also home to the **Villa Kérylos**. Built by archaeologist Théodore Reinach to resemble an ancient Greek villa, the building took inspiration from Delos, Pompeii, Rome and Egypt, and took over six years to complete. Authentic techniques and precious materials were used to create lavish mosaics, frescoes and inlaid furniture. There are also numerous original Greek ornaments, and an antique sculpture gallery.

←

The pretty town of Villefranche-sur-Mer, set around a natural harbour

Villa Kérylos
🖐 🏠 Impasse Gustave Eiffel 🕐 Daily 🌐 villa kerylos.fr

24
Èze

🅰G4 🚉🚌 ℹ Place du Général de Gaulle; www. eze-tourisme.com

Èze, a dramatic eagle's nest *village perché*, is a cluster of ancient buildings on a high peak. Its warm climate allows tropical plants such as date palms, banana plants, orange and lemon trees to grow here. The **Jardin Exotique**, built around the ruins of a 14th-century castle, offers stunning views as far as Corsica.

Flower-bedecked, car-free narrow streets, shady squares and stone archways lead to an 18th-century church, which contains a bust of Christ made from olive wood that survived the terrible fires that raged close by in 1986.

Jardin Exotique
 🏠 Rue du Château 🕐 Daily 🚫 Christmas week 🌐 jardinexotique-eze.fr

25 Peillon

🅰G4 ℹ️ 4 carriera Centrale;
www.tourismepaca.fr

At a height of 373 m (1,225 ft), this pretty *village perché* is said by locals to mark the extremity of the inhabited world. Its streets are stepped and narrow, with houses that have scarcely changed since the Middle Ages. There is an attractive cobbled square with fine views, and the 18th-century parish church has an unusual octagonal lantern. But the most impressive sights of all are Giovanni Canavesio's frescoes in the Chapelle des Pénitents Blancs.

Peillon is ideally placed for pretty woodland walks, which will lead visitors to both Peille and La Turbie.

26 Trophée d'Auguste à La Turbie

🅰G4 🚌 ℹ️ 2 Place Detras;
www.ville-la-turbie.fr

There's an unforgettable view of Monaco and the coast from 480 m (1,575 ft) below the terraces of the grandiose Trophée d'Auguste, which crowns the hilltop village of La Turbie. The Romans built this huge triumphal rotonda, which can be seen from miles around, from white local stone in around 6 BC to mark the division between Italy and newly conquered Gaul.

Originally the Trophée stood on a square podium on which stood a circular colonnade topped by a stepped cone. Inscriptions on its base bear the names

> **The Romans built this huge triumphal rotonda, which can be seen from miles around, from white local stone in around 6 BC.**

of the 44 Ligurian tribes subjugated by the Emperor Augustus in 13 BC, and the original colonnade included niches that once housed statues of each of Augustus's victorious generals.

Stairs once led to every part of the structure, which was topped by a 6-m (20-ft) statue of the Emperor. When the Romans left, the original 50-m (164-ft) monument was gradually dismantled. Early Christian leaders like the 4th-century missionary St Honorat despised it as an object of pagan worship, and its masonry was pillaged to be reused in later buildings. What remained served as a fortress, and it was further demolished in the 17th century on the orders of Louis XIV, who feared it would fall to the invading Savoyards during their invasion of Provence in 1705.

Today, the **Musée du Trophée d'Auguste** documents the history of the building, with fragments of statuary, inscriptions, drawings, and a scale model that shows how it looked in its imperial heyday.

Huddled beneath this imposing relic, La Turbie is an appealing stop on a stretch of the Grande Corniche that crosses ravines and tunnels through mountains. Two medieval gateways lead to a village centre where narrow streets are splashed with purple bougainvillea.

The 18th-century Nice Baroque church Église St-Michel was built with stones plundered from the Trophée. Inside, there is an altar of multi-coloured marble and a 17th-century onyx and agate table, which was used for

↓ Remains of the imposing Trophée d'Auguste in La Turbie

Houses clustered together on the hillside in medieval Peille

communion. The church also contains two paintings by Jean-Baptiste van Loo, a portrait of St Mark attributed to Paolo Veronese, and a Pietà from the Bréa School.

Musée du Trophée d'Auguste

 Ave Albert 1er Tue–Sun trophee-auguste.fr

㉗ Peille

G4 **i** 15 rue Centrale; www.peille.fr

Peille is a charming medieval village with a view from its war memorial across the Peillon Valley and as far as the Baie des Anges. Behind the village looms the massive Pic de Baudon, which rises to a height of 1,264 m (4,160 ft).

The town is filled with cobbled alleyways and covered passages. At the end of place André Laugier, beyond a Gothic fountain, two arches beneath a house rest on a Romanesque pillar.

The Counts of Provence were lords of the castle, and the 12th-century church of Ste-Marie has a picture of Peille in the Middle Ages. There is also a fine 16th-century altarpiece by Honoré Bertone. The Hôtel de Ville is in the domed 18th-century former Chapelle St-Sébastien, and there is a museum in rue de la Turbie.

㉘ Lucéram

G4 **i** Maison de Pays, place Adrien Barralis; www.luceram.fr

In the middle of this pretty, Italianate village is the 15th-century Église Ste-Marguerite. The church contains art by Nice's Primitive masters, notably Louis Bréa, the artist of the 10-panelled altarpiece, who made Lucéram a centre for religious painting. Treasures include a silver statue of the Tarascon dragon and Ste Marguerite (p146). Villagers decorate the streets with pine branches in December, and the church is the setting for a Christmas service, where shepherds, accompanied by flutes and tambourines, bring lambs and fruit as offerings.

EAT

Café de la Fontaine

This bistro, run by the owners of the acclaimed Hostellerie Jérôme, serves Provençal dishes such as rabbit with olives.

G4 4 ave du Général de Gaulle, La Turbie hostellerie-jerome.com

€€€

Auberge de la Madone

Elegant Niçois cooking, made using all local ingredients (including produce from the restaurant garden), is served alfresco here.

G4 3 place Auguste Arnulf, Peillon 04 93 79 91 17

€€€

Boccafina

An informal village bar-restaurant with a quirky grotto setting, Boccafina offers salads, pizzas and some regional specialities.

G4 4 place Adrien Barralis, Lucéram 04 93 79 51 54

€€€

29
Roquebrune-Cap-Martin

⚑ G4 🚗🚆 🛈 218 ave Aristide Briand; www.rcm-tourisme.com

Roquebrune is said to have the earliest feudal château in France, the sole example of the Carolingian style. **Château Grimaldi de Roquebrune** was built in the 10th century by Conrad I, Count of Ventimiglia, to ward off Saracen attack, and was remodelled by the Grimaldis *(p72)*. Englishman Sir William Ingram bought the château in 1911 and added a mock medieval *tour anglaise*.

In the early 1900s, Cap Martin was Provence's smartest resort, attracting the era's glitterati. Impératrice Eugénie, wife of Napoléon III, wintered here. In the 20th century, Coco Chanel, Winston Churchill, and Irish poet W B Yeats frequently visited, while the famous architect Le Corbusier tragically drowned off the cape in 1965.

Some important prehistoric remains have been found in caves such as the Grotte du Vallonnet. On the Menton road, is the *olivier millénaire*, an olive tree thought to be at least 1,000 years old.

Every August since 1467, in gratitude for being spared

💬 INSIDER TIP
Bags of style

There are no border formalities between France and Italy, so visiting Ventimiglia's colourful Friday market is easy from Menton. Leather accessories are a good buy, but beware of fake designer brands.

from the plague, Roquebrune's inhabitants have celebrated the Passion with a procession and concert.

Château Grimaldi de Roquebrune

⚐ 🏛 Place William Ingram 📞 04 93 35 07 22 🕐 Mon-Thu (Feb-Oct: daily) 🚫 Public hols

30
Menton

⚑ G4 🚗🚆 🛈 Palais de l'Europe, 8 ave Boyer; www.tourisme-menton.fr

Menton straddles the frontier between France and Italy, with only a road tunnel separating the town from the Italian resort of Ventimiglia. The beaches on Baie du Soleil are pebbly, but you'll find sandier stretches on the Baie de Garavan.

The town's mellow microclimate is perfect for growing citrus fruits. The annual Fête du Citron, held for two weeks every February, features sculptures created from vast heaps of lemons, and are paraded through the streets.

Menton has several fine sub-tropical gardens. Bougainvillea, palms, and other tropical plants flourish in the Jardin Botanique, in the grounds of Villa Val Rahmeh. Above the town is the Jardin des Colombières designed by artist and writer Ferdinand Bac (1859–1952). This private garden has France's oldest carob tree and can be visited in the summer by appointment.

The jetties offer views of the old town, and steps lead to Parvis St-Michel, where summer concerts are held.

← View from the Château Grimaldi de Roquebrune, over a jumble of rooftops

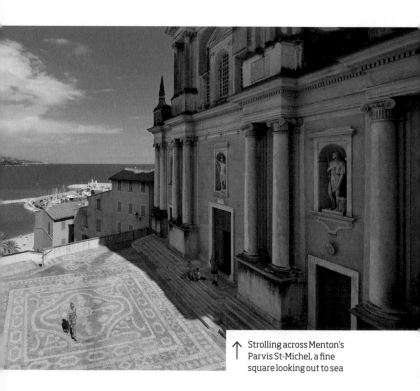

↑ Strolling across Menton's Parvis St-Michel, a fine square looking out to sea

Once the summer residence of the princes of Monaco, **Musée des Beaux-Arts** features 13th- to 18th-century Italian, French and Flemish art, and 20th-century works by Utrillo, Dufy and Graham Sutherland.

Two museums are dedicated to the career of Jean Cocteau, who loved this town: the **Musée Jean Cocteau Le Bastion** in a 17th-century fort, and the **Collection Séverin Wunderman** in a modern annexe that opened in 2021. Between the two museums, the collection spans more than 2,000 works by the artist.

Musée des Beaux-Arts

⊛ 🅰 Palais Carnolès, 3 ave de la Madone 🅲 04 93 35 49 71 🅴 For renovation until further notice

Musée Jean Cocteau Collection Séverin Wunderman

⊛ 🅰 2 quai de Monléon 🅴 For renovation until further notice 🆆 museecocteaumenton.fr

Musée Jean Cocteau Le Bastion

⊛ 🅰 Quai Napoléon III, Bastion du Vieux Port 🅾 Wed-Mon 🅴 Public hols 🆆 museecocteaumenton.fr

> **The town's mellow micro-climate is perfect for growing citrus fruits.**

JEAN COCTEAU

Born near Paris in 1889, Cocteau spent much of his very public life around the Côte d'Azur. A man of powerful intellect and great energy, he became a member of the Académie Française in 1955. Among other talents, Cocteau was a dramatist (*La Machine Infernale*, 1934); the writer of *Les Enfants Terribles* (1929); and a surrealist film director. *Orphée* (1950) was partly shot against the barren landscape at Les Baux-de-Provence (*p148*). He died in 1963, before his museum opened.

VAR AND ÎLES D'HYÈRES

The Var is a region of rolling lands, rocky hills, thick forests and swathes of vineyards. To the north, Provençal villages are thinly scattered by mountain streams, on hilltops and in valleys; to the south, a series of massifs slopes down to the coast, making this stretch of the Côte d'Azur the most varied and delightful shore in France.

The A8 autoroute runs through the centre of the Var, dividing it roughly into two sections. To the south of this artery the influence of the sea is unmistakable. Toulon, the departmental capital, occupies a fine deep-water harbour that is home to the French Mediterranean fleet. Beyond it are the pleasant resorts of Bandol and Sanary, where Jacques Cousteau first put scuba-diving to the test. To the east are the sandy beaches beneath the great slab of the Massif des Maures. The Var's most famous resort, St-Tropez, facing north in the crook of a bay, lies in a glorious landscape of vineyards. Beyond it, just past Fréjus, the first Roman settlement in Gaul, the land turns blood red in the twinkling inlets and coves below the beautiful Corniche de l'Estérel, which heads east towards the Riviera. The more remote areas to the north of the autoroute have always provided a retreat from the bustling activity of the coast. This is where the Cistercians built their austere Abbaye du Thoronet. Today, visitors escape inland from the summer traffic around St-Tropez to the sparsely populated Haut Var, where towns seem to grow from tufa rock.

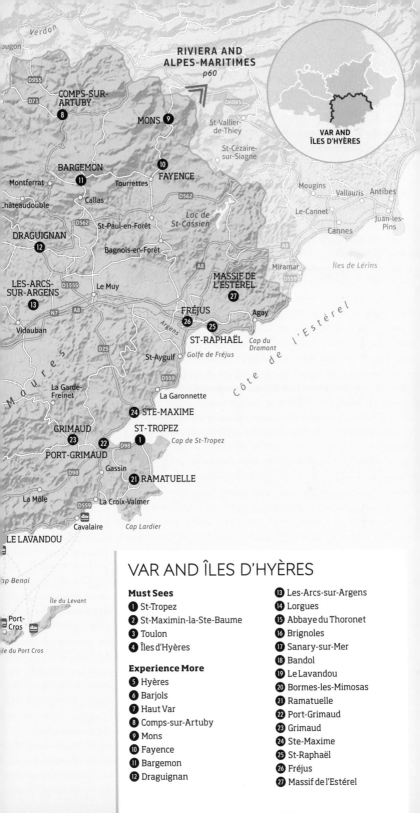

RIVIERA AND
ALPES-MARITIMES
p60

VAR AND
ÎLES D'HYÈRES

VAR AND ÎLES D'HYÈRES

Must Sees

1. St-Tropez
2. St-Maximin-la-Ste-Baume
3. Toulon
4. Îles d'Hyères

Experience More

5. Hyères
6. Barjols
7. Haut Var
8. Comps-sur-Artuby
9. Mons
10. Fayence
11. Bargemon
12. Draguignan
13. Les-Arcs-sur-Argens
14. Lorgues
15. Abbaye du Thoronet
16. Brignoles
17. Sanary-sur-Mer
18. Bandol
19. Le Lavandou
20. Bormes-les-Mimosas
21. Ramatuelle
22. Port-Grimaud
23. Grimaud
24. Ste-Maxime
25. St-Raphaël
26. Fréjus
27. Massif de l'Estérel

↑ Colourful boats docked at the harbour of the coastal town of St-Tropez

1

ST-TROPEZ

🗺E5 **✈Toulon-Hyères, Nice** **🚉St-Raphaël-Fréjus** **⛴from Cannes and Nice** **ℹ8 Quai Jean Jaurès; www. saintropeztourisme.com**

St-Tropez conjures up images of glamorous beach life, celebrity yachts and upmarket shopping, but there's more than frivolity and hedonism here. The ochre-painted walls and terracotta rooftops of the old town evoke a time before tourism. The many great artists who worked here are celebrated in a world-class art museum, while the imposing hilltop citadel is a reminder of a more turbulent past.

①

Musée de l'Annonciade

🏛2 place Georges Grammont **🕐Jan-Mar & Nov-Dec: 10am-5pm Tue-Sun (Apr-Jun & Oct: to 6pm; Jul-Sep: to 7pm daily)** **🔒1-17 May, 15-30 Nov, public hols** **🌐saint-tropez.fr/culture/musee-de-lannonciade**

Painters of the Pointillism and Fauvism movements have pride of place in this gallery, which showcases works by some of the greatest artists of the 20th century. Wealthy art collector Georges Grammont funded the transformation of the 16th-century Chapelle de l'Annonciade by architect Louis Süe in the 1950s. The core of the collection comprises works by Paul Signac, the painter who first popularized St-Tropez when he moved here in 1892, and his Pointilliste colleagues (including Georges Seurat). Seek out paintings by the Les Nabis group, including Pierre Bonnard's *Nu Devant la Cheminée* (1919). Also look out for Signac's *L'Orage* (1895), with its bravura use of swirling brushwork to depict St-Tropez harbour. Matisse, Braque, Dufy and Delauney are among the many other artists whose work is on display.

② Place des Lices

Locals still play pétanque beneath the plane trees on this pretty square as they have done for over a century, watched by spectators seated at the café tables which line each side. The Place des Lices is St-Tropez's social hub, and is at its liveliest on Tuesday and Saturday mornings, when it is transformed into a thronged marketplace where locals shop for fresh produce and visitors browse art and antiques stalls.

③ Église Notre-Dame-de-l'Assomption

🏛 Rue de l'Église 🕐 Times vary, check website 🌐 paroisse-saint-tropez.com

A garishly painted bust of Saint Torpès, the Christian martyr after whom St-Tropez is named, is the pride of this church, built in faux-Baroque style in the late 18th century. According to legend, Torpes was a Roman gladiator and an early convert to Christianity who was beheaded as a heretic on the orders of the Emperor Nero. His headless corpse was put in a boat with a dog and a cockerel, which were expected to devour and desecrate the corpse. Miraculously, it washed up unmolested here in AD 68. The saint's bust is paraded through the streets on 16 May during the traditional *bravades*, an annual religious festival.

④ Musée de la Citadelle

🏛 Montée de la Citadelle 📞 04 94 97 59 43 🕐 10am–5:30pm daily (Apr–Sep: to 6:30pm) 🚫 Public hols

Peacocks patrol the wooded precincts of the sturdy Citadelle de St-Tropez, the early 17th-century fortress that squats on the hilltop east of the harbour. It's worth making your way to its multi-angled ramparts just for the view of the coast. Within, you can discover the maritime history of the area and learn about the lives of some of the port's most famous citizens, such as Pierre-André de Suffren, a leading admiral during France's 18th-century wars with Britain.

ST-TROPEZ'S BEACHES

St-Tropez's famed beaches stretch for 9 km (5.6 miles) in a long, golden crescent along the Baie de Pampelonne, starting 5 km (3 miles) south of St-Tropez. Lined with posh beach clubs and bar restaurants, Pampelonne attracts up to 30,000 visitors a day, but finding a space on its sands can be costly. For a quick dip, you'll find smaller beaches with free access north of the old town centre at Plage de la Glaye and Plage de la Fontanette. Those seeking an all-over tan can find "clothing optional" stretches along Plage de Pampelonne.

A SHORT WALK
ST-TROPEZ

Distance 1 km (half a mile) **Time** 15 minutes

Clustered around the old port and nearby beaches, the centre of St-Tropez, partly rebuilt in its original style after World War II, is full of pretty pastel-coloured old fishermen's houses. In the port itself, traditional fishing boats are still to be seen moored side by side with sleek luxury cruisers. Behind the port-side cafés of the quai Jean Jaurès, the narrow, bustling streets are packed with boutiques and restaurants.

La Fontanette *beach leads to a coastal walk with views over Ste-Maxime.*

The **Ponche Quarter** *is a comparatively quiet and unspoiled area of St-Tropez.*

STA

The **Tour Vieille** *separates the Port de Pêche from La Glaye beach next door.*

Place de la Ponche

LA GLAYE

RUE DE LA PONCHE

Tour du Portalet

PLACE DE L'HÔTEL DE VILLE

↑ The 15th-century Tour du Portalet, part of the city's original defences

QUAI FRÉDÉRIC MISTRAL

RUE SIBILLE

Môle Jean Réveille

QUAI

Did You Know?

St-Tropez first attracted the jet set after Brigitte Bardot filmed *And God Created Woman* here in 1956.

The attractively painted houses and packed cafés lining the **quai Jean Jaurès** *have enticed visitors and inspired artists for over a century.*

Ochre-coloured rooftops of the
Old Town, seen from the Citadelle

*The **Église Notre-Dame-
de-l'Assomption** is
known for its prized bust
of St Torpès, the patron
saint of St-Tropez.*

RUE FONTANETTE

RUE DES PÊCHEURS

REMPARTS

RUE DE L'ORMEAU

RUE DU CLOCHER

L'ÉGLISE

CITADELLE

RUE DE LA

RUE VICTOR LAUGIER

QUAI SUFFREN

0 metres 50

0 yards 50

N

*Statue of
Pierre André
de Suffren*

The narrow streets
of St-Tropez lined with
restaurants and shops

FINISH

ST-MAXIMIN-LA-STE-BAUME

↑ Exterior of the 14th-century apse at Ste-Marie-Madeleine

EXPERIENCE Var and îles d'Hyères

🅰D5 🄰Place de l'Hôtel de Ville 🄲Basilica: 7:30am-7:30pm daily (except during services) 🅆lesamisdelabasilique.fr

Surrounded by hills and vineyards, St-Maximin-la-Ste-Baume is dominated by Provence's finest example of Gothic architecture, the basilica Ste-Marie-Madeleine and its attached former monastery.

According to Provençal tradition, Ste-Marie-Madeleine was built on the site of the tombs of St Mary Magdalene and of St Maximin, the legendary first bishop of Aix. The saints' remains, hidden from the Saracens (*p55*), were rediscovered in 1279. The basilica appears unfinished from the outside (there is no belfry) but within, the sense of balance is stunning. So too are the treasures, notably a 16th-century altarpiece depicting the Passion of Christ, and a renowned 17th-century organ. Mary Magdalene's remains are in a reliquary in the crypt.

The adjoining 13th-century Royal Monastery, so called because the French kings were its priors, was abandoned by Dominican friars in 1957.

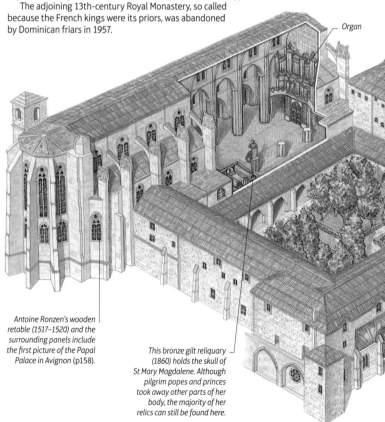

Organ

Antoine Ronzen's wooden retable (1517–1520) and the surrounding panels include the first picture of the Papal Palace in Avignon (p158).

This bronze gilt reliquary (1860) holds the skull of St Mary Magdalene. Although pilgrim popes and princes took away other parts of her body, the majority of her relics can still be found here.

C.1130
△ Ramon Berenguer, Count of Provence, establishes the town of St-Maximin under his governance.

1279
▽ The town becomes a popular pilgrimage site when Charles II, Count of Provence, rediscovers the tombs of St Mary Magdalene and St Maximin.

1295
Charles II founds a cathedral on the site of the tombs, and control of the monastery is granted to the Dominican order.

1316
The cathedral is consecrated, and marble tombs from the Roman era are placed in the newly completed crypt.

1532
▽ Work on the cathedral is abandoned, leaving the building incomplete and lacking a finished frontage or bell towers.

→
Cloisters overlooking the courtyard of the monastery

St-Maximin-la-Ste-Baume's town hall was formerly the pilgrims' hostelry.

Discovered along the Roman Aurelian Way (p125), this 1st-century milestone is now on display at the entrance to the cloisters.

Former refectory

↑ Illustration of Ste-Marie-Madeleine and its attached monastery

↑ The magnificent high altar, set in the apse of Ste-Marie-Madeleine

↑ Toulon's impressive natural harbour and urban sprawl

3

TOULON

🗺D6 ✈Toulon-Hyères 24 km (15 miles) E 🚉Gare SNCF, blvd de Tessé 🚌Gare Routière, blvd de Tessé ⛴Ferries to/from Corsia, Sardinia, Majorca 🛈12 place Louis Blanc; www.toulontourisme.com

Toulon has a rough-edged charm that is quite at odds with the coastal resorts to its east and west and the tranquil villages of the Var hinterland. Sited on a superb natural harbour, it is steeped in maritime history and has for centuries been home to France's Mediterranean fleet. Badly damaged during World War II, and a byword for urban deprivation in following decades, it has transformed itself in the 21st century to become a vibrant, rejuvenated city that remains true to its roots and makes an interesting contrast to the chicer stretches of Provence's coastline. For foodies, it offers a menu that stretches from authentic seafood to imaginative Mediterranean-fusion.

①

Vieille Darse

You'll still see smartly uniformed matelots taking a break from their duties (aboard the frigates of France's Mediterranean fleet) in the cafés and bars along the Vieille Darse, a small sheltered harbour built to protect ships from the elements in 1604–10. For centuries, these quaysides were the beating heart of Toulon, and up until the end of the 19th century, the port employed more than 10,000 dock workers. The traditional fishing boats known as *pointus* still moor here, but these days dockers, fishermen and sailors are usually outnumbered by crowds of strolling visitors who have just disembarked from the giant cruise ships which make Toulon a regular port of call.

②

Musée National de la Marine

🏛Place Monsenergue 🚌7, 23, 40 to Préfecture Maritime 🕙10am-6pm Wed-Mon (Jul-Aug: daily) 🌐musee-marine.fr

Colossal statues of Mars and Bellona, god and goddess of war, flank the grand gateway that leads into Toulon's former royal naval shipyard. Built in the 17th century, the arsenal where France's galleys and galleons were built stretched for more than 240 ha (595 acres) and aimed to make France a major Mediterranean sea power.

Now a museum, the arsenal gatehouse shows exhibits spanning centuries of French maritime history, from early models like that of the 17th-century galley Dauphine to 21st-century nuclear sub-marines, aircraft carriers and other warships. Wooden figure-heads carved by Louis XIV's naval sculptor Pierre Puget 1620–94) and antique naviga-tional instruments provide context to the big ships on display. A special exhibition focuses on the French Navy's darkest hour, the scuttling of the pride of its fleet at Toulon in November 1942.

③

Cathédrale Ste-Marie-de-la-Seds

◨ 55 place de la Cathédrale
◷ 8am-7pm Mon-Sat,
8am-noon & 4-6pm Sun
🔔 For cathedral services
🌐 cathedrale-toulon.fr

Works by Pierre Puget and Jean-Baptiste Van Loo (1684–1745) are among the main attractions of the city's 11th-century cathedral, which is behind a 17th-century Classical façade that belies its early medieval roots. Puget's nephew and disciple Christophe Veyrier (1637–1689) contributed the alabaster reredos in the chapel to the south of the Baroque high altar.

↑ Interior of the 11th-century Cathédrale Ste-Marie-de-la-Seds

④

Musée d'Art de Toulon

◨ 113 blvd Général Leclerc
☎ 04 94 36 81 01 ◷ Noon-6pm Tue-Sun 🔔 Mon, public hols

Founded in the latter half of the 19th century, this museum grew in the 1970s into an outstanding collection of more than 1,000 works by cutting-edge 20th-century artists like Yves Klein, Christo, and other American and European Minimalists, Nouveau-Realists and Conceptualists. It also houses a collection of more than 400 photographs by Henri Cartier-Bresson and other pioneers of photography. The museum reopened in 2021 following a multi-year renovation programme.

💬 INSIDER TIP
Toulon beaches

To find sandy stretches beyond Toulon and enjoy a budget journey across its sheltered bay (the Petit Rade), hop on a water-bus from the ferry terminal at Quai Cronstadt to beaches at Les Sablettes, La Seyne and St Mandrier.

⑤
Musée d'Histoire de Toulon

🏠 10 rue Saint Andrieu
📞 04 94 62 11 07 🚌 15
🕐 2-6pm Mon-Sat

Set in the heart of the old town, this small museum offers a glimpse into multiple aspects of the history of the city and its surrounding region. It houses maps, models, sketches and paintings, as well as busts of famous Toulon residents. The collection also includes works by the prolific sculptor Pierre Puget, who was in charge of decorating Toulon's port and its grand public buildings during the reign of Louis XIV. The library on the first floor has thousands of books.

⑥
Marché du Cours Lafayette

🏠 Cours Lafayette 🚌 15
🕐 7:30am-12:30pm Tue-Sun

Cours Lafayette, next to the Cathédrale Ste-Marie-de-la-Seds, is the venue for this lively market where locals shop for colourful fresh produce and household goods. Alongside stalls selling everyday necessities, visitors will discover vendors of antiques and curios, souvenirs and arts and crafts. The market bustles with life every morning, but is at its busiest and most interesting on Saturdays and Sundays, when it spills over into the neighbouring petit cours, place Paul Comte, place Louis Blanc and rue de Lorgues.

⑦
Rue des Arts

🏠 Rue Pierre Sémard
🌐 ruedesarts.fr

This formerly run-down district in the heart of the old town has been reborn as a chic artists' and artisans' quarter, filled with designer studios and small galleries, showcasing the work of adventurous young local creative talents. Trendy shops and lively café-bars line the area's tree-shaded squares, where an array of street musicians provide a spirited soundtrack.

EAT

Le St Gabriel
Grilled octopus is the signature dish at this bright modern brasserie by the harbour.

🏠 334 ave de la République 📞 04 94 09 32 82

€€€

O Bistro les Artistes
The emphasis here is on clean, sharp flavours and fresh local produce, with a menu that features dishes like salmon carpaccio, steak tartare and foie gras.

🏠 10 rue Dumont d'Urville 🌐 obistrodesartistes.com

€€€

Le Bistrot du Boucan
This vibrant restaurant offers a menu that ranges from favourites like seared duck breast to light dishes such as gravlax with blinis, all beautifully presented.

🏠 223 rue Jean Jaurès 🌐 lebistroduboucan.com

€€€

Carré 2 Vigne
Located close to the opera house, this smart restaurant serves creative modern Mediterranean dishes.

🏠 14 rue de Pomet 🌐 estaurant-toulon.com

€€€

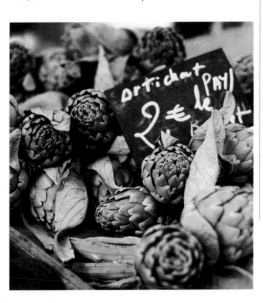

← Artichokes on sale at the Marché du Cours Lafayette

← Café on a narrow street in Toulon's old town

Also at the top of the mountain is the **Mémorial du Débarquement et de la Libération en Provence**, a memorial to the 1944 Allied landings in Toulon. A fascinating multi-media exhibition illustrates the landings by Free French troops and their US allies that began the liberation of Provence.

Mémorial du Débarquement et de la Libération en Provence
⊗ ⌂ Mont Faron
◷ 10am–12:30pm & 1:15–5:15pm Wed–Mon (Apr–Sep: to 7:15pm) ⊗ Public hols, last two weeks in Dec
ⓦ cheminsdememoire. gouv.fr

---

⑧
Mourillon

Toulon's seaside quarter is an attractive jumble of colourful old houses rising from a long stretch of sand and pebbles, around 2 km (1.5 miles) southeast of the city centre. It's a pleasant spot for a day at the beach or a seafood lunch, and also worth the trip for the **Musée des Arts Asiatiques**, dedicated to Asian sacred and decorative art, where visitors will find delicate paintings on silk depicting scenes from the life of the Buddha, bronze gui vases from China and beautiful porcelain used in age-old Japanese tea ceremonies. Many were brought home by French mariners, while almost 500 pieces in jade and metal from China, Japan and India were donated in 1961 by the journalist and collector Hippolyte Fauverge de French.

Musée des Arts Asiatiques
⊗ ⌂ Villa Jules Verne, 169 littoral Frédéric Mistral
☎ 04 94 36 83 13 ⊕ 3
◷ Noon–3pm & 3:30–6pm Tue–Sat

⑨ ⊗ ⊡
Téléphérique du Mont Faron

⌂ Blvd Amiral Vence ⊕ 40
◷ 10am–4:30pm daily (Mar: to 6pm; Apr & Oct: to 6:30pm; May, Jun & Sep: to 7pm; Jul–Aug: to 7:45pm; Nov: to 5:30pm) ⊗ Jan–mid-Feb, Dec ⓦ telepherique-faron.fr

It's worth taking the cable car ride from street level to the summit of Mont Faron, 584 m (1,916 ft) above sea level, just for the stunning view which allows you to appreciate the sheltered natural harbour. There is a restaurant right at the top of the mountain where you can buy a range of refreshments and soak up the view.

↑ Spectacular view of Toulon from Téléphérique du Mont Faron

HARBOUR BOAT TOUR

For an insight into how Toulon became one of the world's greatest naval bases, take a boat tour of the harbour, where grey-painted leviathans like the aircraft carrier Charles de Gaulle, pride of the French Navy, can be seen looming above pleasure craft and fishing boats. One-hour cruises with Bateliers de la Côte d'Azur leave from Quai Cronstadt, next to the ferry terminal (www.bateliersdelacotedazur.com).

4

ÎLES D'HYÈRES

A E6 **X** Toulon-Hyères **🚗🚌🚆** From Hyères **ℹ** Rotonde du Park Hotel, 16 ave de Belgique; www.hyeres-tourisme.com

Not for nothing are the Îles d'Hyères also known as the "Îles d'Or" or "Golden Isles". Each of these three tiny islets, which lie 10 km (6 miles) off the Var coast, has its own charms. They have a chequered history thanks to their strategic position; occupiers have included Greeks, Romans, Saracens and pirates.

Porquerolles

Porquerolles, the largest of the trio, is a car-free paradise of sandy beaches, pine-scented woods and olive groves, with a network of easy-going trails to explore on foot or with a rented bike.

The newest jewel in its crown is the Villa Carmignac, opened in 2018, where a collection of radical contemporary and modern art can be explored in a 1980s villa and an underground labyrinth of galleries where visitors walk barefoot. Above ground, giant masks and boulders are scattered around the wooded estate. The permanent collection includes works by Basquiat, Lichtenstein, Warhol and other 20th- and 21st-century giants.

> A marine national park extends to the seabed, where brightly coloured rainbow wrasse swim and octopuses lurk among the rocks.

Port-Cros

Port-Cros is a delight for nature lovers. Around it, a marine national park extends to the sea-bed, where brightly coloured rainbow wrasse swim and octopuses lurk among the rocks. An underwater trail leads snorkellers around the island's shores. On land, the Circuit des Crêtes leads through pine and arbutus woods to the island's highest point. The prosaic walls and barracks of the 18th-century Fort du Moulin overlook the harbour.

Le Levant

To visit Le Levant, visitors must either be naked or in uniform. Most of the island is a French naval base, and so is off-limits to civilians. The other 10% is occupied by Heliopolis, Europe's first naturist resort.

Beach on Porquerolles, and (inset) diver on a marine trail in Port-Cros ↓

JACQUES-YVES COUSTEAU

Godfather of scuba diving, Jacques-Yves Cousteau (1910–97) dedicated his career to undersea exploration and to raising awareness of the plight of the oceans. He patented the first successful self-contained underwater breathing apparatus, the Aqua-Lung, in 1946. He also directed the 1956 documentary film version of his book *The Silent World*, which won a Palme d'Or at the Cannes Film Festival.

Pretty, flower-filled back streets in the town of Hyères ↑

EXPERIENCE MORE

⑤ Hyères

🅐D6 ✈Toulon-Hyères
� icons 🛈Rotonde du Park Hotel, 16 ave de Belgique; www.hyeres-tourisme.com

The town of Hyères is one of the most agreeable on the Côte d'Azur, and the oldest of the south of France winter resorts. Hyères lies at the centre of well-cultivated land that provides fresh fruit and vegetables all year. It has three leisure ports, 25 km (16 miles) of sandy beach and a peninsula facing the Îles d'Hyères.

A palm-growing industry was established here in 1867, soon becoming the largest in Europe. The industry is still important and thousands of palms line the boulevards of the new town.

Hyères' main church is St-Louis in place de la République. Romanesque and Provençal Gothic, it was completed in 1248. From place Massillon, rue St-Paul leads past the 11th-century Église St-Paul, full of 17th-century ex-votos. The road continues to the ruined 12th-century Château St-Bernard, which has good views.

A must-see is the stunning **Villa Noailles** (1924), high above the pedestrianized old town. A great attraction for 20th-century artists, the villa was where Man Ray filmed *Les Mystères du Château de Dé*; it has also hosted the likes of Dalí, Miró and Picasso.

Villa Noailles
🅐🅐🅐 🅐Montée Noailles ⏰Times vary, check website 🚫Public hols 🌐villanoailles.com

Fontaine du Monument aux Morts in place Victor Hugo, Barjols

❻

Barjols

🄰D5 🚍 🅸 Blvd Grisolle; www.barjols.fr

Once renowned for its busy tanneries, Barjols now lies peacefully among woods and fast-flowing streams. In 1983, after almost 400 years, the leather industry folded. The abandoned factories have now become artisans' studios.

Two traditional Provençal instruments, the three-holed flute (*galoubet*) and the narrow drums (*tambourins*), were still made in Barjols until recently. These instruments resound each January at the annual *fête* of St Marcel, the town's patron saint.

St Marcel's relics can be seen in the 11th-century church of Notre-Dame-de-l'Assomption. A mixture of Romanesque, Byzantine and Gothic architectural styles, the church also contains a beautiful organ dating from 1656. There are good views of the surrounding countryside from the bell tower.

Of the many stone fountains dotted around the town, the most famous is the mossy *Champignon* in place Capitaine Vincens. It stands under what is reputed to be the largest plane tree in Provence. Between the church and the old tanneries are the restored buildings of the old quartier du Réal. Exotic porticoes, particularly on the Renaissance Hôtel de Pontevès, add spice to otherwise drab streets.

---

❼

Haut Var

🄰E4 🚏 Toulon-Hyères, Nice 🚊 Les Arcs 🚌 Aups 🅸 Place Martin Bidouré, Aups; www.aups-tourisme.com

The most remote and unspoiled lands of the Var are situated between Barjols and Comps-sur-Artuby, up towards the Gorges du Verdon (*p192*). Much of the land here has been taken over by the military.

Aups, set among undulating hills on the plateau edge, is the region's centre. Epicureans may be drawn by the local honey and olive oil, or by the truffle market each Thursday morning in winter. It is an attractive town with a grand old square and castle ruins. The 15th-century St-Pancrace church has a Renaissance doorway. Also worth a visit is the excellent **Musée Simon Segal**, which is housed in a former Ursuline convent.

The museum contains works by Segal and Paris painters, as well as local scenes.

About 5 km (3 miles) northwest on the D9 is the village of Moissac-Bellevue. Many of its buildings date from the 16th and 17th centuries and its church was mentioned in a papal edict of 1225. South from Aups is Villecroze, set against the dramatic backdrop of the **Grottes Troglodytiques**. These are natural caves on three levels, which local lords in the 16th century turned into dwellings. The arcaded streets and the keep of the feudal castle give the town a medieval flavour. A short drive from Villecroze leads up to Tourtour, a smaller, prettier and more popular village. Renowned French expressionist painter Bernard Buffet lived his last days here. Two of his creations – large, metal-built insect sculptures – are still displayed in the village.

The valley town of Salernes lies in the opposite direction, 10 km (6 miles) west on the D51. Smoke pumps from the kilns of its 15 ceramic factories. Salernes is one of the best-known Provençal tile-making centres, noted for *tomettes* – hexagonal terracotta floor-tiles.

 Gushing cascades at the Grottes Troglodytiques waterfall, near Villecroze

TRUFFLES

This richly flavoured fungal delicacy of the Var is traditionally sniffed out by trained pigs. The golfball-sized truffles are collected during the winter, when they are at their most fragrant, from underground near the roots of oak trees. Local markets specialize in truffles when they are in season, though their rarity means that they tend to be extremely expensive to buy.

18th-century paintings, artifacts, tapestries and furniture. The garden, by Le Nôtre, is publicly owned.

Musée Simon Segal

 Rue Albert Premier 🌐 04 94 70 01 95 🕐 Jun–Sep: Wed–Mon

Grottes Troglodytiques

🌐 Villecroze 🌐 04 94 67 50 00 🕐 Times vary, call ahead

Château d'Entrecasteaux

🌐 83570 Entrecasteaux 🕐 Easter–mid-Jun: Sun & public hols; mid-Jun–Sep: Sun–Fri 🌐 chateau-entrecasteaux.com

---

Cotignac, west of Salernes, is an echo of Villecroze, with a cave-pocked cliff behind it. Behind the *mairie* (town hall), a river springs from the rocks, and beyond is an open-air theatre. The intriguing **Château d'Entrecasteaux** lies 15 km (9 miles) east of Cotignac. The 17th-century castle is filled with 17th- to

Did You Know?

The Grottes Troglodytiques were formed 700,000 years ago.

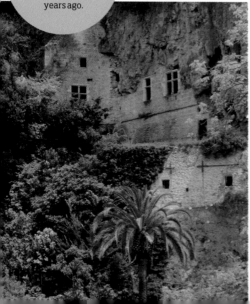

8
Comps-sur-Artuby

🇫🇷 E4 🚌 🅸 2 ave Lazare Carnot, Draguignan; 04 98 10 51 05

The eastern approach to the Gorges du Verdon *(p192)* passes through Comps-sur-Artuby. The village nestles at the foot of a rock topped by the 13th-century chapel of St-André, which has been restored. From the church there are grand views of the Artuby Gorges.

↑ Chapel of St-André, overlooking the Artuby Gorges

To the east lies Bargème, a village of steep streets with a population of 196. At 1,094 m (3,589 ft) it is the highest community in the Var. The village is closed to traffic.

Dominating Bargème is a large, well-preserved 14th-century castle. There is also the 13th-century Romanesque Église St-Nicolas with a carved, wooden altarpiece depicting Saint Sebastian.

9
Mons

🇫🇷 F4 🚌 🅸 Place St-Sébastien; 04 94 76 39 54

Situated on a rock-spur, Mons, with its tiny lanes and overhanging arches, has an almost magical appeal. The place St-Sébastien looks out across the coast, with views from Italy to Toulon.

Originally a Celtic-Ligurian settlement, its Château-Vieux quarter dates from the 10th century, but was mainly built by Genoese who repopulated the village after the plague in the 14th century. The first families came from Figounia; their legacy is the local dialect, *figoun*, which survives thanks to the isolated position of the village. Nearby is the *roche taillée*, a Roman aqueduct carved from solid rock.

Fayence

🅐 E3 🚌 ℹ️ Place Léon Roux; www.paysdefayence.com

The hillside town of Fayence is the largest between Grasse and Draguignan and is an international centre for local crafts as well as gliding. Dominated by a wrought-iron clock tower, it still has a few remains of its 14th-century defences, including a Saracen-style gate.

The Église St-Jean-Baptiste was built in the 18th century with a Baroque marble altar (1757) crafted by a local mason, Dominique Fossatti.

On the hillside opposite, in the community of Tourettes, there is a striking château. Part modelled on the Cadet school in St Petersburg, it was built in 1824 for General Alexandre Fabre, who once worked as a military engineer for Tsar Alexander I of Russia. He originally intended to make the building a public museum, but failed to finish the task and so it remains private.

There are several attractive villages nearby. Among the best are Callian and Montauroux to the east, and Seillans, 5 km (3 miles) to the west, where the German-born painter Max Ernst (1891–1976) chose to spend his last years. The prestigious Quatuors à Cordes en Pays de Fayence festival in September brings string quartets who perform in the charming local churches.

Bargemon

🅐 E3 🚉 Les Arcs 🚌 ℹ️ Ave Pasteur; www.ot-bargemon.fr

This medieval village, fortified in AD 950, has three 12th-century gates and a tower from the mid-16th century. The village is laid out around a number of squares with fountains, shaded by plane trees.

The angels' heads on the high altar of the 15th-century church, St-Étienne, now the Musée-Galerie Honoré Camos, are attributed to the school of Pierre Puget, like those in the Chapelle Notre-Dame-de-Montaigu. The chapel contains an oak-wood carving of the Virgin brought here in 1635. The Museum of Fossils and Minerals on rue de la Résistance displays over 3,000 pieces.

The adjoining library houses a lavishly illuminated 14th-century manuscript of the *Roman de la Rose*, considered to be the most important book of courtly love in France.

Draguignan

🅐 D4 🚌 ℹ️ 2 ave Lazare Carnot; www.tourisme-dracenie.com

The former capital of the Var *département* has the busy air of a small market town. Baron Haussmann, planner of modern Paris, laid out Draguignan's 19th-century boulevards. At the end of his plane-tree-lined allées d'Azémar, there is a Rodin bust of the prime minister Georges Clémenceau (1841–1929), who represented Draguignan for 25 years. The pedestrianized old town has a Provençal atmosphere, from its market square to its narrow alleyways. A major landmark is the 24-m (79-ft) clockless clock tower, built in 1663, on the site of the original keep. Get to the top: there is a good view from its wrought-iron campanile. The Église St-Michel contains a statue of St Hermentaire. In the 5th century he slew a dragon, giving the town its name.

Draguignan has two good local museums. The **Musée des Arts et Traditions Populaires** deals with the region's social and economic history. It occupies buildings that date back to the 17th century. Regional country life is shown using reconstructed kitchens and barns.

The **Musée des Beaux-Arts** shows paintings, sculptures, ceramics and furniture, as well as archaeological artifacts. The adjoining library (by appointment only) houses a lavishly illuminated 14th-century manuscript of the *Roman de la Rose*, considered to be the most important book of courtly love in France.

Northwest of the town on the D955 is the enormous prehistoric dolmen Pierre de la Fée, or Fairy Stone.

↑ Neat hedges in the formal garden at the Château de Villeneuve, Les Arcs-sur-Argens

Musée des Arts et Traditions Populaires
♿🖼️📷 🅰️ 75 place Georges Brassens 📞 04 94 47 05 72 🕐 Tue–Sat 🚫 Public hols

Musée des Beaux-Arts
🖼️📷 🅰️ 9 rue de la République 📞 04 98 10 26 85 🚫 Times vary, phone ahead

___

⑬

Les-Arcs-sur-Argens

🅰️D4 🏢🚌 ℹ️ Place du Général de Gaulle; www.tourisme-dracenie.com

Wine centre for the Côtes de Provence, Les Arcs has a medieval quarter, Le Parage, set around the 13th-century Château de Villeneuve. The Église St-Jean-Baptiste (1850) contains a screen by Louis Bréa (1501).

To the east of Les Arcs, in a former 11th-century abbey, is the **Chapelle Ste-Roseline**, named after Roseline de Villeneuve, daughter of the Baron of Arcs. Legend has it that when her father stopped

← Looking out over the rooftops of Bargemon to the green hills beyond

her from taking food to the poor, the food turned into roses. Roseline de Villeneuve entered the abbey in 1300, later becoming its abbess. The chapel contains the body of the saint in a glass shrine, as well as a Chagall mosaic.

Chapelle Ste-Roseline
🅰️ Route de Ste-Roseline 📞 04 94 73 37 30 🕐 Tue–Sun pm 🚫 Mid-Dec-Jan, public hols

PIERRE DE LA FÉE

The massive stone slab that crowns this 2.5-m- (8-ft-) high dolmen is 6 m (20 ft) long and estimated to weigh 60 tonnes. It was built around 2,500–2,000 BC, and is the only true prehistoric dolmen in Provence. Rock carvings suggest the region was first inhabited about a million years ago.

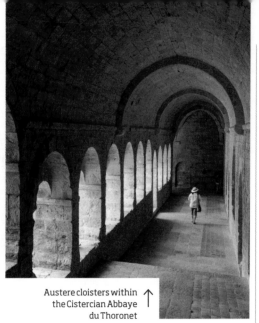

Austere cloisters within the Cistercian Abbaye du Thoronet ↑

⑭ Lorgues

Ⓐ E5 🚌 ℹ️ 12 rue du 8 mai 1945; www.lorgues-tourisme.fr

Near oak and pine woodland, Lorgues is surrounded by vineyards and olive groves. Its old town was fortified in the 12th century. Two 14th-century gates and city wall remains can be seen, along with 18th-century municipal buildings and monuments.

In the centre of town is the stately Collégiale St-Martin, consecrated in 1788. Its organ, dating from 1857, is the finest example of the work of the Augustin Zeiger factory, Lyon. A marble Virgin and Child (1694) here is attributed to the school of Pierre Puget.

⑮ Abbaye du Thoronet

Ⓐ E5 🏠 83340 Le Thoronet Ⓞ Daily 🗓 1 Jan, 1 May, 1 & 11 Nov 🌐 le-thoronet.fr

Founded in 1146, Le Thoronet was the first Cistercian building in Provence. It occupies a remote site in deep woodland. Along with the Romanesque abbeys of Sénanque (*p170*) and Silvacane (*p152*), it forms one of the three "Cistercian sisters" of Provence.

The cool geometry of the church, cloister, dormitory and chapter house reflects the austerity of Cistercian principles. Only the bell tower breaks with the order's strict building regulations: instead of wood, it is made of stone, to enable it to withstand the strong Provençal winds.

Dilapidated by the 1400s, the abbey was abandoned in 1791. Its restoration, like that of many medieval Provençal buildings, was instigated by Prosper Mérimée, Napoleon III's Inspector of Historic Monuments, who visited in 1834. Just beside the

Did You Know?

Every year in June, the fishermen of Sanary-sur-Mer prepare a bouillabaisse for up to 3,000 people.

abbey is the modern Monastère de Bethléem, home to Cistercian nuns.

⑯ Brignoles

Ⓐ D6 🚌 ℹ️ Carrefour de l'Europe; www.la-provence-verte.net

Bauxite mines have stained the Brignoles countryside red: over a million tonnes of metal are mined here annually. The medieval town remains above it all, quiet and empty for most of the year. An unexpected delight is the **Musée du Pays Brignolais** in a 12th-century castle that was built as a summer retreat for the Counts of Provence. The eclectic collection includes the La Gayole marble sarcophagus, which is carved with both pagan and Christian images; a boat made of cement designed by J Lambot (1814–87), who gave the world reinforced concrete; and a collection of votive offerings. St Louis, bishop of Toulouse and patron of Brignoles, was born in a palace beside the Église St-Sauveur in 1274.

Musée du Pays Brignolais

🎨 🎟️ 🏠 2 place des Comtes de Provence Ⓞ Times vary, check the Brignoles tourism website 🗓 21 Dec-Jan, public hols

⑰ Sanary-sur-Mer

Ⓐ D6 🚉 Ollioules-Sanary 🚌 ℹ️ 1 quai du Levant; www.sanary-tourisme.com

In the agreeable, clear blue waters of Sanary-sur-Mer, the diver Jacques Cousteau's

→

Boats at dusk in the yachting harbour at Bandol

experiments to develop the modern aqua-lung took place *(p115)*. Diving and fishing (mainly for tuna and swordfish) are still popular pursuits in this delightful resort, where rows of pink and white houses line the bay. Its name derives loosely from St-Nazaire; the lovely local 19th-century church took the saint's name. Dating from about 1300, the landmark medieval tower in the town still contains the cannon that saw off an Anglo-Sardinian fleet in 1707. It is now part of a hotel.

Sanary-sur-Mer has enticed visitors for many years. Once the home of the British writer Aldous Huxley (1894–1963), it was a haven between the wars for innumerable other authors. Bertolt Brecht (1898–1956) and Thomas Mann (1875–1955) fled here from Nazi Germany. To the east of Sanary, the coast becomes dramatic and rocky. By the peninsula's extremity at the Cap Sicié is the Notre-Dame-du-Mai chapel, built in the 17th century and now a pilgrimage destination full of votive offerings. Its stepped approach offers a

wonderful panorama over the coast and surrounding hills. Outside the town, **Zoa**, a zoo and botanic garden, is home to wildlife including monkeys, small cats and some rare and tropical plants.

Zoa

⊗ ⓨ ⊙ ⓐ ⓐ ❑131 ave Pont d'Aran, Sanary-sur-Mer ⏲Feb–Oct: 9:30am–6pm daily (Apr–Sep: to 7pm); Nov–Jan: 9:30am–5:30pm Wed, Sat & Sun ❑Public hols ⓦzoaparc.com

---

CÔTES DE PROVENCE VINEYARDS

The slopes of the Côtes de Provence wine-growing region stretch from the Haut Var to the coast, and produce luscious red, white and above all rosé wines, around 80 per cent of the region's vintages. Cinsaut, Carignan, Mourvèdre, Grenache and Tibouren are the main grape varieties grown. To sample some of the 800 regional wines, visit the Maison des Vins Côtes de Provence at Les Arcs *(www.maison-des-vins.fr)*.

 18

Bandol

❑D6 ☐ **i**Allée Alfred Vivien ⓦbandoltourisme.fr

Tucked away in a bay, this cheerful resort has a tree-lined promenade (with plenty of shops and restaurants), a casino and a yachting harbour. The shelter of encircling hills provides excellent grape-growing conditions. Indeed, Bandol has produced superb wines since 600 BC.

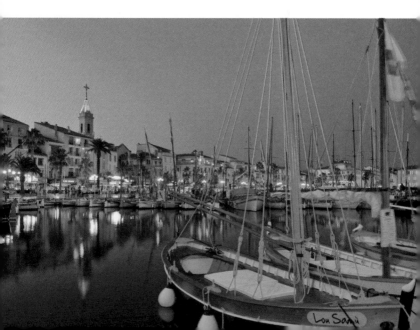

Did You Know?

In 2000, the Mayor of Le Lavandou passed a by-law making it illegal to die in the town.

Le Lavandou

E6 🚌 🚢 ℹ️ Quai Gabriel Péri; www.ot-lelavandou.fr

An embarkation port for the nearby Îles d'Hyères, Le Lavandou is a fishing village now almost entirely given over to tourism. This is due to its 12 sandy beaches, each with its own character. It is a centre for watersports and offers moorings for luxury yachts. Full of bars, nightclubs and restaurants, Le Lavandou is a favourite of younger, less well-heeled visitors.

The village takes its name not from the lavender fields in the hills, but from a *lavoir* (wash-house) depicted in a painting of the town in 1736 by Charles Ginoux. During the 19th century, when it was no more than a fishing village,

Le Lavandou was popular with artists. The most famous was Ernest Reyer (1823–1909), a composer and music critic after whom the main square is named. From this square there is a view over the Îles du Levant and Port-Cros.

Much of nearby Brégançon is in the hands of the military, and the French president has a summer residence there.

Bormes-les-Mimosas

E6 🚌 Hyères ℹ️ 1 place Gambetta; www.bormesles mimosas.com

Bormes is a medieval hill village on the edge of the Dom Forest, bathed in the scent of oleander and eucalyptus, with a flower-lined walk around its castle. "Les Mimosas" was added to its name in 1968, a century after the plant was first introduced from Mexico. A pretty and popular village, Bormes serves a marina of more than 800 berths. Plummeting streets such as rue Rompi Cuou lead to lively cafés and coastal views.

A statue of St Francis di Paola stands in front of the 16th-century Chapelle

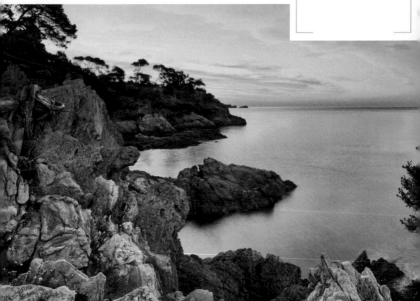

St-François-de-Paule, commemorating the saint's timely arrival during a plague outbreak in 1481. The 18th-century church of St-Trophyme has restored 18th-century frescoes. The works of local painter Jean-Charles Cazin (1841–1901) are well represented in the **Musée Arts et Histoire**.

Musée Arts et Histoire

🏠 103 rue Carnot 📞 04 94 71 56 60 🕐 Tue–Sun

 21

Ramatuelle

🅰 E6 🚌 *i* **Place de l'Ormeau; www.ramatuelle-tourisme.com**

Surrounded by vineyards, and dotted with fig trees, this attractive hilltop village was called "God's Gift" (Rahmatu 'llah) by the Saracens who left behind a gate, now restored. It is one of three particularly quaint villages on the St-Tropez peninsula (with Grimaud and Gassin). Gérard Philipe (1922–59), the leading young French actor during the 1950s, is buried here. Theatre and jazz festivals take place here annually.

 Visible from afar, the pretty village of Grimaud spreading down the hillside among the trees

Nearby, Les Moulins de Paillas (322 m, 1,056 ft) offers a fine panorama, as does Cap Camarat, with its lighthouse, at the tip of the peninsula, 7 km (4 miles) east of Ramatuelle.

22

Port-Grimaud

🅰 E5 🚌 *i* **Les Terrasses, rue de l'Amarrage; www.grimaud-provence.com**

This beautiful port village was dreamed up entirely by the renowned Alsace architect François Spoerry (1912–99). In 1962 he bought up the marshy delta lands of the River Giscle west of the Golfe St-Tropez. Four years later, work began on a mini-Venice of 2,500 canal-side houses with moorings covering 90 ha (222 acres).

There are now three "zones", a marina and a beach. Its church, St-François-d'Assise, in the place de l'Église, contains some stained glass by Victor Vasarely (1908–97), and offers a sweeping view of the port from the top of its tower.

 ←

Soft dawn light illuminating the rugged coastline of Le Lavandou

The port is traffic-free and the *coche d'eau* offers a water-taxi service. Port-Grimaud has about one million visitors a year.

23

Grimaud

🅰 E4 🚌 *i* **679 route nationale; www.grimaud-provence.com**

The medieval, fortified, traffic-free *village perché* of Grimaud dates back to the Gallo-Roman days. During the 11th century, its steep summit allowed Grimaud to dominate the Gulf of St-Tropez (also known as the Golfe de Grimaud) and control access to the town from the North and Maures mountains. Grimaud has no connection to the ubiquitous Grimaldi family; it can instead be associated with the much older Grimaldo dynasty. The 11th-century castle of Grimaud was ruined in the Wars of Religion (*p56*). The view of the coast made it an ideal vantage point from which to watch for invasion.

The rue des Templiers is the town's oldest street, lined with arcades designed to be battened down in case of attack. Legend has it that the Knights Templar stayed here.

Golden sunlight over the port of Ste-Maxime in the bay of St-Tropez

Ste-Maxime

AE5 **St-Tropez, St-Raphaël **21 place Louis Blanc; www.sainte-maxime.com

Facing St-Tropez across the Gulf, Ste-Maxime is protected by hills. Visitors come year-round – attracted by the resort's watersports, nightlife, beaches and casino – but numbers peak in the summer.

Ste-Maxime was once protected by the monks of Lérins, who named the port after their patron saint and put up the defensive Tour Carrée des Dames. Nearby, the traditional *sardinade*, or grilled sardine feast, is held every June during the village's jolly Fête de la St-Pierre.

St-Raphaël

AF5 ****99 quai Albert Premier; www.saint-raphael.com

This staid family resort dates to Roman times when rich families came to stay near where the modern seafront casino now stands. Napoleon put the town on the map when he landed here in 1799

on his return from Egypt, and 15 years later when he left St-Raphaël for exile on Elba.

Popularity grew when the Parisian satirical novelist Jean-Baptiste Karr (1808–90) publicized the town's delights. In the old part is the 12th-century church of St-Raphaël and the **Musée Archéologique**, which contains Greek amphorae and other important finds.

Musée Archéologique

**Parvis de l'Église **04 94 19 25 75 **Nov-Feb: 2-5pm Tue, 9am-12:30pm & 2-5pm Wed-Fri, 9am-12:30pm Sat; Mar-Jun & Oct: 2-5pm Tue, 9am-12:30pm & 2-5pm Wed-Sat; Jul-Sep: 10am-6pm Tue-Sat **Public hols

Fréjus

AF5 **St-Raphaël **249 rue Jean-Jaurès; www.frejus.fr

Visibly wealthy in history, Fréjus is one of the highlights of the coast. The oldest Roman city in Gaul, it was founded by Julius Caesar in 49 BC and greatly expanded by Augustus. Lying on the Aurelian way – a huge road built in the reign of Augustus from Rome to Arles – it covered 40 ha (100 acres), had a population of 30,000–40,000 and, as a port, was second in importance only to Marseille.

Although substantial sections of the Roman city were decimated by the Saracens in the 10th century, a few parts of their walls remain, including a tower of the western Porte des Gaules. The opposite eastern entrance, the Porte de Rome, marks one end of a 40-km (25-mile) aqueduct.

Just to the north of here lie the remains of the semicircular, 1st-century theatre, where

→
The imposing 12th-century Cathédrale St-Léonce in Fréjus

performances are still held. The praetorium or Plateforme – military headquarters that formed the eastern citadel – lie to the south. North of the Porte des Gaules, on the road to Brignoles, stands the large 1st–2nd-century **Arènes de Fréjus**, built to hold 12,000 spectators, now used for music and dance.

The spectacular **Cathédrale St-Léonce et Cloître** houses a Musée Archéologique with finds from all around Fréjus. The Chapelle Notre-Dame, decorated by Cocteau, and Musée d'Histoire Locale are also well worth a visit.

South of the town is the Butte St-Antoine citadel, which once overlooked the harbour. The canal linking the harbour to the sea began silting up in the 10th century; by the 1700s it was entirely filled in, forming a new land mass that later became Fréjus-Plage. A little over 2 km (1 mile) from the town's centre, this modern resort stretches along a sandy beach towards the town of St-Raphaël.

Arènes de Fréjus

⊘ 🏛296 rue Henri Vadon 📞04 94 51 83 83 🕓Apr-Sep: Tue–Sun; Oct–Mar: Tue–Sat 🕓Public hols

Cathédrale St-Léonce et Cloître

⊘⊘🏛 🏛58 rue du Cardinal Fleury 🕓Cathedral: daily; Cloisters: Tue–Sun (May–Aug: daily) 🕓Public hols 🌐cloitre-frejus.fr

---

27

Massif de l'Estérel

🅰F5 ✈Nice 🚌🚆Agay, St-Raphaël 🛈Quai Albert Premier, St-Raphaël; www.esterel-cote dazur.com

The Estérel, a mountainous volcanic mass, is a wilderness compared with the bustling coast. Although it rises to no more than 620 m (2,050 ft), and a succession of fires have destroyed its forests, its innate ruggedness and the dramatic colours of its porphyry rocks remain intact.

Until the mid-1800s, it was a popular refuge for highwaymen and escaped convicts from the Bagne prison in Toulon. Indeed, after being fêted on arrival in St-Raphaël, Napoleon and his coach were robbed of all their valuables on the Estérel while on their way to Paris.

The north side of the massif is bounded by the DN7 which runs through the Estérel Gap. To reach Mont Vinaigre, take the road to the Malpey *maison forestière* (ranger station), and walk the final 45 minutes to the highest point on the massif, where there is a fine panorama from the Alps to the Massif des Maures.

On the seaward side of the massif, the D559 from St-Raphaël twists along the top of startlingly red cliffs to Agay.

Round the bay is Pointe de la Baumette, where there is a memorial to French writer and World War II aviator, Antoine de St-Exupéry.

At La Napoule is the 14th-century **Château de la Napoule**, refurbished by American sculptor Henry Clews (1876–1937), who left his work scattered about the estate. The château is now an art centre, the Clews Center for the Arts.

Château de la Napoule

⊘⊘🏛🏛 🏛1 blvd Henry Clews, Mandelieu-La Napoule 🕓Early Feb-early Nov: 10am–6pm daily; early Nov–early Feb: 2–5pm Mon–Fri (from 10am Sat & Sun) 🌐chateau-lanapoule.com

> ## Did You Know?
>
> The scrubland on the Massif de l'Estérel is blanketed with iris flowers in spring.

BOUCHES-DU-RHÔNE AND NÎMES

This southwestern corner of Provence has a feel that's unique in the region. It is the land of Van Gogh, brightly patterned materials and beaches of shifting sands. Many inland towns reflect the region's Greek and Roman past. The Greeks first settled in France in around 600 BC and founded Marseille. The Romans, who arrived after them, built the theatre at Arles and the amphitheatre at Nîmes, and left the remains of Classical houses at the archaeological site of Glanum. They also built the huge aqueduct Pont du Gard, a great feat of engineering, which runs beween a spring at Uzès to a water tower at Nîmes.

Bloodthirsty warriors ruled in the Middle Ages from an extraordinary eyrie in Les Baux-de-Provence. This former fief was paradoxically famous as a Court of Love during the 13th century. In the 15th century, Good King René held his court in the castle of Tarascon and in Aix-en-Provence, the ancient capital of Provence. Aix's university, founded by René's father, Louis II of Anjou, in 1409, is still the hub of this lively student town.

Today, France's second largest city prides itself on being truly cosmopolitan. As Emmanuel Macron said, while visiting Marseille on his presidential campaign trail, "When I see Marseille, I see Armenians, Cormorians, Italians, Algerians, Moroccans, Tunisians, I see Malians, Senegalese, Ivorians… But what do I see? I see citizens of Marseille – I see citizens of France."

BOUCHES-DU-RHÔNE AND NÎMES

Must Sees

1. Nîmes
2. Aix-en-Provence
3. Marseille
4. Arles
5. Camargue
6. Aigues-Mortes

Experience More

7. Barbentane
8. Abbaye St-Michel de Frigolet
9. Beaucaire
10. St-Gilles-du-Gard
11. Tarascon
12. St-Rémy-de-Provence
13. Les Alpilles
14. Les Baux-de-Provence
15. Fontvieille
16. Abbaye de Montmajour
17. Martigues
18. Salon-de-Provence
19. Aubagne
20. Abbaye de Silvacane
21. Cassis
22. Les Calanques

BOUCHES-DU-RHÔNE
AND NÎMES

L'Isle-sur-
la-Sorgue

Roussillon

Gordes

Apt

Cavaillon

VAUCLUSE
p154

Orgon

Petit Luberon

Cucuron

Lourmarin

Cadenet

La Tour
d'Aigues

Sénas

Durance

Pertuis

Mirabeau

Eyguières

Mallemort

20

Caderache

**ABBAYE DE
SILVACANE**

Durance

Meyrargues

Jouques

**SALON-DE-
PROVENCE**

Lambesc

Rognes

St Cannat

Pélissane

Venelles

Miramas

Lançon-Provence

18

Coudoux

D7N

RHÔNE

Chamas

D113

D10

Ventrabren

A6

2 **AIX-EN-PROVENCE**

Istres

Berre-l'Etang

A7

D113

Gardanne

Fuveau

Trets

**Étang
de Berre**

Les Pennes-
Mirabeau

MARTIGUES

17

Marignane

**Aéroport de
Marseille Provence**

Mimet

A52

Peypin

Auriol

D96

Châteauneuf-les-
Martigues

Le Rove

Septemes-les-
Vallons

A55

Ensués-la-Redonne

Roquevaire

La Couronne

Carry-le-Rouet

Allauch

A52

AUBAGNE

Gemenos

MARSEILLE

3

A50

19

*Rade de
Marseille*

Cuges-les-Pins

*Château
d'If*

Roquefort-la-
Bédoule

Îles du Frioul

D6N

Ceyreste

Cap Croisette

Plages du Prado

21

CASSIS

**VAR
AND ÎLES
D'HYÈRES**
p98

A50

D559

**LES
CALANQUES** **22**

*M e d i t e r r a n e a n
S e a*

0 kilometres   10

0 miles   10

N

❶
NÎMES

🅰 A4 ✈ Nîmes-Arles-Carmargue 🚆🚌 Pl de l'ONU
ℹ 6 blvd des Arènes; www.nimes-tourisme.com

The Romans left their mark on Nîmes more firmly than on any other city in Provence. In the 21st century, their vast amphitheatre, Les Arènes, is still the cultural hub of a city of broad boulevards and airy squares, dotted with architectural relics of the Roman era. The city is also famous for developing denim (de Nîmes), the tough material used for blue jeans and traditionally worn by Camargue cowboys.

① Les Arènes (L'Amphithéâtre)

🏛 Blvd des Arènes 📞 04 66 21 82 56 🕐 Times vary, check website 🔒 Ferias (fairs) & performance days 🌐 arenes-nimes.com

At 130 m (427 ft) by 100 m (328 ft) and with seating for 24,000, Nîmes' amphi-theatre is only slightly smaller than the arena at Arles (p134). It was built as a venue for gladiatorial combat, but after Rome's collapse in AD 476 it became a fortress, a knights' head-quarters, and eventually a slum, housing 2,000 people. Restored in the 19th century, it is thought to be one of the best preserved of all Roman amphitheatres. Today, it is used for rock concerts rather than for gladiatorial contests.

② Cathédrale Notre-Dame-et-St-Castor

🏛 9 rue St-Castor 📞 04 66 67 27 72 🕐 Times vary, call ahead

Nîmes's cathedral dates from the 11th century but was extensively rebuilt in the 19th century. The west front has a partly Romanesque frieze with scenes from the Old Testament.

③ Maison Carrée

🏛 Place de la Maison Carrée 📞 04 66 21 82 56 🕐 Times vary, check website 🌐 arenes-nimes.com

The Maison Carrée ("square house") is the world's best preserved Roman temple. Built by Marcus Agrippa, this beautiful structure captivates visitors with its harmonious proportions. It is Hellenic with Corinthian columns around the main hall. A multimedia film – *Nemausus, the birth of Nîmes* – that chronicles the heroic past of Nîmes is shown inside the temple.

↑ Façade of the well-preserved Roman temple Maison Carrée

← Exterior of Les Arènes, Nîmes's well-preserved Roman amphitheatre

and zoology. Visitors can see collections on birds and mammals, botany, geology, mineralogy, palaeontology and even prehistoric archaeology.

---

⑤ Les Jardins de la Fontaine

🏛 Quai de la Fontaine
🕐 Times vary, check website 🌐 nimes.fr; arenes-nimes.com

The city's main park is named after an underground spring harnessed in the 18th century. The park's 2nd-century Temple of Diana is today in ruins.

Another highlight is the octagonal Tour Magne. Dating from 15 BC, it is the earliest surviving Roman building in France. Climb the tower's 140 steps for spectacular views.

④ Musée d'Histoire Naturelle

🏛 13 blvd Amiral Courbet
📞 04 66 76 73 45 🕐 10am-6pm Tue-Sun 🔒 1 May, 1 Nov

Set around a cloister and 17th-century chapel, this museum covers three themes: the pre-historic period, ethnography

⑥ Carré d'Art (Musée d'Art Contemporain)

🏛 Place de la Maison Carrée
🕐 10am-6pm Tue-Sun
🌐 carreartmusee.com

On the opposite side of the square from the Maison Carrée, this modern, light-flooded art complex opened in 1993 and was designed by Norman Foster.

---

⑦ Musée des Beaux-Arts

🏛 Rue de la Cité Foulc 📞 04 66 76 71 82 🕐 10am-6pm Tue-Sun 🔒 1 May, 1 Nov

A diverse collection in the Fine Art Museum includes paintings by Boucher, Rubens and Watteau. The ground floor displays a large Roman mosaic, *The Marriage of Admetus*, found in 1883 in Nîmes's former covered market.

↑ Visitors roam the markets at Aix-en-Provence's bustling place Richelme

2

AIX-EN-PROVENCE

🅰C5 🚉Ave Victor Hugo 🚌Ave de l'Europe 🛈300 ave Giuseppe Verdi; www.aixenprovencetourism.com

Provence's former capital is an international students' town, with one of the region's most cosmopolitan streets of restaurants and bars, rue de la Verrerie. The university was founded by Louis II of Anjou in 1409 and flourished under his son, Good King René. Another wave of prosperity transformed the city in the 17th century, when the mansion-lined cours Mirabeau was built. Aix's fountains were added in the 18th century.

①

Old Town

North of the cours Mirabeau, between the Cathédrale St-Sauveur and the place d'Albertas, lies the town's old quarter. Sights include the Musée du Palais de l'Archevêché, housed in the former Bishop's palace, and the 17th-century Hôtel de Ville. Built around a court-yard by French architect Pierre Pavillon, it stands in a square now used as a flower market. Nearby is the 16th-century clock tower.

②

Cathédrale St-Sauveur

📍34 place des Martyrs de la Résistance ⏰Times vary, check website 🌐cathedrale-aix.net

The cathedral at the top of the old town creaks with history. The main door has solid walnut panels sculpted by Jean Guiramand (1504). On the right there is a fine 4th–5th-century baptistry, with a Renaissance cupola standing on 2nd-century Corinthian columns. The jewel of the church is the triptych of *The Burning Bush* (1476) by Nicolas Froment.

③

Musée du Vieil Aix (Musée Estienne de Saint-Jean)

📍17 rue Gaston de Saporta 📞04 42 91 89 78 ⏰Wed-Mon

Gain insight into Aix's fascinating heritage and traditions in the town's history museum, housed in a former aristocratic townhouse. The eclectic collection includes a 19th-century *crèche parlante* (puppet show) and figures from the Corpus Christi parade that was first celebrated during the medieval reign of King René.

④

Musée Granet

📍Pl St-Jean de Malte ⏰Tue-Sun 🚫1 Jan, 1 May, 25 Dec 🌐museegranet-aixenprovence.fr

The city's main museum sits in a 17th-century former priory of the Knights of Malta.

L'Atelier de Cézanne
600 m (650 yd)

BOULEVARD A. BRIAND

PLACE BELLEGARDE

AVENUE SAINTE-VICTOIRE

Cathédrale St-Sauveur ②

Parc Rambot

BOULEVARD JEAN JAURÈS

RUE DES ÉTUVES

PLACE DE L'UNIVERSITÉ

Musée des Tapisseries

NEUF

COURS ST-LOUIS

COURS DES ARTS ET MÉTIERS

Thermes Sextius

Pavillon de Vendôme

RUE DU BON PASTEUR

PLACE DES MARTYRS DE LA RÉSISTANCE

Musée du Vieil Aix ③

RUE PAUL BERT

Église de la Madeleine

RUE VENEL

RUE SUFFREN

RUE PORTALIS

BOULEVARD CARNOT

Hôtel de Ville

PLACE DE L'HÔTEL DE VILLE

Ancienne Halle aux Grains

PLACE DES PRÊCHEURS

PLACE DES CARDEURS

RUE DES CORDELIERS

RUE RICHELME ①

RUE MONCLAR

Palais de Justice

Old Town

PL. DE VERDUN

Hôtel Boyer d'Eguilles

PLACE FORBIN

Granet XXe

PLACE NIOLLON

PLACE JEANNE D'ARC

COURS MIRABEAU

St-Jean-de-Malte

PLACE FRANÇOIS VILLON ℹ

PLACE DU GÉNÉRAL DE GAULLE

Hôtel de Caumont Centre d'Art

RUE CARDINALE

Musée Granet ④

Fondation Vasarely
km (1.5 miles)

BOULEVARD DU ROI RENÉ

COURS GAMBETTA

AVE A. FRANCE

🚍 Bus Station

Gare (TGV) 15 km (9 miles)

Aix-en-Provence Gare (SNCF)

| 0 metres | 250 |
| 0 yards | 250 |

N ↑

François Granet (1775–1849), a local artist, bequeathed his collection of French, Italian and Flemish paintings to Aix, including Ingres' *Portrait of Granet* and *Jupiter and Thetis*. There is also a room devoted to Granet's own paintings. The museum also features works by other Provençal painters, such as Van Gogh and Pablo Picasso, as well as eight canvases by Paul Cézanne, plus artifacts from Roman Aix.

⑤

Fondation Vasarely

🏠 1 ave Marcel Pagnol
🕐 Daily 🔒 1 Jan, 24–26 Dec
🌐 fondationvasarely.org

Op Art master Victor Vasarely's peculiar hexagonal complex of steel cubes, adorned by black and white circles, houses a permanent collection of his monumental works and a calendar of temporary exhibitions, concerts and conferences starring local, national and international talents. The building was fully refurbished in 2018.

---

⑥

L'Atelier de Cézanne

🏠 9 ave Paul Cézanne
🕐 Tue–Sat 🔒 1 May, 25 Dec
🌐 cezanne-en-provence.com

Ten minutes' walk uphill from the Cathédrale St-Sauveur is the house of renowned artist Paul Cézanne (*p36*), seen by many as the father of modern art (although he was jeered at in his hometown during his lifetime). The studio is much as he left it when he died in 1906. Not far from here you can see the scenic Montagne Ste-Victoire, a favourite subject of the painter.

↑ Fondation Vasarely's unique modern structure

❸

MARSEILLE

🅐 C5 ✈ 25 km (15 miles) NW Marseille 🚊 Pl Victor
🛈 11 La Canebière; www.marseille-tourisme.com

Marseille, founded more than 2,500 years ago, may be France's oldest city, but it's busily re-inventing itself as a vibrant 21st-century community around its bustling waterfront. It's dotted with stunning examples of modern architecture – from Le Corbusier's Cité Radieuse, opened in 1952, to Norman Foster's literally dazzling Ombrière at the rejuvenated Vieux Port – as well as other powerhouses of the city's cultural renaissance.

 ①

La Vieille Charité

🏛 2 rue de la Charité
Ⓜ Joliette ⏰ 9am-6pm Tue-Sun 🌐 vieille-charite-marseille.com

With its serene arcades and courtyards, this 17th-century almshouse is one of the finest buildings in the old town and is worth visiting for its architecture alone. Begun in 1671, the building was designed by Pierre Puget, court architect to Louis XIV, and was originally intended to house rural migrants. It now houses the Musee d'Archéologie Méditerranéenne, a rich collection of ancient Egyptian artifacts. Those with more

contemporary tastes can also enjoy a changing schedule of exhibitions by 20th- and 21st-century artists.

---

②

Cathédrale de la Major

🏛 Place de la Major 🚌 60
⏰ 10am-5:30pm Wed-Mon (Apr-Sep: to 6:30pm)
🌐 marseille.catholique.fr

The pompous, colossal Neo-Byzantine cathedral, completed in 1893, is a landmark on the west side of the old town. Bishops of Marseille are interred in its crypt. Next to it is the 11th-century Ancienne Cathédrale, with a 1073 reliquary altar.

 ③

Musée des Civilisations de l'Europe et de la Méditerranée (MUCEM)

🏛 7 promenade Robert Laffont 🚌 82, 60, 49
⏰ Wed-Mon 🌐 mucem.org

Art from all around the shores of the Mediterranean and from every era since Neolithic times to the present day is on show in a striking Post-Modern building, and in the adjacent Fort St-Jean. These buildings are connected by a roof-level bridge suspended over the sea.

 Visitors relax by the waterfront outside the MUCEM

←

Marseille's stunning harbour port and impressive city skyline

Between Notre-Dame and the port, it was founded in the 5th century and belonged to one of the most powerful religious foundations in Provence. Its patron, the hermit St Victor, was martyred in the 3rd century, and within his cave, crypts and sarcophagi.

④ (cycling) (metro) (building)

Abbaye St-Victor

🏛 Place St-Victor 🚌 55, 60, 61, 80, 82, 83 Ⓜ Vieux Port 🕐 9am-7pm daily

The fortress-like basilica of St Victor is Marseille's finest piece of religious architecture.

⑤ (cycling)

Palais Longchamp

🏛 Blvd Jardin Zoologique 🚌 81 Ⓜ Cinq avenues Longchamp 🚊 T2 Longchamp 🕐 9am-6pm Tue-Sun 🌐 musees.marseille.fr

This 19th-century palace, surrounded by green gardens and gushing fountains, is home to the Musée des Beaux-Arts, the Musée d'Histoire Naturelle

and the Observatoire de Marseille, with its planetarium and Foucault telescope.

⑥ (cycling) (metro)

Musée d'Histoire de Marseille

🏛 2 rue Henri Barbusse 🚌 83, 55 Ⓜ Vieux Port 🕐 9am-6pm Tue-Sun 🚫 1 Jan, 1 May, 25 Dec 🌐 museehistoire-marseillevoie-historique.fr

Visitors to this museum follow remnants of a paved Roman road through the Jardin des Vestiges, site of Marseille's oldest port. The most fascinating exhibits are the hulls of ancient Greek and Roman vessels retrieved from the seabed, and sarcophagi unearthed at nearby archaeological sites.

④

ARLES

🅐B4 ✈Nîmes-Ales-Camargue 🚉Ave P Talabot 🚌Ave P Talabot
🛈Blvd des Lices; www.arlestourisme.com

Like a miniature version of Rome, charming Arles spreads out around a massive arena and remnants of its Roman heyday are scattered all around its narrow streets. It's even better known for its connection with Vincent Van Gogh, who, inspired by its bright light and rich colours, enjoyed the most creative period of his tragically short life here. On the east bank of the Rhône, it's also the gateway to the unique wetlands of the Camargue (p140), with its flamingos and distinctive herds of black cattle and white horses. Most guided tours and safaris into the wilds of the delta start here.

① ✒ 🅼
Les Arènes

🅐Rond-point des Arènes
🕐Times vary, check website
🎫Events 🌐arenes-arles.com

The largest Roman building in Gaul is as impressive now as when it was built around 90 AD, with seats for 20,000 spectators to watch chariot races and bloody gladiatorial battles. Today, it is used for concerts and other spectacles. The top tier of seating provides an excellent panoramic view of Arles. Just to the southwest of the amphitheatre is the elegant Théâtre Antique, another beautifully preserved Roman-era stadium with 2,000 tiered seats.

② ✒
Cryptoportiques

🅐Hôtel de Ville, place de la République 🕐9am-7pm Wed-Mon 🚫Tue and public hols 🌐patrimoine.ville-arles.fr

Beneath the site of the Roman Forum, these huge, horseshoe-shaped underground galleries – up to 10 m (33 ft) wide and ventilated by air shafts – were probably used as granaries. Constructed in the 1st century AD, then buried beneath later church buildings, they were left forgotten and inaccessible until archaeologists began the task of re-opening them in 1935.

Les Thermes de Constantin are all that remains of Constantine's Palace, built in the 4th century AD.

④ *Fondation Vincent Van Gogh Arles (50 m; 55 yd)*

② *RUE DE LA REPUBLIQUE*

RUE MOLIERE

BOULEVARD GEORGES CLEME

⑥ *Musée Départemental Arles Antique (1 km; half a mile)*

↑ Sunset over the Roman obelisk in place de la République

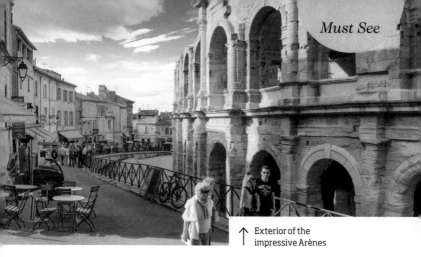

↑ Exterior of the impressive Arènes

One of Provence's most impressive monuments, Les Arènes was the largest Roman building in Gaul.

INSIDER TIP
City Passes

The tourist office offers sightseeing passes that cover visits to museums and monuments. Visit the website *(www.arles tourisme.tickeasy.com)* to buy the Advantage Pass, or the cheaper Liberté Pass.

Église Notre-Dame-de-la-Major is dedicated to Saint George, patron saint of the Camargue gardians (cowboys).

The Théâtre Antique, constructed at the end of the 1st century BC, was incorporated into the fortified enclosure surrounding the city in the Middle Ages; its stones were later used for other buildings.

The cloister of Église St-Trophime features some exquisite examples of Romanesque carving.

(5) Luma
(500 m; 550 yd)

(7) Les Alyscamps
(300 m; 330 yd)

A Roman obelisk with fountains at its base stands in the place de la République. It came from the Roman circus across the Rhône.

← Aerial illustration of the historic centre of Arles

135

↑ The Fondation Vincent Van Gogh Arles garden, and *(inset)* museum exterior

in context and highlights the artist's influence on his contemporaries and successive generations of painters.

Luma

🏠 **45 chemin des Minimes, 33 ave Victor Hugo**
🕐 **10am-7:30pm daily**
🌐 **luma-arles.org**

Soaring above the old town like a starship ready for lift-off, Frank Gehry's gleaming metallic landmark opened in summer 2018, endowing Arles with a brand-new venue for world-class contemporary art and performance. The Luma cultural centre, led by Swiss art collector Maja Hoffmann, forms a 20-acre complex of

↑ Extraordinary metallic exterior of the Luma cultural centre

galleries, theatres, studios and workshops dedicated to producing new and adventurous work in photography and conceptual art. The collection is split between Gehry's new building and six former factory and warehouse spaces. It also hosts events and exhibitions during the annual Rencontres d'Arles photography festival.

Musée Réattu

🏠 **10 rue du Grand Prieuré**
🕐 **10am-5pm Tue-Sun (Mar-Oct: to 6pm)** 🌐 **musee reattu.arles.fr**

The work of local artist Jacques Réattu (1760–1833) and his contemporaries form the basis of this collection. A Picasso donation and a photographic display are among the other 20th-century pieces exhibited.

Fondation Vincent Van Gogh Arles

🏠 **35 rue du Dr Fanton**
🕐 **11am-6pm Tue-Sun (Apr-Oct: from 10am daily)**
🌐 **Between exhibitions, check website** 🌐 **fondation-vincentvangogh-arles.org**

Housed in a 15th-century mansion, the Hôtel Léautaud de Donines, this foundation aims to put Van Gogh's work

SHOP

Les Indiennes de Nimes

Buy colourful Camargue outfits here (as worn by the famous *gardians*) in traditional patterns with a modern twist.

🏠 **14 place de la République** 🕐 **Sun**
🌐 **indiennes de nimes.fr**

Christian Lacroix

Shop for high style from this world-famous Arles-born designer.

🏠 **52 rue de la République** 🕐 **Sun**
🌐 **christian-lacroix.com**

Musée Départemental Arles Antique

🏛 Presqu'île du Cirque Romain 🕐 10am–6pm Wed–Mon 🚫 25 Dec 🌐 arles-antique.cg13.fr

A marble statue of the Emperor Augustus, a statue of Venus and a massive altar dedicated to Apollo are among the highlights of this museum's collection of Roman sculptures, which dates from pre-Christian times to the period that followed the Christian conversion of the Empire in AD 312. A new wing opened in 2013 to house the Arles-Rhône 3, a fantastically well-preserved Roman 31-m-(102-ft-) long flat-bottomed wooden river barge that was retrieved from the bed of the the Rhône.

Les Alyscamps

🏛 Ave des Alyscamps 🕐 Daily

Christ is claimed to have appeared to early Christians who met in secret at this vast necropolis, which was one of the largest and most famous cemeteries in the Western world. An avenue of marble sarcophagi marks the site where many of the city's dignitaries were buried. Superstitious pagan Romans shunned the place at night, making it an ideal rendezvous for clandestine Christian worshippers under their early teacher, St Trophime. Later, Christians were often honoured by burial next to the tomb of Genesius, a beheaded Christian martyr.

Église St-Trophime

🏛 Place de la République 🕐 Daily 🌐 patrimoine.ville-arles.fr

This is one of Provence's great Romanesque churches. The portal and cloisters are decorated with biblical scenes.

St Trophime, thought to be the first bishop of Arles in the early 3rd century, appears with St Peter and St John on the carved northeast pillar.

Les Thermes de Constantin

🏛 Rue du Grand-Prieuré 🕐 Daily 🌐 patrimoine.ville-arles.fr

Built by the Roman emperor Constantine in 306 AD, these once vast public baths were partially restored at the end of the 19th century. The three remaining original buildings attest to the ingenuity of Roman engineering.

📷 PICTURE PERFECT
In the Footsteps of Van Gogh

Visit the atmospheric place du Forum in the evening for a snap of the Restaurant-Café Van Gogh, still painted just as it was when it inspired his *Café Terrace at Night* (1888).

↑ Carved figures of St John *(left)* and St Peter *(right)* at Église St-Trophime

→ Flamingos wading through the lagoons of the Carmargue

5

CAMARGUE

 A5-B5 Bouches-du-Rhône Nîmes, Marseille Arles parc-camargue.fr

The mighty Rhône meets the Mediterranean in the Camargue, a delta of reedbeds, wetlands and marshland pastures where half-wild white horses and black cattle roam. At its heart is the vast Étang de Vaccarès, part of a network of channels and lagoons edged by a seemingly endless arc of beaches, such as the Plage de Beauduc.

① St-Gilles-du-Gard

🛈 1 place F Mistral; www. tourisme.saint-gilles.fr

Perched on the northern edge of the delta, the small town of St-Gilles-du-Gard is the 12th-century gateway to the Camargue. It's noted for its many festivals devoted to local music, culture, produce (including fruit from its famed apricot and peach orchards) and black bulls. In the heart of the old town, the Abbaye de St-Gilles is a UNESCO-listed *étape* on the Saint-Jacques-de-Compostelle pilgrimage route. The lovely carved façade is all that remains of the original building, which was founded by Raymond IV, Count of Toulouse, in the 12th century.

② Saintes-Maries-de-la-Mer

🛈 5 avenue Van Gogh; www.saintesmaries.com

Miles of long sandy beaches stretch either side of this easy-going seaside village, which is full of restaurants serving local produce, and shops selling colourful Camargue ceramics and textiles.

The 9th-century Église Notre-Dame-de-la-Mer, with its black Madonna, is the focus of a huge gypsy festival in May. Parades, horse races, and flamenco dances celebrate the village's three patron saints, Mary Magdalene, Mary Jacobe (sister of the Virgin) and Mary Salome (mother of the apostles James and John). According to local legend, all three washed up here in AD 40 and first brought Christianity to Provence.

 ③

Parc Ornithologique du Pont de Gau

📍 RD570, Pont-de-Gau ⏰ Ticket office: 9am–6pm daily 🚫 25 Dec 🌐 parc ornithologique.com

Wooden walkways and viewing platforms let visitors get close to flocks of wading flamingos, herons and many other waterfowl

↑ Visitors on the roof of Église Notre-Dame-de-la-Mer

in the wild. Visit in the evening to admire and photograph the Provençal coast's most spectacular sunsets.

④ 🗺 🛍

Musée de la Camargue

🏠 Mas du Pont de Rousty, D570, Arles ⏰ Oct–Mar: 10am–5pm daily; Apr–Sep: 9am–5:30pm daily ⏰ Weekends in Nov–Jan, 1 Jan, 1 May, 25 Dec 🌐 museedela camargue.com

The customs and lifestyles of the Camargue are the focus of this museum, housed in the huge barn of a traditional Provençal *mas* or farmhouse. Displays, including video footage and slide shows, provide an excellent introduction to the people, environment and wildlife of the wetlands. Among the many subjects covered are the lives of the Camargue cowboys, and the history of the *grand* and *petit* Rhône rivers which once flowed far to the east of Nîmes. Many of the dis-

↑ Spectacular sunset over the wetlands of the Camargue

plays are focused the story of Frédéric Mistral, a local man who won the Nobel Prize for literature in 1904.

A signposted 4-km (2-mile) walking trail leads out from the museum to the Marais de la Grand Mare, and back again in a pleasant circular route. An observation tower at the end of the walk affords great views over the surrounding countryside.

Did You Know?

The salt pans in the southeast corner of the Camargue produce 800,000 tonnes of salt a year.

in this 24-ha (60-acre) expanse of lagoons, pastures and reedbeds. Aviaries dotted around the marshland house unusual birds that are very usually difficult to spot

STAY

L'Auberge Cavalière du Pont des Bannes

Stay in luxury rooms in these lovely waterside farmhouse-style villas. Perks include swimming pools, a spa, riding stables and an excellent restaurant.

🏠 Rte d'Arles, Saintes-Maries-de-la-Mer 🌐 auberge cavaliere.com

€€€

Mas Saint Germain

Accommodation in spacious self-catering gîtes and guesthouse rooms among Camargue fields and pastureland.

🏠 Villeneuve-Camargue, Arles 13200 🌐 massaint germain.com

€€€

Étang du Fangassier

🛈 Rte d'Arles, 13129 Salin-de-Giraud ⏰ Apr-Sep: for guided tours only 🚫 Oct-Mar 🌐 guide-nature.fr

The Étang du Fangassier is home to France's only breeding colony of flamingos. Between 10,000 and 15,000 pink-plumaged pairs raise their young on and around a lagoon island that was used for salt production until 2008. The flamingos feed on shrimp and other tiny creatures that thrive in the lagoon, and during the breeding season you can hear the birds from hundreds of metres away.

Domaine de la Palissade

🏠 13129 Salin-de-Giraud ⏰ 9am-5pm Wed-Sun (Mar-Oct: daily) 🚫 Dec-Jan, 1 May, 11 Nov 🌐 palissade.fr

This lovely, richly bio-diverse estate is one of the last expanses of the delta to survive untouched by the land reclamation projects, drainage channels and saltpans that have gradually altered the face of the Camargue over centuries. It comprises a dozen different habitats, each home to colourful wild-flowers and butterflies. Rare birds such as bitterns, terns, avocets and other waders nest and roost here. Vast expanses of dunes and marshland can be explored on foot or on a half-wild white Camarguais horse, with guided tours lasting from 30 minutes to 3 hours.

Start your expedition at the nature centre, which provides free maps of the three walking tours on the estate, and binocolars to hire.

Maison du Riz

🏠 Mas de la Vigne, Chemin de Figares, 13123 Albaron ⏰ Apr-Nov: 9:30am-12:30pm & 2-6pm Sun-Fri, (book in advance) 🚫 Dec-Mar 🌐 maisonduriz.com

Generations of the Rozière family have grown rice at their farm in the heart of the Camargue wetlands, and their mission is to bring this agricultural tradition to life. Visit in spring and early summer to help with planting the fields, or in September and October to take part in the harvest. To immerse yourself fully in the life of the farm, you can stay in one of the farm's five self-catering gîtes, and buy gourmet rice products from the shop there.

> 💬 INSIDER TIP
> **Mosquitoes**
>
> Don't forget to pack mosquito repellent if venturing off the beaten track – Camargue mosquitoes are noto-riously bloodthirsty.

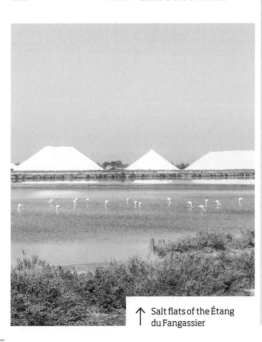

↑ Salt flats of the Étang du Fangassier

BIRDS AND BEASTS OF CAMARGUE

The Camargue's extensive areas of salt marshes, lakes, pastures and sand dunes – covering a vast 1,000 sq km (386 sq miles) – provide shelter and nutrients to a varied array of wildlife. Native horses and black bulls roam the green pastures; migrating seabirds and wildfowl shelter in the wetlands.

CAMARGUE BIRDS

The Camargue is a paradise for birders, particularly in spring when migrant birds visit on their journey north. This is the only French breeding site of the slender-billed gull, and the red-crested pochard, rarely seen in Europe, also breeds here.

HORSES

The half-wild, free-roaming white horses of the Camargue *(below)* are a primitive breed. Descended from wild horses that roamed Provence in prehistoric times, they are dark brown at birth and gradually turn white between four and seven years of age.

GREATER FLAMINGOS

The icons of the Camargue, wild flamingos stalk the delta's shallow lagoons. The Camargue is home to more than 20,000 of these fabulous pink birds, but multiple threats, such as climate change, pollution and illegal hunting, place their future at risk.

CAMARGUE BULLS

Raised on ranches called *manades* and herded by *gardians*, Camargue bulls are bred for the *course Camarguaise*, a type of bloodless variant on the bullfight. Under the name *raço di biòu*, the meat of Camargue bulls has AOC status and features in many local dishes.

CAMARGUE GARDIANS

The native white horses and black bulls of the Camargue have been herded, branded and tended to by the region's cowboys, or *gardians* since the 16th century. There are around 2,500 active *gardians*, working across the region – of whom around 10 per cent are women – but social and economic pressures are taking their toll on the profession and making it harder to maintain.

6

AIGUES-MORTES

 A5 30 km (15 miles) W Montpellier Rte de Nîmes Tour de
Constance Pl St-Louis; www.ot.aiguesmortes.com

A sturdy sentinel set among the salt marshes of the Camargue,
Aigues-Mortes ("dead waters" in Provençal) looks much as it
must have done when it was completed in around 1300. Then,
however, the Rhône had not yet deposited the silt which now
landlocks the town, and canals transported the vast blocks used
to make its walls from quarries in Beaucaire. Only the Hundred
Years' War saw the town's ramparts breached: now its gates
are always open to the besieging armies of admiring visitors.

Tour de la
Poudrière
Porte de
l'Arsenal

The 1,634-m (1-mile)
long ramparts are
punctuated by ten
gates, most notably
the Porte de la Reine,
named for Queen Anne
of Austria, who visited
the town in 1622.

RUE DE L'ARSENAL
RUE HOCHE
RUE HOCHE
RUE ROGER
SALENGRO
RUE EMI
RUE BAUDIN
BOULEVARD GAMBETTA
RUE DE LA REPU

Tour de
la Mèche

Chapelle des
Pénitents Blancs

Tour du Sel

←
Aigues-Mortes
harbour, seen next to
the Tour de Constance

①
Chapels of the Grey and White Penitents

Founded around 1400,
the Chapelle des Pénitents
Gris is still used by the "grey
penitents", a Catholic monastic
order founded in 1400. Named
for their grey cowls, they
walk with the white-cowled
Pénitents Blancs in the annual
Palm Sunday procession.
Built in 1668, the Chapelle
des Pénitents Blancs has an
outstanding mural depicting
the descent of the Holy Spirit.

②
The Towers

The Tour de Constance, at the
northwest corner, often held
religious prisoners such as the
Knights Templar, condemned
as heretics by Philip the Fair
in the early 14th century. The
Tour des Bourguignons was
used to keep the salt-pickled

The beautifully preserved medieval city of Aigue-Mortes ↑

Porte de la Marine

Porte des Galions

Lined with cafés, leafy place St-Louis is at the heart of town life. In its centre is a bronze statue of St Louis, on a base carved with the prows of crusader ships.

Porte de l'Organeau

CQUES ROUSSEAU

RUE THEAULON

RUE VICTOR HUGO

RUE P ROLLAND

MARCEAU

RUE DENFERT ROCHEREAU

RUE ALSACE LORRAINE

ST-LOUIS

RUE SADI-CARNOT

③

RUE AMIRAL COURBERT

GRAND RUE JEAN JAURES

Tour des Bourguignons

②

Porte de la Gardette

← Illustration of the streets of Aigue-Mortes

corpses of hundreds of Burgundian troops slain when Gascon troops seized the town, and the Tour de la Mèche or "wick tower" held a constant flame used to light cannon fuses. The Tour de la Poudrière at the southeast corner of the fortifications was the arsenal, where weapons and gunpowder were stored, while the Tour du Sel was used to store the salt that was the town's most highly valued commodity.

③

Notre-Dame des Sablons

The Gothic church of "Our Lady of the Sands", was built in the mid-12th century, before the construction of Aigues-Mortes' rectangle of ramparts. Although it pre-dates most of the town's buildings, it lay derelict for almost a century following the collapse of its bell tower in 1634 and was extensively rebuilt between 1738 and 1744. In the 1960s much of the elaborate 19th-century decoration was removed to return the building to a plainer style more in keeping with its medieval heritage. The interior is beautifully lit by luminously colourful stained-glass windows created in 1991 by Nîmes-born artist Claude Viallat (b. 1936).

EXPERIENCE MORE

7

Barbentane

 B4 Avignon, Tarascon
  3 rue des Pénitents;
www.barbentane.fr

Members of Avignon's Papal court liked to build summer houses in Barbentane, beside the Rhône, 10 km (6 miles) south of the city. One such building, opposite the 13th- to 15th-century Notre-Dame-de-Grâce, was the handsome Maison des Chevaliers, which was owned by the Marquises of Barbentane. Only the 40-m (130-ft) Tour Anglica remains of the town's 14th-century castle. Just outside the medieval quarter is the Château de Barbentane,

> HIDDEN GEM
> ### Massif de la Montagnette
> Just outside Barbentane, the peaceful wilderness of the vast Massif de la Montagnette makes for a great weekend escape. Here, gentle hills cloaked in pine, olive groves and almond trees are crisscrossed by a network of walking, cycling and riding trails.

a finely decorated Italianate mansion, built in 1674 by the Barbentane aristocracy who still own and reside in it.

Also in the town is the 16th- to 17th-century Moulin de Mogador, which was an oil mill and now hosts dinners.

8

Abbaye St-Michel de Frigolet

 B4 8am-6pm daily; check website for tours and group visits frigolet.com

The abbey is situated south of St-Michel de Frigolet, in the La Montagnette countryside. A cloister and small church date from the 12th century, but in 1858 a Premonstratensian abbey was founded, and one of the most richly decorated churches of that period was built. The whole interior is colourfully painted in rich tones of red and green, with golden stars on the ceiling and bright saints on the pillars. The small 12th-century Église St-Michel is on the Abbey road, near the entrance.

After a brief period of exile in Belgium at the beginning of the 20th century, the monks returned to Frigolet. The word *frigolet* is Provençal for thyme.

> **The whole interior is colourfully painted in rich tones of red and green, with golden stars on the ceiling and bright saints on the pillars.**

9

Beaucaire

 B4 Tarascon
 8 rue Victor Hugo;
www.beaucaire.fr

The bullring in Beaucaire occupies the site of one of the largest fairs in Europe. Held every July for the past seven centuries, it attracted up to a quarter of a million people. A smaller version of the fair takes place today, with a procession on 21 July.

It was inaugurated by Raymond VI in 1217, who enlarged the **Château de Beaucaire**. This was later used by the French kings to watch over their Provençal neighbours across the river. It was partly dismantled on the orders of Cardinal Richelieu but the triangular keep and enough of the walls remain to indicate its scale. There is a Romanesque chapel within the walls, and various medieval spectacles take place here, including frequent displays of falconry.

The Abbaye de St-Roman is situated 5 km (3 miles) from Beaucaire. Dating from the 5th century, it is the only troglodyte monastery in Europe.

Château de Beaucaire
  Place Raimond VII
 04 66 59 26 57 Jul-Aug: daily; Sep-May: Wed-Sun

←
Rich colours and detail in the interior of the Abbaye St Michel de Frigolet

PONT DU GARD

The Pont du Gard is a triumph of Roman engineering. Begun around 19 BC, this bridge is part of an the three-tiered aqueduct is made of huge limestone blocks, some of them weighing up to six tonnes. Amazingly, no mortar was used in its construction. Blocks of masonry that supported scaffolding during the construction of the aqueduct can still be seen jutting from its mighty arches.

The Pont du Gard's water channel, covered by stone slabs, was in its uppermost tier, and it is thought that it may have been supplying the citizens of Nîmes with water as recently as the 6th century AD. Until the early 20th century the Pont du Gard was used as a road bridge, but since being declared a UNESCO World Heritage Site its location has been cleared of more recent constructions and it appears once again as it did in Roman times.

Did You Know?

The Pont du Gard could carry 20 million litres (4 million gallons) of water each day.

WATER TRANSPORT SYSTEM

The Pont du Gard was part of a vast system of underground channels and bridges that included the Pont de Bornègre, where the aqueduct emerged from an underground tunnel to cross a triple-arched bridge, and the Pont de la Lône, an overhead arcade carrying the water channel for some 400 m (1,320 ft). The Pont Roupt, a huge bridge that was more than 255 m (840 ft) long (of which 37 arches survive), was also part of this water system. At Sernhac, downstream from the Pont du Gard, you can explore two tunnels, each about 60 m (197 ft) long, which carried the stream onwards towards Nîmes.

↑ Water tunnels at Sernhac, part of the water transport system fed by the Pont du Gard

The triple-tiered arched design ensures the heavy water load is supported.

Water channel, covered by stone slabs

Protruding stones for supporting scaffolding during construction

Skilfully designed cutwaters have ensured the bridge has resisted many violent floods.

↑ The beautifully preserved Roman Pont du Gard

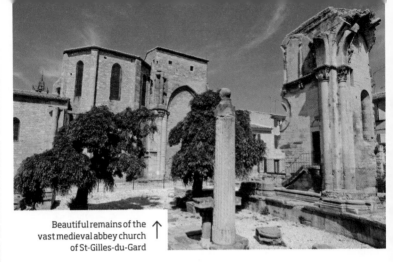

Beautiful remains of the vast medieval abbey church of St-Gilles-du-Gard ↑

 10

St-Gilles-du-Gard

A4 **Nîmes** **1 place Frédéric Mistral; www. tourisme.saint-gilles.fr**

Known as the "Gateway to the Camargue", St-Gilles is famous for its Abbaye de St-Gilles. The building was damaged in 1562 during the Wars of Religion, and all that remains are the west façade, chancel and crypt. The carved façade is the most beautiful in all Provence. It includes the first sculpture of the Passion in Christendom, from the late 12th century.

Founded by Raymond VI of Toulouse, the abbey church was the Knights of St John's

LEGEND OF THE TARASQUE

According to legend, the tarasque – a man-eating monster with a lion's head and mane, a snake's tail, the claws of a bear and a turtle-like shell – terrorized Tarascon until it was killed by St Martha. An effigy of the beast is paraded though the streets during the last weekend in June in an annual celebration that has taken place since the 15th century.

first priory in Europe. It soon became one of the key destinations on the pilgrimage route to Santiago de Compostela in Spain, and a port of embarkation for the Crusades. The crypt houses the tomb of Saint Gilles, a hermit who arrived by raft from Greece.

The bell tower of the original abbey contains *La Vis*, a spiral staircase which is a masterpiece of stonemasonry.

 11

Tarascon

B4 **62 rue des Halles; www.tarascon.fr**

The gleaming white vision of the **Château de Tarascon** is one of the landmarks of the Rhône. Little is left of the glittering court of Good King René, who finished the building his father, Louis II of Anjou, began early in the 15th century (p50). Following René's death in 1480, Provence fell to France, and the castle became a prison until 1926. A drawbridge leads to the poultry yard and garrison quarters. Beside it rises the impressive main castle, centred on a courtyard from where two spiral staircases lead to royal apartments in its sturdy towers. Prisoners' graffiti and some painted ceiling panels remain, but the only adornment is a handful

of borrowed 17th-century tapestries which depict the deeds of Roman general Scipio (237–183 BC).

The Collégiale Ste-Marthe nearby has a tomb in the crypt to the monster-taming St Martha (p46), who rescued the inhabitants from the Tarasque, a man-eating monster, which gave the town its name.

In the old town is the 16th-century Cloître des Cordeliers where exhibitions are held. On the rue des Halles is the 17th-century town hall, with a carved façade and balcony.

The traditional life of the area and its hand-printed fabrics is seen in the **Musée Souleïado**. The ancient textile industry was revived in 1938, under the name *Souleïado*, meaning "the sun passing through the clouds" in Provençal. The museum has a huge collection of woodblocks, many of them still used for the company's colourful prints.

The **Musée d'Art et d'Histoire**, housed in the Couvent des Cordeliers, covers the history of the Fête de la Tarasque, and also holds temporary art exhibitions.

→

Enjoying a break under the trees in place Favier, St-Rémy

Château de Tarascon

◈ ◈ ◐ 🅰 Blvd du Roi René 🕒 Apr–Sep: daily; Oct–Mar: Tue–Sun 🚫 1 Jan, 1 May, 1 & 11 Nov, 25 Dec 🌐 chateau.tarascon.fr

Musée Souleïado

◈ ◈ 🅰 39 rue Charles Deméry 🕒 Mon–Sat 🚫 1 Jan, 1 & 11 Nov, 25 Dec 🌐 souleiado.com

Musée d'Art et d'Histoire

🅰 Place Frédéric Mistral ☎ 04 90 91 38 71 🕒 May–Aug: Tue–Sat; Sep–Apr: Mon–Fri

---

🕧

St-Rémy-de-Provence

🅰 B4 🚌 Avignon 🛈 Place Jean-Jaurès; www.alpille senprovence.com

St-Rémy is ideal for exploring the Alpilles countryside where the plants for its traditional *herboristeries* (herb shops) grow.

One of the town's most attractive 15th- to 16th-century mansions is now a museum. The **Musée des Alpilles** has a fine ethnographic collection. The well-known 16th-century physician and astrologer, Nostradamus, was born in a house in the outer wall of the rue Hoche, in the old quarter of St-Rémy.

The **Musée Estrine**, in the 18th-century Hôtel Estrine, houses modern and contemporary art. Temporary exhibits pay tribute to Van Gogh's relationship with

40,000

The number of 18th-century woodblocks that are kept at the Musée Souleïado.

St-Rémy. In May 1889, after he had mutilated his ear, Van Gogh arrived at the **Cloître et Cliniques de St-Paul de Mausole**, which is situated between the town and Glanum. The grounds and the 12th-century monastery house a museum and culture centre in which an entire wing is dedicated to the painter's stay. You can visit a reconstruction of Van Gogh's room and the field that he painted 15 times.

Just behind the clinic is Le Mas de la Pyramide, a farmstead half-built into the rock, which was once a Roman quarry. The remains of the earliest Greek houses in Provence, from the 4th-century BC, are in the **Site Archéologique de Glanum** *(p44)*, a Greco-Roman town at the head of a valley in the Alpilles. The ancient statuary unearthed here is preserved at the **Hôtel de Sade**, a

15th-century mansion in the heart of St-Rémy. The hotel also has a fascinating display of the different stages of archaeological research. Along the roadside stands a triumphal arch from 10 BC, celebrating Caesar's conquest of the Greeks and Gaul, and a mausoleum dating from about 30 BC.

Musée des Alpilles

◈ 🅰 Place Charles Favier ☎ 04 90 92 68 24 🕒 Tue–Sun (Nov–Apr: Tue–Sat pm only)

Musée Estrine

◈ ◐ 🅰 8 rue Lucien Estrine 🕒 Tue–Sun (Mar & Nov: pm only) 🚫 Dec–Feb 🌐 musee-estrine.fr

Cloître et Cliniques de St-Paul de Mausole

◈ 🅰 Chemin St-Paul 🕒 Mar–Dec: daily 🚫 Public hols 🌐 saintpauldemausole.fr

Site Archéologique de Glanum

◈ ◈ ◐ 🅰 Ave Vincent Van Gogh 🕒 Daily (Oct–Mar: Tue–Sun) 🚫 1 Jan, 1 May, 1 & 11 Nov, 25 Dec 🌐 site-glanum.fr

Hôtel de Sade

◈ ◈ ◐ 🅰 1 rue du Parage 🕒 Mid-Jun–mid-Sep: Tue–Sun 🌐 hotel-de-sade.fr

13

Les Alpilles

B4 **Arles, Tarascon, Salon-de-Provence** **Les Baux-de-Provence, St-Rémy-de-Provence, Eyguières, Eygalières** **St-Rémy-de-Provence; www.alpillesenprovence.com**

St-Rémy-de-Provence is on the western side of the limestone massif of Les Alpilles, a 24-km (15-mile) chain between the Rhône and Durance rivers. A high point is La Caume, at 387 m (1,270 ft), which can be reached from St-Rémy, just beyond Glanum.

East of St-Rémy, the road to Cavaillon runs along the north side of the massif, with a right turn to Eygalières. The painter Mario Prassinos (1916–85) lived here. Just beyond the village is the 12th-century Chapelle St-Sixte.

The road continues towards Orgon where there are views across the Durance Valley and the Luberon. Orgon skirts the massif on the eastern side. A right turn leads past the ruins of Castellas de Roquemartine and Eyguières, a pleasant village with a Romanesque church. It is a two-hour walk to Les Opies, a 493-m (1,617-ft) hill crowned by a tower. This forms part of the GR6 which crosses the chain to Les Baux-de-Provence, one of the best walking routes in Provence. From Castellas de Roquemartine the road heads back west towards Les Baux.

The countryside of Les Alpilles is filled with olive trees and vast green fields with the Montmajour abbey visible in the distance from the D17, en route to Les Baux-de-Provence.

14

Les Baux-de-Provence

B4 **La Maison du Roy, rue Porte Mage; www.lesbauxdeprovence.com**

The attractive and popular town of Les Baux-de-Provence sits on a spur of the Alpilles (*bau* in Provençal means escarpment). The majestic fortified **Château des Baux-de-Provence** offers breathtaking views of the surrounding region from Aix to Arles and across to the Camargue (*p138*). The most dramatic fortress site in the region, it is extremely popular, welcoming nearly two million visitors every year, so avoid midsummer, or go early

in the morning to avoid the crowds. The pedestrianized town has a car park beside the Porte Mage gate. When the Lords of Baux built their fine citadel here in the 10th century, they claimed one of the three wise men, King Balthazar, as an ancestor and took the star of Bethlehem as their emblem. These fierce warriors originated the troubadour Courts of Love, and wooed noble ladies with poetry and songs. This became the medieval convention known as courtly love and paved the way for a literary tradition.

The citadel ruins lie on the heights of the escarpment. Their entrance is via the 14th-century Tour-du-Brau. A plateau extends to the end of the escarpment, where there is a monument to the French farmer and poet Charloun Rieu (1846–1924).

In the town centre there are two other museums of local interest. At the **Fondation Louis Jou**, medieval books are housed in the beautifully restored Renaissance home of Spanish typographer and engraver Louis Jou, after whom the museum is named, along with a collection of prints and drawings by Dürer, Goya and Jou. At the **Musée des Santons**, located in the town's 16th-century old town hall, a traditional Provençal crib scene has been created, representing the nativity at Les Baux. Exquisite handmade clay *santons*, or figurines

←
The walls of the Château des Baux-de-Provence rise up above the landscape

↑ The modest 1814 Moulin de Daudet lies near Fontvieille

> **When the Lords of Baux built their fine citadel here in the 10th century, they claimed one of the wise men, King Balthazar, as an ancestor.**

representing saints and local figures, show the evolution of Provençal costume.

Next door to the imposing 12th-century Église St-Vincent is the Chapelle des Pénitents Blancs, decorated in 1974 by renowned local artist Yves Brayer.

Located on the D27 road to the north of Les Baux, and within walking distance of the main car park in Les Baux, is the Val d'Enfer, or the Valley of Hell. This jagged gorge, said to be inhabited by witches and spirits, may have inspired some of Dante's poetry. It is also the site where bauxite was discovered in 1821 by the geologist Berthier, who named it after the town.

It was in this large quarry that the Cathédrale d'Images, or the **Carrières de Lumières** as it is presently known, was established. Here, the imaginative art exhibitions featuring

the works of painters such as Klimt, Chagall and Van Gogh are projected not only onto the white limestone walls of the natural theatre, but also onto the floor and ceiling, creating a dramatic three-dimensional effect. Accompanied by captivating music, the exhibitions are truly an extraordinary audio-visual experience.

Château des Baux-de-Provence

⊛ ⊘ 🕐 Times vary, check website 🌐 chateau-baux-provence.com

Fondation Louis Jou

⊛ 🏠 Hôtel de Brion, Grande rue 🕐 Times vary, check website 🌐 fondation louisjou.org

Musée des Santons

🏠 Place Louis Jou 📞 04 90 54 34 39 🕐 10am–5pm daily (winter: 9am–7pm)

Carrières de Lumières

⊛ ⊘ 🕐 🏠 Route de Maillane 🕐 Times vary, check website 🌐 carrieres-lumieres.com

---

Fontvieille

🅰 B4 🚆 🚌 *i* Ave des Moulins; www.alpillesen provence.com

Fontvieille is an agreeable country town in the flat fruit and vegetable lands of the irrigated Baux Valley. There is a market here every Monday and Friday. Halfway between Arles and Les Alpilles, the town makes an excellent centre from which to explore the area. Until the French Revolution in 1789, the town's history was bound up with the Abbaye de Montmajour. The oratories that stand at the four corners of the small town were erected in 1721 to celebrate the end of the plague.

To the south on the D33 is the Moulin de Daudet and the remarkable remains of a Roman aqueduct at Barbegal.

16

Abbaye de Montmajour

🅐 B4 🚗 Route de Fontvieille ⏱ Daily (Oct-Apr: Tue-Sun) 📅 1 Jan, 1 May, 1 & 11 Nov, 25 Dec 🌐 abbaye-montmajour.fr

Standing out like Noah's ark on Mount Ararat, situated 5 km (3 miles) northeast of Arles, this Benedictine abbey was built in the 10th century. At the time, the site was an island refuge in marshland. The handful of monks in residence spent all their spare time draining this area of marshland between the Alpilles chain and the Rhône.

The abbey is an imposing place, though all the Baroque buildings were destroyed by fire in 1726 and were never restored. The original church is said to have been founded by Saint Trophime as a sanctuary from the Romans. It grew rich in the Middle Ages when thousands of pilgrims arrived at Easter to purchase pardons. After 1791, the abbey was broken up by two successive owners who

→

Imposing tower at the abbey of St Pierre at Montmajour

bought it from the state. The abbey was largely restored in the 19th century.

The Église Notre-Dame is one of the largest Romanesque buildings in Provence. Below, the 12th-century crypt has been built into the sloping hill. The cloister has double pillars ornamented with beasts, and lies in the shadows of the 26-m (85-ft) tower, built in the 1360s. It is worth climbing the 124 steps to the tower platform to see the stunning view across to the sea.

Also carved into the hillside is the atmospheric Chapelle de St-Pierre. It was established at the same time as the abbey and is a primitive place of worship. There are a number of tombs in the abbey grounds, but the principal burial area is the 12th-century Chapelle Ste-Croix. It lies not far to the east and is built in the shape of a Greek cross.

17

Martigues

🅐 B5 🚉🚌 ℹ Rond-Point de l'Hôtel de Ville; www.martigues-tourisme.com

The Étang de Berre, situated between Marseille and the Camargue, has the largest petroleum refinery industry in

France, which dominates the landscape. However, on the inland side of the Canal de Caronte is the former fishing port and artists' colony of Martigues, which still attracts a holiday crowd.

Martigues lies on both banks of the canal and on the island of Brescon, where the Pont St-Sébastien is a popular place for artists to set up their easels. Félix Ziem (1821–1911) was the most ardent admirer of the canals, bridges and docks of this "little Venice"; his paintings, as well as works by a variety of contemporary artists, can be viewed in the **Musée Ziem**.

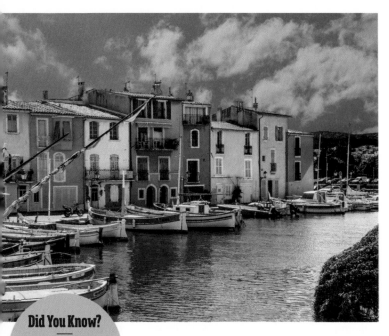

Musée Ziem

🏛 Blvd du 14 Juillet 🕐 Wed-Sun pm (Jul-Aug: Wed-Mon)

 18

Salon-de-Provence

🅱 B4 🚃 ℹ 249 pl Morgan; www.visitsalonde provence.com

Known for its olives (the olive oil industry here was established in the 1400s) and soap, Salon-de-Provence is dominated by the castellated **Château de l'Empéri**, which overlooks the Crau plain. Standing on its rocky base, the château was once home to the archbishops of Arles, and it now contains the Musée de l'Empéri, which has a large collection of militaria dating from the time of Louis XIV up to World War I. Near the château is the 13th-century Église St-Michel and in the north of the old town stands the Gothic St-Laurent, where the French physician and astrologer Nostradamus, Salon's most famous citizen, is buried. Here, in his adopted home, he wrote *Les Centuries*, his book of predictions, published in 1555. It was banned by the Vatican, as it foretold the diminishing power of the papacy. However, his renown was widespread and in 1560 he became Charles IX's physician.

Salon is the host of a two-week chamber music festival, which takes place from late July to August, with concerts in the château, Église St-Michel, Abbaye de Sainte-Croix and the town's theatre.

From the place Crousillat, you can admire the Tour de l'Horloge clock tower and the mushroom-shaped, moss-covered Fontaine Moussue.

Château de l'Empéri

🖼 🏛 Montée du Puech 📞 04 90 44 72 80 🕐 Tue-Sun 🚫 1 Jan, 1 May, 1 Nov, 24-25 & 31 Dec

↑ Rainbow-coloured houses overlooking the harbour at Martigues

GAME FISHING FROM MARTIGUES

Straddling the channel that links the Étang de Berre with the open sea, Martigues is famous among anglers hoping to hook prized trophy fish like marlin, tuna and even shark. But game fishers are aware of conservation issues. Many release their catch after winning their battles, and ethical "no-kill" skippers no longer return to Martigues with their catch dangling from the rigging. These days, the trophies are selfies and video footage, even though chartering a boat and skipper costs around €1,200 per day (€220 for those willing to share a boat with other anglers).

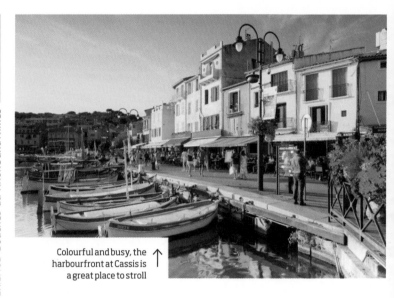

Colourful and busy, the harbourfront at Cassis is a great place to stroll ↑

19

Aubagne

⚑C5 🚌🚐 *i* 8 cours Barthelémy; www. tourisme-paysdaubagne.fr

Marcel Pagnol's life and work are the main attractions of this simple market town. A plaque at No. 16 cours Barthélemy marks the birthplace of the much-loved Provençal writer and filmmaker. The town also has a tradition of making ceramics and *santons* (figurines). The town's tableaux can be seen in the Petit Monde de Marcel Pagnol display on the Esplanade de Gaulle, about 300 m from the tourist office.

Just outside the town is the headquarters of the French Foreign Legion, moved here from Algeria in 1962. The headquarters is home to the **Musée de la Légion Étrangère** with memorabilia on display from a variety of campaigns ranging from Mexico to IndoChina.

Musée de la Légion Étrangère

⚑Chemin de la Thuilière 🕙10am–12pm & 2–6pm Tue–Sun 🌐legion-etrangere.com

20

Abbaye de Silvacane

⚑C4 🚗RD 561 🚌 🕙Daily (Oct–May: Tue–Sun) 🚫1 Jan, 1 May & 25 Dec 🌐abbaye-silvacane.com

Like her two Cistercian sister abbeys, Sénanque and Le Thoronet, Silvacane is a harmonious 12th-century monastery tucked away in the countryside. A bus from Aix-en-Provence travels regularly to La Roque-d'Anthéron, the nearest village.

The abbey was founded on the site of a Benedictine monastery, in a clearing of a "forest of reeds" *(silva canorum)*. It adheres to the austere Cistercian style, with no decoration. The church, with nave, two aisles and a high, vaulted transept, is solid, bare and echoing. The cloisters, arcaded like a pigeon loft, are 13th century, and the refectory dates from the 14th century. Shortly after the refectory was built, all the monks left and the church served the parish. After the Revolution, it was sold as state property and became a farm until it was transformed back into an abbey.

21

Cassis

⚑C6 🚌🚐 *i* Quai des Moulins; www.ot-cassis.com

A favourite summer resort of artists such as Derain, Dufy and Matisse, Cassis is a delightful port, tucked into limestone hills. The Romans admired it, too, and built villas here, and when Marseille prospered during the 17th century a number of mansions were erected. It was also a busy fishing centre in the 19th century, and is still

---

PAINTERS INSPIRED BY CASSIS

Cassis, its landscapes, rich hues and brilliant light, inspired painters such as André Derain, Raoul Dufy and Henri Matisse, all three of whom painted scenes from the village in the early 20th century. It also lured artists from as far away as Scotland, including Colourists who visited in the 1920s.

known for its seafood. The local delicacy is sea urchins, enjoyed with a glass of Cassis's reputed AOC white wine.

The **Musée Municipal Méditerranéen** has items dating back to the Greeks, some rescued from the seabed. It shows Cassis to have been a substantial trading port until World War II. Other items include paintings by Félix Ziem and other early 20th-century artists who were equally drawn to Cassis.

There are three good beaches nearby, notably the Plage de la Grande Mer. The red cliffs of Cap Canaille, between Cassis and La Ciotat, offer a 4-hour walk (one-way) along Route des Crêtes.

Musée Municipal Méditerranéen d'Art et Traditions Populaires

 ⌂ Place Baragnon ☎ 04 42 01 88 66 ◷ Wed-Sat

22

Les Calanques

⌂ C6 🚉🚌⛴ Cassis, Marseille ⓦ calanques-parcnational.fr

Between Marseille and Cassis, the coast is broken up by calanques – fjord-like inlets lying between vertical white cliffs. Deep under the blue waters, they offer safe natural harbours and fascinating aquatic life, with glorious views from the high clifftops. The precipitous cliff face provides a challenge for keen climbers. The Parc National des Calanques is the only national park in Europe to include land, marine and semi-urban areas. Opened in 2012, it is home to over 200 protected animal, plant and marine species.

From Cassis, it is possible to walk to the nearest *calanque*, Port-Miou. Beyond it lies Port-Pin, with occasional pine trees and a shady beach, but the most scenic is En-Vau, which has a sandy beach and needle-like rocks rising from the sea. Walking paths often close in summer, due to the risk of fire. On the western side, the Sormiou and Morgiou inlets can be reached by road.

In 1991, the entrance to a cave was found 100 m (350 ft) under the sea at Sormiou. It is decorated with pictures of prehistoric animals resembling the ancient cave paintings at Lascaux in the Dordogne. Bear in mind when visiting the area that the main car parks serving Les Calanques beaches are notorious for theft.

EAT

La Villa Madie
Enjoy idyllic sea views and spectacular seafood at this fine-dining restaurant.

 C6 ⌂ Ave de Revestel, Cassis ☎ 04 96 18 00 00 ◷ Tue-Wed, Jan-mid-Feb

€€€

La Vieille Auberge
This family-run bistro has a seafood-heavy menu and a harbour-side terrace.

 C6 ⌂ 14 quai Jean-Jacques Barthélemy, Cassis ☎ 04 42 01 73 54 ◷ Wed

€€€

L'Hemisphere
Family-run seafood bistro on the quayside, serving squid with pimento and roast cod.

 B5 ⌂ 6 quai Lucien Toulmond, Martigues ☎ 04 42 80 63 23 ◷ Tue

€€€

Breathtaking Calanque d'En-Vau, with its turquoise waters and dramatic cliffs ↑

VAUCLUSE

The jewel of Vaucluse is the fortified riverside city of Avignon, home to the popes during their "Babylonian exile" from 1309 to 1377, and now host to one of the greatest music and theatre festivals in France. The popes' castle at Châteauneuf-du-Pape is now a ruin, but the village still produces stupendous wines. The Rhône valley wine region is justly renowned, and its vineyards spread as far northeast as the slopes of the towering giant of Provence, Mont Ventoux.

The Roman legacy in Vaucluse is also remarkable. It is glimpsed in the great theatre and triumphal arch in Orange, and in the ruins of Vaison-la-Romaine which were preserved by successive civilizations. Carpentras was also a Roman town, but its claim to fame is its possession of France's oldest synagogue. The story of the Jews, who were given papal protection in Vaucluse, is one of many religious histories which can be traced through the region. Another is the Baron of Oppède's brutal crusade against the Vaudois heretics in 1545, when many villages were destroyed.

Near Oppède, at Lacoste, a path leads to the château of France's notorious libertine Marquis de Sade. Perhaps a more elevated writer was Petrarch, who also made Fontaine-de-Vaucluse his home.

VAUCLUSE

Must Sees

1 Avignon
2 Villeneuve-lès-Avignon
3 Orange
4 Abbaye de Sénanque
5 Vaison-la-Romaine
6 Mont Ventoux
7 Le Colorado Provençal

Experience More

8 L'Harmas de Fabre
9 Bollène
10 Carpentras
11 Caderousse
12 Châteauneuf-du-Pape
13 Fontaine-de-Vaucluse
14 L'Îsle-sur-la-Sorgue
15 Gordes
16 Château de Saumane
17 Roussillon
18 Cavaillon
19 Cadenet
20 Apt
21 Ansouis
22 Pertuis
23 La Tour d'Aigues

❶

AVIGNON

🅰B4 ✈8 km (5 miles) Avignon-Caumont 🚉🚌Blvd St-Roch; Gare TGV (pl de l'Europe, Courtine) ℹ41 cours Jean-Jaurès; www.avignon-tourisme.com

With its beautifully preserved medieval centre set along the Rhône and surrounding the magnificent Palais des Papes, Avignon attracts millions of visitors, so its main sights bustle for much of the year, especially during the summer Avignon Festival. To experience the city like a local, venture a couple of blocks from the focal place du Palais and place de l'Horloge to discover lively open-air markets and café terraces.

①

Palais des Papes

🅰Place du Palais 🕙10am–5pm daily 🌐palais-des-papes.com

The white stone walls of this 14th-century palace complex soar above Avignon's historic heart, a reminder of the power and wealth of the seven French popes who lived here after Pope Clement V moved the papacy from Rome to Avignon (p55). Pope Benedict XII was responsible for the sober, Cistercian architecture of the Palais Vieux; his successor, Clement VI, added the Palais Neuf in Gothic style, creating a flamboyant ensemble of turrets and hefty stone walls.

Entrance to this miniature Vatican is by means of the Porte des Champeaux, beneath the twin pencil-shaped turrets of the Palais Neuf. Inside, highlights include the Chambre du Pape, the Grande Chapelle, and the main court-yard, La Cour d'Honneur, which makes a grand central setting for the summer festival.

---

②

Place de l'Horloge

Café tables clutter Avignon's main square, overlooked by

↑ Wooden horses prancing round on the carousel in place de l'Horloge

←
Café tables spilling out onto place Crillon, shaded by plane trees

museum in 1976, and houses Avignon's medieval collection, which includes works by Simone Martini and Botticelli, as well as works from the Avignon School.

④ 🍽 🖥 🛍

Les Halles

🏠 Place Pie ⏰ 6am–2pm
Tue–Sun 🌐 avignon-leshalles.com

Savvy locals shop for fine produce at this state-of-the-art covered market. There are stalls where you can stand and sip a coffee or a glass of fizz, and booths where you can sit down to a seafood platter. The outer wall, facing place Pie, is an amazing vertical garden.

AVIGNON FESTIVAL

France's greatest theatre event is really two festivals. The official one takes over the Palais des Papes' Cour d'Honneur and other venues for both modern and classical drama. However, it is the unofficial "off" festival that enlivens the town, with street performers and up to 400 shows a day, from dance to burlesque comedy.

the Gothic clock tower that gives it its name. Built on the site of the city's ancient forum, the square is home to the 19th-century town hall and opera house. During the Avignon festival, the square becomes a stage for lively street performers. At other times of the year, the main attraction is the traditional *belle époque* carousel, where colourful wooden horses provide some excellent photo opportunities for families with children.

③ 🏛

Musée du Petit Palais

🏠 Palais des Archevêques, place du Palais ⏰ 10am–1pm & 2–6pm Wed–Mon
🌐 petit-palais.org

Set around an arcaded courtyard, the "little palace", built in 1318, was modified in 1474 to suit Michelangelo's patron Cardinal Rovere, later Pope Julius II. It became a

EAT

Restaurant Sevin

This fine-dining restaurant has a good-value lunch menu, while dinner features costlier items like oysters and lobster.

🏠 10 rue de Mons
🌐 restaurantsevin.fr

€€€

La Vieille Fontaine

The menu here is dazzlingly eclectic, with options like Brittany scallops with truffles, shrimp ceviche with coriander and garden cherries, and cold garden pea soup.

🏠 Hôtel d'Europe, 12 place Crillon
🌐 heurope.com

€€€

La Cabane d'Oléron

Tucked away in a corner of Avignon's extraordinary covered market, this restaurant has a handful of tables and a surprisingly affordable connoisseur's choice of seafood.

🏠 Rue de l'Olivier, Les Halles 📞 06 98 29 10 88

€€€

Carré du Palais

The two-course menu at this restaurant and wine bar in a historic building on place du Palais is a bargain. The *Grand Menu* is more indulgent, and the wine list is long and ever-changing.

🏠 1 place du Palais
🌐 carredupalais.fr

€€€

Musée Calvet

🏠 65 rue Joseph Vernet
🕐 10am-1pm & 2-6pm Wed-Mon 🌐 musee-calvet.org

Works by Soutine, Manet and Dufy are highlights of the Victor Martin collection of 19th- and 20th-century art in this gracious 18th-century townhouse, which also houses fine art, faïences and bronzes, and a new collection of ancient Egyptian art.

Pont St-Bénézet

🏠 Blvd de la Ligne
🕐 Daily

Angelic voices heard by a shepherd boy inspired the building of the first bridge here in 1185. Its arches were so often washed away by floods that in the early 17th century the townsfolk gave up rebuilding them, so it now ends abruptly in the middle of the river. Just four of the original 22 arches remain, as well as the gatehouse at the Avignon end of the bridge, and the Tour Philippe-le-Bel, the western terminus in Villeneuve-lès-Avignon that once connected Avignon's papal enclave with the rest of France (p164).

Cathédrale Notre-Dame-des-Doms

🏠 Place du Palais 🕐 Daily
🌐 metropole.diocese-avignon.fr

Founded in the 12th century and rebuilt several times since then, Avignon's cathedral stands next to the Palais des Papes, a larger-than-life golden Madonna poised atop its tower since the 19th century. Inside, the basilica is embellished with murals and paintings, and a chapel holds the tomb of Pope John XXII. Next to the cathedral, the gardens of the

43 BC

△ Avignon flourishes as it becomes a Roman colony.

1177–1185

▽ Pont St-Bénézet is built (for the first time).

1309–52

△ Pope Clement V moves the papacy from Rome to Avignon; Palais Vieux and Petit Palais are built to hold the papal court.

1947

▽ The first Avignon festival is held at the Palais des Papes.

Rocher des Doms offer a pleasant escape from busy city streets.

Collection Lambert

📍 5 rue Violette 🕐 11am–6pm Tue–Sun (Jul–Aug: to 7pm daily) 🌐 collection lambert.fr

The Collection Lambert is located in an 18th-century mansion, next to the School of Art, and houses an outstanding collection of contemporary art on loan for 20 years from gallery-owner Yvon Lambert. Paintings date from the 1960s and include all the major art movements since then. Highlights include ground-breaking works by Jean-Michel Basquiat, Louise Bourgeois, Carl Andre, Anselm Kiefer and Cy Twombly. The museum also runs creative courses for children.

Musée Angladon

📍 5 rue Laboureur 🕐 1–6pm Tue–Sat (Apr–Oct: also Sun) 🔒 Jan, 25 Dec 🌐 angladon.com

This dazzling hi-tech museum cleverly combines modern science with the intimacy of a private home. It displays a fine private collection of art dating from the 18th to the 20th centuries, including works by Degas, Van Gogh, Picasso, Modigliani and other greats. Temporary exhibitions feature contemporary guest stars like David Hockney.

Musée Lapidaire

📍 27 rue de la République 🕐 Tue–Sun 🔒 1 Jan, 1 May, 25 Dec 🌐 musee-lapidaire.org

Once a 17th-century Baroque Jesuit college, this museum houses a fascinating selection of Celtic-Ligurian, Egyptian, Gallic and Roman artifacts, including a 2nd-century Tarasque monster (*p148*). In the summer, the museum holds temporary exhibitions relating to the collection.

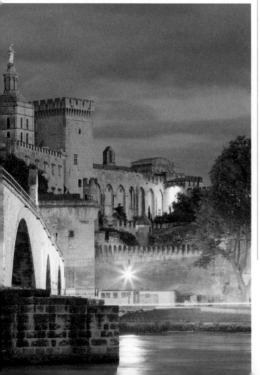

←

The remaining arches of Pont St-Bénézet over the Rhône

A SHORT WALK
AVIGNON

Distance 2 km (1 miles) **Nearest station**
Gare d'Avignon Centre **Time** 30 minutes

Bordered to the north and west by the Rhône, the medieval city of Avignon is the chief city of Vaucluse and the gateway to Provence. Its walls cover nearly 5 km (3 miles) and are punctuated by 39 towers and seven gates. Within the walls thrives a culturally rich city with its own opera house, university, several foreign-language schools and numerous theatre companies.

Chapelle St-Nicolas was named after the patron saint of bargemen and is a 16th-century building on a 13th-century base. Entrance is via Tour du Châtelet.

The **Pont St-Bénézet** was begun in 1177 by shepherd boy Bénézet. The bridge is the subject of the famous song Sur le Pont d'Avignon.

The historic **Porte du Rhône**

START

FINISH

You can access the 14th-century **ramparts** from the entrance to the Pont St-Bénézet.

Did You Know?

The Palais des Papes is the biggest Gothic palace in the world.

RUE FERR

RUE DE LIMAS

RUE GRANDE FUSTERIE

RUE DES GROTTES

RUE DE LA BALANCE

RUE ST-ETIENNE

RUE PETITE FUSTERIE

RUE RACINE

PLACE DE L'HORLOGE

Place de l'Horloge, the main square, was laid out in the 15th century. Many of today's buildings date from the 19th century.

The façade of the **Hôtel des Monnaies**, the former mint, built in 1619, bears the arms of Cardinal Borghese.

↑ Visitors stroll past the carousel in Avignon's place de l'Horloge

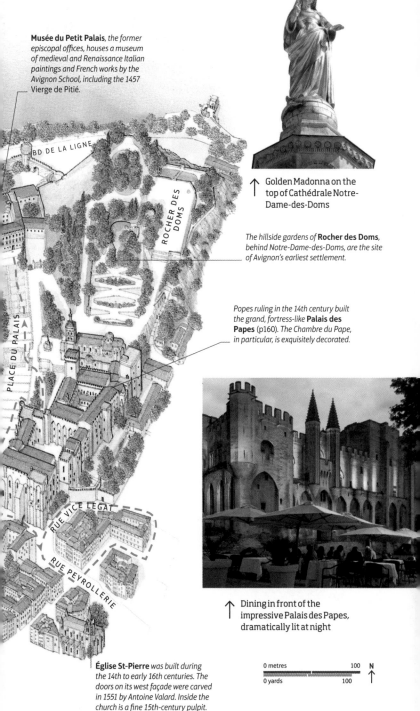

Musée du Petit Palais, *the former episcopal offices, houses a museum of medieval and Renaissance Italian paintings and French works by the Avignon School, including the 1457 Vierge de Pitié.*

BD DE LA LIGNE

ROCHER DES DOMS

PLACE DU PALAIS

RUE VICE LEGAT

RUE PEYROLLERIE

↑ Golden Madonna on the top of Cathédrale Notre-Dame-des-Doms

*The hillside gardens of **Rocher des Doms**, behind Notre-Dame-des-Doms, are the site of Avignon's earliest settlement.*

*Popes ruling in the 14th century built the grand, fortress-like **Palais des Papes** (p160). The Chambre du Pape, in particular, is exquisitely decorated.*

↑ Dining in front of the impressive Palais des Papes, dramatically lit at night

Église St-Pierre *was built during the 14th to early 16th centuries. The doors on its west façade were carved in 1551 by Antoine Valard. Inside the church is a fine 15th-century pulpit.*

| 0 metres | 100 | N |
| 0 yards | 100 | ↑ |

VILLENEUVE-LÈS-AVIGNON

🅰B4 ✈**8 km (5 miles) Avignon-Provence** 🚇🚌 **Ave de la Gare**
ℹ **Place Charles David; www.tourismegard.com**

This tranquil town on the west bank of the Rhône is within sight of
Avignon *(p160)*, but even in high season it seems a world away from
the tourism-thronged streets of its high-profile big sister.

With some lovely places to stay and a central
square lined with budget-friendly eateries,
Villeneuve-lès-Avignon is a fabulous base for
exploring Avignon, and has some important
sights that make it a destination in its own right.

The connecting bridge between Avignon
and Villeneuve-lès-Avignon, Pont St-Bénézet,
was at one time guarded by the Tour Philippe-
le-Bel, built in 1307. Its rooftop terrace, 176
steps up, gives a fine panorama of the papal
city. Even better is the view from the two giant
40-m (130-ft) round towers at the entrance
to the impressive 14th-century Fort St-André,
which originally enclosed a small town,
monastery and church.

Between these two bastions lie the Église
Collégiale Notre-Dame and the Musée
Pierre-de-Luxembourg, both spectacular
14th-century buildings containing prize
collections of medieval and Renaissance art.

Another major sight is the Chartreuse du
Val-de-Bénédiction, a vast former monastery
with some lovely gardens.

For a stroll in the countryside and views
of Villeneuve-lès-Avignon and the Avignon
skyline, head for the Île de la Barthelasse.
This long, narrow island in the Rhône is
said to be Europe's largest river island, and
stretches of its shoreline are listed as special
zones of ecological interest.

💬 INSIDER TIP
Evening kayak

Take a moonlit kayak and float down the Rhône beneath the famous arches of the Pont St-Bénézet for a truly unforgettable nocturnal experience.

1 Imposing towers dominating the entrance to the impressive 14th-century Fort St-André.

2 *Coronation of the Virgin* (1454) by Enguerrand Quarton, in the Musée Pierre de Luxembourg.

3 Stunning view of Fort St-André and Villeneuve-lès-Avignon from the top of Tour Philippe-le-Bel.

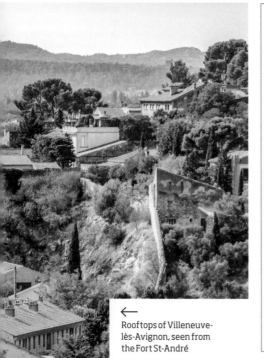

← Rooftops of Villeneuve-lès-Avignon, seen from the Fort St-André

TOP 4 SIGHTS IN VILLENEUVE-LÈS-AVIGNON

Tour Philippe-le-Bel
🏠 Montée de la Tour
This 14th-century tower guarded the west end of the Pont St-Bénézet.

Fort St-André
🏠 Rue Montée du Fort
🌐 fort-saint-andre.fr
A vast fortress that once contained a village and monastic community.

Chartreuse du Val-de-Bénédiction
🏠 58 rue de la République
🌐 chartreuse.org
A former monastery with elegant gardens.

Musée Pierre-de-Luxembourg
🏠 3 rue de la République
Treasures of medieval art are housed here.

❸

ORANGE

🅐 B3 ✈ Avignon 37 km (23 miles) 🚆 Vaucluse 🚌 Ave Frédéric Mistral 🚏 Blvd Daladier 🛈 5 cours Aristide Briand; www.orange-tourisme.fr

The revered vineyards of the Côtes du Rhône surround Orange, part of a lush patchwork of fields, orchards and olive groves. Olives, fragrant honey and truffles find their way to stalls in the lively market on place Georges Clémenceau, but its big attractions are two of the finest Roman monuments in Europe, the Théâtre Antique d'Orange *(p168)* and the Arc de Triomphe.

①
Parc de la Colline St-Eutrope

🏠 148 allée du Dr Rassat

There's a bird's eye view of Orange's vast Roman theatre, from the top of the Colline St-Eutrope, and a sweeping panorama of the surrounding countryside stretching all the way to the heights of Mont Ventoux. The scanty remnants of a 17th-century castle, built by Prince Maurice of Nassau and later blown up on the orders of Louis XIV, can be seen on its summit. The leafy park also has plenty of places for a picnic.

②
Musée d'Art et d'Histoire d'Orange

🏠 1 rue Madeleine Roch
🕑 Times vary, check website
🌐 theatre-antique.com

The exhibits found in the courtyard and on the ground floor of this museum reflect the history of Orange. They include more than 400 marble fragments which, when assembled, proved to be plans of the area, based on three surveys dating from AD 77. Also on display are portraits of members of the Royal House of Orange and paintings by the British artist, Sir Frank Brangwyn (1867–1956). One room demonstrates how printed fabrics were made in 18th-century Orange.

③
Arc de Triomphe

🏠 Ave de l'Arc de Triomphe

Originally dedicated to the victories of Julius Caesar and the Roman II Augusta legion, this triple triumphal arch was redesigned in the reign of the

Did You Know?

The Dutch dynasty of Nassau inherited Orange in 1544 and ruled until 1713.

←

Orange's monumental
Arc de Triomphe, one
of its star attractions

Emperor Tiberius to celebrate
victories in Germany and at
sea. Look out for the ropes
and anchors that form a
recurrent decorative theme,
and for the defeated Gauls
and Teutons that are shown
chained and naked on the
elaborately carved east face.

Almost 20 m (65 ft)
in height, the monument
was later built into the city's
defensive ramparts, and so
escaped the fate of many of
Orange's Roman buildings,
which were demolished
during the Middle Ages so
that their stone could be reused. However, it was not left
completely unscathed: the
visible pockmarks that cover
the arch are believed to have
been made by medieval cross-
bowmen practising their aim.

The arch is the oldest
surviving example of a design
that would later be used in
Rome for the Arch of Septimius
Severus and the Arch of
Constantine. It is now listed as
a UNESCO World Heritage Site.

CHORÉGIES D'ORANGE

On sultry summer evenings, the perfect acoustics
of Orange's Roman theatre provide a superb setting
for France's oldest music festival, which celebrated its
150th anniversary in 2019. The seven-week festival
takes place between mid-June and early August each
year and its programme of opera and choral music
features some of the world's greatest voices and
classical ensembles. To enjoy it for free, take a picnic
to the lower slopes of Colline St-Eutrope, immediately
above the Théâtre Antique.

④
Cathédrale Notre-
Dame-de-Nazareth

🏛 Rue Notre Dame
🕐 Daily

Orange's cathedral, with its
crumbling Romanesque portal,
has had a turbulent history.
Built in the 12th century, it
was damaged during the

16th-century Wars of Religion,
then restored between 1584
and 1599. It was again damaged during the Revolution,
when for some years it served
as a "Temple to Reason and the
Supreme Being" as part of the
Revolution's attempt to replace
Christianity. It was returned to
the Catholic church in 1795, but
ceased to be the seat of the
Bishopric of Orange in 1801.

⑤ 🖌️ Ⓜ️ 🖥️ 🛍️

THÉÂTRE ANTIQUE ET MUSÉE D'ORANGE

📍1 rue Madeleine Roch 📞04 90 51 17 60 🕐Jan-Feb & Nov-Dec: 9:30am-4:30pm daily; Mar & Oct: 9:30am-5:30pm daily; Apr, May & Sep: 9am-6pm daily; Jun-Aug: 9am-7pm daily 🚫1 Jan, 25 Dec 🌐theatre-antique.com

Orange's Roman theatre, a UNESCO World Heritage site, is one of the best preserved in Europe. It still retains its original stage wall, the only Roman stage wall to remain intact, and it continues to be a popular venue for concerts and performances.

The highlight of the Parc de la Colline St-Eutrope (*p166*), this theatre was built at the start of the Christian era. Its stage wall was designed to ensure perfect acoustics, while its hollow stage doors amplified the voices of actors who stood in front of them. The *cavea*, or tiered semicircle, originally held up to 7,000 spectators. From the 16th to 19th centuries, the theatre was filled with squalid housing, traces of which can still be seen.

Today, the theatre hosts rock concerts, operas and ballets. A new roof covers the stage, and a fascinating multimedia presentation of great moments in the theatre's history is shown in four grottoes behind the tiers of the amphitheatre. Some parts of the theatre may be closed for restoration, so check the website before you visit.

Still visible on the exterior walls are corbels which held the huge velum-bearing masts.

A canvas awning, known as a velum, protected the theatre-goers from sun or rain.

Did You Know?

The productions performed here in Roman times were totally free to attend and open to all.

Reconstruction showing how the theatre looked in Roman times ↑

←
Fête de la Musique concert at the Théâtre Antique in Orange

Stage wall of the Théâtre Antique, with fragments of its original marble decoration

The inner face of the stage wall still bears fragments of marble friezes and mosaics.

This 3.5-m (11-ft) statue of Emperor Augustus, with a hand raised in greeting, dominates the stage at the third level.

Side rooms, or parascaenia, were where actors could rest when not required on stage.

Statue of Emperor Augustus, set in the stage wall

Built of red limestone, this massive wall is 103 m (338 ft) long and 36 m (117 ft) high.

Each strip of velum awning could be rolled individually to suit the direction of the sunlight.

The stage wall had three levels. The wall's columns and varied surfaces broke up sound waves, so that the actors could speak without their voices having an echo.

Winched capstans held and tightened the ropes supporting the velum.

The stage curtain was lowered to reveal the stage. It was operated by machinery beneath the floor of the stage.

Must See

4 ⊘ Ⓜ 🛍

ABBAYE DE SÉNANQUE

🅰C4 🄳D117, Gordes 🚌Gordes 🕒9:45am–5pm Mon–Sat, 1–5pm Sun for guided tours only (advance booking highly recommended) 🌐senanque.fr

Swathes of purple lavender surround this serene 12th-century Cistercian abbey, built of pale grey stone and roofed with limestone slabs. This is one of three Romanesque monasteries in Provence and, like its Cistercian siblings at Silvacane (p152) and Le Thoronet (p118), its austere architecture reflects the simple ideals of the order. It was founded in 1148 by an abbot and 12 monks, who came to this isolated plateau to pray and contemplate. The monks today continue this legacy, dedicating their lives to prayer and to maintaining the abbey and its land.

Lavender Gardens

When the acres of immaculately groomed lavender fields that surround the Abbaye de Sénanque are in full flower in July, they are loud with the humming of bees gathering lavender pollen, which in turn gives a distinctive perfume to their honey. The Cistercians built a system of channels to carry water from the nearby Sénancole to irrigate their gardens, turning the native garrigue into cultivable land. Nevertheless, lavender is one of the few crops that is hardy enough to flourish in this harsh climate terrain. The monks harvest the lavender to make honey, soap, perfume, nougat and essential oils, all of which are available to buy in the Abbey's boutique.

HISTORY OF THE ABBEY

Although initially founded on simple ideals, Sénanque grew wealthy in medieval times. Its monks yielded to earthly temptations and the abbey was sacked by the Protestant Vaudois in 1544. Plague struck in 1580, and by the 17th century only two monks remained in the tumbledown abbey. The abbey was restored in 1854, and since 1988 it has once again been home to a small monastic community.

↑ The Abbey cloisters, adorned with exquisite carvings of vines and foliage

→ Austere church interior, stripped bare in 1544 by Protestants

Abbey Church

Building work on the beautifully proportioned abbey church began in 1160, 12 years after the foundation of the abbey, and one of its four altars dates from that time. Beneath an octagonal dome, the barrel-vaulted nave is five bays long, with three stone steps connecting nave and transept. A modest tombstone in the transept marks the tomb of the 13th-century Lord of Venasque, the Abbey's former patron.

Cloister, Scriptorium and Chapterhouse

Delicate carvings of flowers, leaves and vines adorn the dove-grey limestone columns which support the arcades around Sénanque's square central cloister, which forms the core of abbey. These superb works of craftsmanship date from between 1180 and 1220.

On the north side of the cloister is the scriptorium, the only room which was permitted to be heated under the order's austere regime. This enabled the monks to read and write in relative comfort. It is no longer in use for this purpose. Next to it is the chapterhouse, lined with stone seats where monks gathered to hear the abbot read from the Bible, or from the Rule of St Bernard, founder of the Cistercian order.

← Vibrant lavender fields surrounding the Abbey

5

VAISON–
LA-ROMAINE

🅰 B3 ✈ Aéroport Avignon Provence 60 km (37 miles) 🚌 From Orange Gare SNCF
🅦 vaison-ventoux-tourisme.com

Straddling a steep-sided gorge of the river Ouvèze, Vaison-la-Romaine
is a picturesque town featuring a magnificent array of Roman relics.
The modern town sits beside two Roman sites, the Puymin and Villasse
quarters, opposite the medieval Haute Ville on the other side of the river.

Founded by the Celtic Vocontti tribe, the town
was named Vasio Vocontiorum after the Roman
conquest, and for four centuries it flourished
until the collapse of the empire, when the
original site was abandoned for the walled
Haute Ville and its castle. The Roman city
was excavated between 1907 and 1955.

Roman Remains

The biggest of the two Roman sites, the
Puymin quarter, contained the courthouse,
temples, shops and noble townhouses. The
star attraction is the extraordinary Théâtre
Antique. Carved out of the living rock by Gallo-
Roman craftsmen, this 1st-century AD theatre is
a dazzling display of Roman building skill, with
34 semi-circular rows of stone benches seating
up to 7,000 spectators.

The Villasse quarter, the second Roman
site, is home to the remains of an array of villas
and shops, some featuring elegant mosaic
floors. The site is dotted with copies of original
statues that are now kept in the excellent
Musée Théo Desplans.

EAT

Le Moulin à Huile
Set in a former oil mill, this restaurant has a pretty terrace for alfresco dining. Truffles are a menu highlight here when in season.

📍 1 quai Maréchal Foch
🕐 Tue & Wed 🌐 lemoulin ahuile84.fr

€€€

La Table
Exceptional food made with local produce and served with carefully selected wines.

📍 Rue Gaston Gevaudan
🕐 Sun & Mon
🌐 maisonsduo.com

€€€

← Vaison's medieval Haute Ville and the Pont Romain, a 2,000-year-old bridge

Haute Ville

Vaison's 2,000-year-old Roman bridge connects the north bank with the upper town on the south bank. The pretty old quarter, with its 17th-century townhouses, courtyards and fountains, is ringed by ramparts and entered through a massive 14th-century gateway. At the highest point stands the dramatic castle, built in 1194 by the Count of Toulouse.

← Ancient Roman statue among the ruins

↑ Excavation of the Puymin quarter of the Roman city

6

MONT VENTOUX

🅰 C3 ✈ Avignon 48 km (30 miles) SW of Vaucluse 🅸 Ave de la Promenade, 84390 Sault; www.ventoux-en-provence.com

Swept by the mistral winds that blow down the Rhône valley, the "Giant of Provence" looms high above the hills, fertile plains and vineyards that surround it. Snow-capped in winter, its treeless limestone summit also gleams white in the summer.

Soaring 1,912 m (6,242 ft) into the blue sky of Provence, Mont Ventoux is all the more impressive because it stands lonely and aloof above the foothills that surround it. It has awed and inspired artists and adventurers for centuries, from the Renaissance poet Petrarch (1304–74), who made the first recorded ascent to the top in 1336, to competitive road cyclists, for whom the mountain is one of the most gruelling climbs in the world, frequently featuring in the legendary Tour de France race. Keen walkers can make it to the summit in around five hours on well-marked roads starting from Sault, on the east side of the mountain, Bedoin to the south and Malaucène on the southern slopes.

But you don't need to be super-fit to enjoy the panorama from the peak, where a viewing table helps you make out the misty ranges of the Cévennes and the Luberon in the distance, and the peak of Ste-Victoire. The lower slopes are idyllic places in which to ramble through oak and beech woodlands and wildflower meadows. At higher levels, conifers rise to the treeline, around 1,000 m (3280 ft), and give way to slopes where alpine poppy and trumpet gentian add colour in early summer.

> ### Did You Know?
>
> Mont Ventoux is popular with unpowered gravity racers. The current speed record is 85.612 mph.

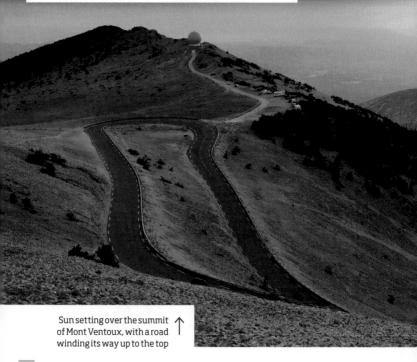

Sun setting over the summit of Mont Ventoux, with a road winding its way up to the top ↑

1 A skier on the slopes at Mont Serein (also called Mont Ventoux-Nord), below the summit of Mont Ventoux.

2 A Zygaena moth settles on a wildflower on the lower slopes of the mountain.

3 Cyclists tackle the ascent to the mountain's summit in one of the many competitive races that take place in the summer. 3

TOP 3 MOUNTAIN ACTIVITIES

Guided Walks
Start before dawn from Malaucène to follow in Petrarch's footsteps, and watch the sun rise from the summit. Walks with an experienced guide also start from Bedoin and Sault.

Winter Sports
Ski and snowboard at Mont Serein (Mont Ventoux-Nord), 5 km (3 miles) below the summit, where there are 20 pistes and 7 lifts. Ski season starts just before Christmas and lasts until late March.

Watch Cycle Racing
Vantage points are hard to find when the mountain is a stage in the Tour de France but you can watch super-fit cyclists battling for supremacy in a packed calendar of races on the mountain's slopes every summer.

LE COLORADO PROVENÇAL

① ⌖ Ⓜ ▣

◉ C4 △ Maison du Colorado, 84400 Rustrel ◷ Times vary, check website ▣ Jan ⓦ coloradoprovencal.fr

The weird landscapes of the old ochre quarries around Rustrel, with their crimson, orange and yellow gulches and pinnacles, immediately trigger the imagination of sci-fi and western movie fans, but sweet-smelling herbs and pines and the sound of shrilling cicadas remind you that this incredible place is still in Provence.

You wouldn't be surprised to encounter Han Solo or Dr Who among the other-wordly scenery of Le Colorado Provençal, a former ochre quarry. Walking trails wind through 30 hectares (74 acres) of human-made spires, ravines and canyons that change colour from pale yellow to deep crimson. The main walking circuit is an easy-going walk that takes around four hours. You'll find shady picnic spots along the way, but don't forget to bring plenty of water with you.

Between the 1880s and 1950s the ochre quarry here employed almost all the population of the nearby village of Rustrel. With its ochre-tinted pink and yellow houses, the village is worth a visit, not least for its sweeping views of the wooded hills and valleys that surround it. There are also a handful of sights to explore, including a 17th-century olive oil mill and a Renaissance château.

Visitor exploring the carved-up landscape of the former ochre quarry

GUIDED TOURS

For a self-guided tour of Le Colorado Provençal, pick up a map of the walking route from the Maison du Colorado visitor centre. There are two routes to choose from. You can also book a tour of Le Lavage des Ocres, where descendants of the local *ocriers* (ochre workers), who owned the land, will show you how ochre was quarried, then washed and dissolved in water in channels and settling ponds before being made into paints, dyes and ceramic glazes.

Hiking trail through the multi-hued ochre cliffs

Did You Know?

At the peak of the ochre industry, the quarries of Luberon produced 40,000 tonnes of ochre a year.

Walking through the ochre quarry in Luberon, Roussillon ↑

EXPERIENCE MORE

L'Harmas de Fabre

B3 445 rte de Orange, Sérignan-du-Comtat Times vary, check website 1 May harmasjeanhenri fabre.fr

Bees buzz, cicadas sing and butterflies flutter by in the half-wild gardens that surround this pretty, traditional farmhouse. It was home to the remarkable Jean-Henri Fabre, scientist, writer and teacher, who bought it in 1879. The estate comprises of some fallow land ("harmas" means fallow land in the Provençal language), providing Fabre with an open-air laboratory for his studies. The hawthorn, lavender and rosemary he planted attracted plenty of insects for him to observe and record in his paintings.

Inside the house, now a museum dedicated to Fabre's life and work, you can see his vast collection of finds from the surrounding countryside, from bones and animal and bird skulls to shards of Roman and medieval pottery. There's also the laboratory where he conducted his entomological studies and a dining room with the harmonium on which he composed his music.

The gardens contain a pond, flower beds of French marigolds and lilies, heirloom vegetables and herbs, as well as an arboretum, with cedar, fig, sweet bay and pine trees.

9
Bollène

B3 32 ave Pasteur; www.provence coterhone-tourisme.com

Despite being spread along the A7 autoroute, Bollène is pleasant, with airy boulevards and walks beside the river Lez, where there is a camping site. The narrow streets of the old quarter lead to the 11th-century Collégiale St-Martin, with its distinctive timber saddleback roof and Renaissance doorway.

The nearby Couvent des Ursulines, built in the 17th century, also has some lovely features, including its magnificent chapel and staircase. Bollène became famous in

↑ Magnificent views from the walls of the Mornas fortress, outside Bollène

1882, when Louis Pasteur stayed here and developed innoculation against swine fever. The Belvédère Pasteur garden above the town has views over the Rhône valley to the Cévennes, the Bollène hydroelectric power station and Tricastin nuclear power plant. The town hosts free open-air concerts from early July to August.

South of Bollène is the clifftop fortress of Mornas, built by the Earl of Toulouse, which was later fought over for its strategic position during the Wars of Religion. The steep climb is rewarded by spectacular views of the Rhône valley.

Between Bollène and Pierrelatte is the troglodyte village of Barry, on the side of a hill looking over Tricastin. Occupied in Neolithic times until the beginning of the 20th century, the caves were gradually extended as the soft rock of the hill was dug out.

JEAN-HENRI FABRE

Renowned naturalist Jean-Henri Fabre (1823-1915) was the very first scientist to study the habits of insects in the wild at a time when entomologists collected dead specimens. With no formal schooling, the self-taught Fabre painstakingly unravelled the weird and wonderful life-cycles of the creatures of his native Provence, from tiny predators such as the praying mantis to shrill song-sters such as cicadas and crickets.

10

Carpentras

🅰B3 🚌 🛈 97 place du 25 Août 1944; www.carpentras-ventoux.com

This market town is in the centre of the Côtes-du-Ventoux wine region. The Porte d'Orange is the only surviving part of the medieval ramparts. In the Middle Ages, the town had a large Jewish community, and the 14th-century **Synagogue** is the oldest in France, now used by some 100 families. While not openly persecuted under papal rule, many Jews changed faith and entered the **Cathédrale St-Siffrein** by its 15th-century south door, the *Porte Juive*. The cathedral is in the centre of the old town. In it are Provençal paintings and statues by local sculptor Jacques Bernus (1650–1728). The town hall has a fine 18th-century pharmacy. It also has 18th-century collections from the **Inguimbertine** library and museum.

Did You Know?

Carpentras's Friday market is reputed to be the oldest in France – it began in the 1st century BC.

Synagogue
🅰Pl Maurice Charretier 📞04 90 63 39 97 🕒Mon–Fri (for guided tours only, by pre-booking) 🚫Jewish feast days

Cathédrale St-Siffrein
🅰3 pl Saint-Siffrein 📞04 90 63 08 33 🕒Mon–Sat

Inguimbertine
🅰Hôtel Dieu, place Aristide Briand 🕒Tue–Sun 🌐inguimbertine.carpentras.fr

←

Crowds in the square outside the Cathédrale St-Siffrein in Carpentras

⑪ Caderousse

Ⓐ B3 **ⓘ La Mairie, rue Berbiguier; www.chateau neuf-du-pape-tourisme.fr**

This bankside village lies at a point where Hannibal is said to have crossed the river Rhône with his elephants on his way to Rome in 218 BC. For centuries, Caderousse has endured the floods of the Rhône, and plaques on the town hall record the high levels of floodwater. By 1856, the villagers took action, and erected a dyke that is still in place. Its four entry points can close if floods should threaten again.

Caderousse has a Romanesque church, St-Michel, to which the Flamboyant Gothic chapel of St-Claude was added during the 16th century.

⑫ Châteauneuf-du-Pape

Ⓐ B3 **ⓡ Sorgues, then taxi** **🚌 ⓘ 3 rue de la République; www.chateauneuf-du-pape-tourisme.fr**

The best-known of the Côtes du Rhone wine labels takes its name from an unassuming yellow stone village on a small hill, filled with cellars and restaurants selling the products of the local growers entitled to the *appellation d'origine contrôlée*. The **Musée du Vin – Maison Brotte** traces the history and current state of the local viniculture.

At the top of the village are the ruins of the Château des Papes, mostly burned down in the 16th-century Wars of Religion. From the remaining walls there is a superb view of Avignon and the vineyard-lined clay fields where smooth stones deposited by the Rhône

↑ Châteauneuf-du-Pape wine displayed in the shop of a local vineyard

reflect the sun's heat onto 13 varieties of grape. The château was built in 1317 by John XXII, an Avignon pope who planted the first vineyards, but it took some 400 years for the wine's reputation to spread. Today, there are 180 Châteauneuf-du-Pape domaines.

The nearby town of Pernes-les-Fontaines is known for its 40 fountains, in particular the 18th-century Fontaine du Cormoran. Until 1914, each of the fountains had an individual keeper.

Musée du Vin - Maison Brotte

Ⓒ **Ⓐ Ave St-Pierre de Luxembourg, Châteauneuf-du-Pape** **Ⓒ 04 90 83 70 07** **Ⓒ Daily** **🔒 1 Jan, 25 Dec**

⑬ Fontaine-de-Vaucluse

Ⓐ C4 **🚌 Avignon** **ⓘ Résidence Jean Garcin, ave Robert Garcin; www.isle surlasorguetourisme.com**

The source of the Sorgue river is one of the natural wonders of Provence. It begins underground, with tributaries that drain the Vaucluse plateau, an area of around 2,000 sq km (800 sq miles). In the closed valley above the town, water erupts from an unfathomable depth to develop into a fully fledged river. Beside the river is the **Moulin à Papier Vallis Clausa**, which produces handmade paper using a 15th-century method. The mill sells maps, prints and lampshades.

→ Mossy waterwheel in the canals that run through L'Îsle-sur-la-Sorgue

The town has an interesting underground museum, **Le Monde Souterrain**, which features the discoveries of French speleologist Norbert Casteret from over 30 years of exploring Sorgue's caves and waterfalls. There is also the **Musée d'Histoire Jean Garcin 1939–1945**, which traces the fate of the Resistance during WWII and daily life under the Occupation. The **Musée-Bibliothèque François Pétrarque** was the house where the poet Francesco Petrarca lived for 16 years.

Moulin à Papier Vallis Clausa

⊛ ⊛ 🅐 Chemin de la Fontaine ⏱ Daily 🚫 1 Jan, 3 weeks in Jan, 25 Dec
🌐 moulin-vallisclausa.com

Le Monde Souterrain

⊛ ⊛ ⊛ 🅐 Chemin de la Fontaine ⏱ Mid-Feb-mid-Nov: daily 🌐 moulin-vallis clausa.com

Musée d'Histoire Jean Garcin 1939-45

⊛ 🅐 Chemin de la Fontaine
☎ 04 90 20 24 00 ⏱ Apr–Sep: Thu–Mon 🚫 1 May

Musée-Bibliothèque François Pétrarque

⊛ 🅐 Rive gauche de la Sorgue
☎ 04 90 20 37 20 ⏱ Apr–Sep: Thu–Mon 🚫 1 May

L'Île-sur-la-Sorgue

🅐 B4 🚌 🚍 ℹ 13 place Ferdinand Buisson; www.islesurlasorgue tourisme.com

This attractive town lies on the river Sorgue, which once powered 70 watermills along its banks. Today, 14 idle wheels remain, and seven of the old buildings that once housed warehouses and weaving mills now house hundreds of antiques and vintage dealerships, making L'Île-sur-la-Sorgue France's biggest antiques trading centre after Paris.

Dealers began to migrate to the area during the 1960s, attracted by affordable spaces for their stores. There were also rich pickings from local castles, farmhouses and village homes when their owners sold off unloved old possessions, which were soon to become pricey collectables. There are now around 300 antiques dealerships around the village.

Other highlights of the village include the ornate 17th-century Notre-Dame-des-Anges, with its attractive clock, and the Musée du Jouet et de la Poupée Ancienne, which displays antique toys and dolls.

↑ Sumptuous interior of the Baroque Notre-Dame-des-Anges

 INSIDER TIP
Antiques hunt

For the best buys and biggest choice of antiques, visit L'Île-sur-la-Sorgue on All Saints' Day or at Easter, when the village turns into one huge antiques fair with a great selection of finds and bargains galore.

The spectacularly sited medieval village of Gordes ↑

15

Gordes

⊞ C3 🛈 Place Genty Pantaly; www.gordes-village.com

Expensive restaurants and hotels confirm the popularity of this hilltop village, which spills down in terraces from a Renaissance château and the church of St-Firmin. Its vaulted, arcaded medieval lanes are also lovely. The village has been popular with artists since the academic Cubist painter André Lhote began visiting in 1938.

The **Château de Gordes** was built in the 16th century on the site of an 11th-century fortress. The château has an ornate 16th-century fireplace in the great hall on the first floor, decorated with shells, flowers and pilasters. Today, the château hosts temporary exhibitions during the summer.

Outside Gordes is the **Village des Bories**, a museum of rural life and dry stone huts.

Château de Gordes
🏠 Place Genty Pantaly 📞 04 90 72 02 08 🕐 Apr-Oct: daily

Village des Bories
⊛ 🏠 Les Savournins 📞 04 90 72 03 48 🕐 Daily 🚫 1 Jan, 25 Dec

16

Château de Saumane

⊞ C4 🏠 Montée du Château 🕐 Times vary, check website 🌐 islesurlasorgue tourisme.com

Looming on a hilltop above the village of Saumane, this impressive medieval fortress has massive walls concealing a lavish interior graced by vaulted corridors, painted ceilings, marble fireplaces and stone stairways. The outer walls are almost 2 m (6 ft) thick, ensuring the interior is pleasantly cool, even in high summer.

Within is a mysterious labyrinth of hidden doorways and secret passages leading to a series of gloomy cellars and dungeons that once stirred the twisted imagination of the young Marquis Donatien de Sade (1740–1814), a notorious libertine and philosopher. He lived here as a guest of his uncle, the Abbé Jacques-François de Sade, between the ages of five and ten. The château was owned by the de Sade family until 1868. It was acquired by the regional council in 1982 and opened to the public.

SHOP

Ocres de France
Discover more than 150 shades of authentic ochre-based paint and plaster on display in this historic factory and showroom.

⊞ C4 🏠 200 chemin des Ocriers, Apt 🕐 Sat & Sun

La Compagnie des Ocres
Paints and pigments made from ochre and a rainbow of other traditional colorants are on sale here. You can ask for items to be sent to your home address.

⊞ C4 🏠 Sentier des Ocres, Roussillon 🌐 lacompagnie desocres.fr

---

→

Striking colourful landscape of the Sentier des Ocres

a 10-minute walk from the tourist information office. **Ôkhra – Écomusée de l'Ocre**, in the old factory, is well worth visiting. It displays a huge collection of natural pigments, and runs day courses on the subject.

A superb panorama to the north can be enjoyed from the Castrum, the viewing table beside the church in the main square.

Ôkhra - Écomusée de l'Ocre

⊛ ⊛ ⊕ 🏠 570 route d'Apt 🕑 Jan: by appointment; mid-Feb-Oct: daily; Nov-Dec: Mon, Tue, Thu & Fri 🌐 okhra.com

---

⑰
Roussillon

🅰 C4 🛈 Place de la Poste; www.otroussillon. pagesperso-orange.fr

The deep ochres used in the construction of this hilltop community are stunning. Its hues come from at least 17 shades of ochre discovered in and around the village, notably in the dramatic former quarries along the Sentier des Ocres. The entrance to the quarries – which are home to a bizarre series of landscapes that would look more at home in Arizona than in Provence – is to the east of the village,

⑱
Cavaillon

🅰 B4 🚉🚌 🛈 Place François Tourel; www.luberoncoeurde provence.com

The viewing table outside the Chapelle St-Jacques at the top of this town shows the Luberon range in perspective against Mont Ventoux and the Alpilles chain. In closer proximity are acres of fruit and vegetable plots, for Cavaillon is France's largest market

garden, an area especially well-known for its melons. Its local market competes with the one in Apt for renown as the most important in Vaucluse.

Colline St-Jacques was the site of the pre-Roman settlement that prospered under Rome. There is a 1st-century Roman arch in place Duclos nearby. Roman finds are on display in the **Musée Archéologique de l'Hôtel Dieu** in the Grand'Rue, which leads north from the church, a former cathedral dedicated to its 6th-century bishop, Saint Véran. The **synagogue** in rue Hébraïque dates from 1772, although there has been one on this site ever since the 14th century. The **Musée Jouves et Juif Comtadin**, on the same road, commemorates its fascinating history.

Musée Archéologique de l'Hotel Dieu

⊛ 🏠 Place Jean Bastide 📞 04 90 71 73 81 🕑 Jun-Sep: Wed-Mon (pm only); Oct-May: daily (pm only)

Synagogue & Musée Jouves et Juif Comtadin

⊛ 🏠 Rue Hébraïque 📞 04 90 72 26 86 🕑 May-Sep: Wed-Mon; Oct-Apr: Mon, Wed-Sat 🚫 1 Jan, 1 May, 25 Dec

⑲ Cadenet

🅰C4 🚌Avignon 🛈11 cours Pourrières, Curcuron; www.luberoncotesud.com

Tucked underneath the hills in the Durance valley, the pretty village of Cadenet has 11th-century castle ruins and a 14th-century church with a square bell tower. Its font is made from a Roman sarcophagus. In the main square, which is used for Cadenet's bi-weekly market, is a statue of the drummer boy, André Estienne, who beat such a raucous tattoo in the battle for Arcole Bridge in 1796 that the Austrian forces thought they could hear gunfire and retreated.

⑳ Apt

🅰C4 🚌🚆Avignon 🛈788 ave Victor Hugo; 04 90 74 03 18

Apt is the northern entry to the Parc Naturel Régional du Luberon. The **Maison du Parc**, in a restored 18th-century mansion, has information on the area, including walks, *gîtes d'étapes* and flora and fauna.

The busy old town of Apt has a square for playing *boules*, and fountains and plane trees. Surrounded by cherry orchards, it claims to be the world capital of crystallized fruit. The **Musée de l'Aventure Industrielle** explains how the production of crystallized fruit, earthenware pottery and the extraction of ochre brought prosperity to Apt in the 18th and 19th centuries. The town is also famous for truffles and lavender essence. The Saturday market offers Provençal delicacies and entertainment, including jazz, barrel-organ music and stand-up comedy. Le Colorado Provençal *(p176)*, the best ochre quarry site by the River Dôa, to the northeast, makes for an interesting excursion.

The medieval **Cathédrale Ste-Anne** lies at the heart of Apt's old town. Legend has it that the veil of St Anne was brought back from Palestine and hidden in the cathedral by Auspice, who is thought to have been Apt's first bishop. Each July her festival is celebrated with a procession. The treasury inside the sacristy contains the saint's shroud and an 11th-century Arabic standard from the First Crusade (1096–9). In the apse is a 15th- to 16th-century

window that depicts the tree of Jesse. Nearby is the 17th-century Hôtel d'Albertas.

The items on display in the **Musée d'Histoire et d'Archéologie** consist of prehistoric flints, stone implements, Gallo-Roman carvings, jewellery and mosaics. Just a few miles from Apt, **L'Observatoire Sirene** has an idyllic location and state-of-the-art technology, ideal for star-gazing.

Maison du Parc
🏠60 pl Jean-Jaurès ⏰Mon-Fri 🌐parcduluberon.fr

Musée de l'Aventure Industrielle
🔷🔷🔷🏠Pl du Postel 📞04 90 74 95 30 ⏰Sep-Jun: Tue-Sat; Jul-Aug: Mon-Sat 🔒Public hols, Jan

Cathédrale Ste-Anne
🔷🔷🏠Place de la Cathédrale 📞04 90 04 85 44 ⏰Tue-Sat

← A street lined with cafés in the centre of the old village of Cadenet

Musée d'Histoire et d'Archéologie

 27 rue de l'Amphithéâtre 📞 04 90 74 95 30 ⏰ By appointment only

L'Observatoire Sirene

D34, Lagarde d'Apt ⏰ Daily by appt 🚫 Public hols 🌐 obs-sirene.com

---

㉑ Ansouis

C4 📍 11 cours Pourrières, Curcuron; www.luberon cotesud.com

One of the most remarkable things about the Renaissance **Château d'Ansouis** is that it was owned by the Sabran family from 1160 until 2008, when it was sold to a new owner. The Sabrans have a proven pedigree: in the 13th century, Béatrice de Savoie and Raymond Bérenger IV's four daughters became queens of France, England, Sicily and Germany. In 1298, Elzéar de Sabran married Delphine de Puy, a descendant of the Viscount of Marseille. But she had resolved to become a nun, so agreed to the marriage, but not to its consummation. Both were canonized in 1369.

The castle's original keep and two of its four towers are still visible. Its gardens include the lovely Renaissance Garden of Eden, built on the former cemetery.

The **Musée Extraordinaire de Georges Mazoyer**, located south of the village, displays the work of artist Georges Mazoyer, as well as Provençal furniture and a re-created underwater cave, all in 15th-century cellars.

Château d'Ansouis

Rue du Cartel ⏰ Apr-Oct: Thu-Sun for guided tours 🌐 chateau ansouis.com

Musée Extraordinaire de Georges Mazoyer

Quartier de Colombier 📞 04 90 09 82 64 ⏰ Daily (Oct-May: pm only)

㉒ Pertuis

C4 🚉 📍 44 place St-Pierre; www.ville-pertuis.fr

Once the capital of the Pays d'Aigues, present-day Pertuis is a quiet town, whose fertile surroundings were gradually taken over by Aix- en-Provence. Pertuis was the birthplace of the philandering Count of Mirabeau's father, and the 13th-century clock tower is located in place Mirabeau. The Église St-Nicolas, re-built in Gothic style in the 16th century, has a 16th-century triptych and two 17th-century marble statues. To the southwest is the battlemented 14th-century Tour St-Jacques.

㉓ La Tour d'Aigues

C4 🚉 Pertuis 📍 Château de la Tour d'Aigues; www.luberon cotesud.com

Nestling beside the grand limestone mountain ranges of Luberon, and surrounded by scenic vineyards and orchards, this beautiful town takes its name from a historic 10th-century tower. The 16th-century castle completes the triumvirate of Renaissance châteaux in the Luberon (the others are Lourmarin and Ansouis). Built on the foundations of a medieval castle by Baron de Central, its massive portal is based on the splendid Roman arch at Orange (p166). The castle was damaged first in a fire in 1780 and then in the French Revolution (1789–9), but has been partially restored.

Château de la Tour d'Aigues

 BP 16 📞 04 90 07 42 10 ⏰ Apr-Jun & Sep: Tue-Sat; Jul & Aug: Mon-Sat

← Imposing entrance to the Château de la Tour d'Aigues

A CYCLING TOUR
IN VAUCLUSE

Length 48 km (30 miles) **Level** Easy
Start/finish point: Bédoin

Allow four hours in the saddle for this easy-going ride on country roads and waymarked cycle trails lined with yellow broom and wild almond, pine and oak trees. With plenty of time for picnic stops, restorative coffees and a leisurely lunch break in one of the pretty, red-tiled villages along the way, this tour is a full day out from Avignon, Orange or Carpentras.

Locator Map
For more detail see p156

← Scenic view over Mazan, with Mont Ventoux in the distance

Medieval townhouses line the narrow streets of the village of **Mazan**, where the aristocratic dynasty that spawned the infamous Marquis de Sade (p182) had its roots.

Olive groves and cherry orchards surround **Malemort-du-Comtat**, where you can stretch your legs by ambling around the tumbledown remnants of medieval towers and ramparts.

Did You Know?

Werewolves supposedly preyed on Mazan's ancient cemetery until a chapel was built to protect villagers.

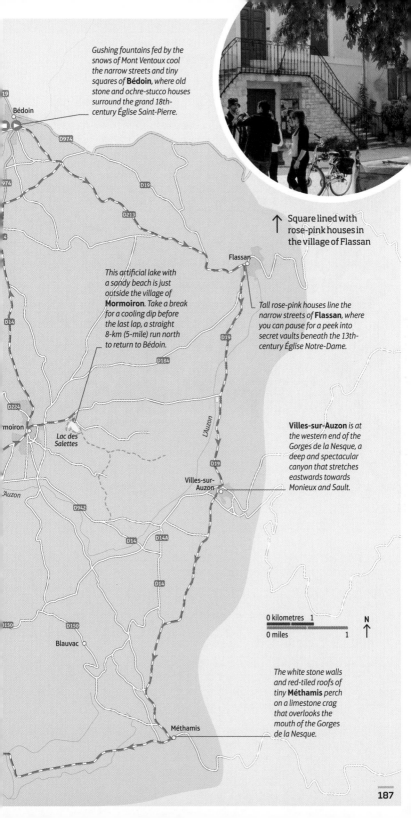

Gushing fountains fed by the snows of Mont Ventoux cool the narrow streets and tiny squares of **Bédoin**, where old stone and ochre-stucco houses surround the grand 18th-century Église Saint-Pierre.

Bédoin

↑ Square lined with rose-pink houses in the village of Flassan

Flassan

This artificial lake with a sandy beach is just outside the village of **Mormoiron**. Take a break for a cooling dip before the last lap, a straight 8-km (5-mile) run north to return to Bédoin.

Tall rose-pink houses line the narrow streets of **Flassan**, where you can pause for a peek into secret vaults beneath the 13th-century Église Notre-Dame.

Mormoiron

Lac des Salettes

Villes-sur-Auzon is at the western end of the Gorges de la Nesque, a deep and spectacular canyon that stretches eastwards towards Monieux and Sault.

L'Auzon

Villes-sur-Auzon

Blauvac

0 kilometres 1
0 miles 1

N ↑

The white stone walls and red-tiled roofs of tiny **Méthamis** perch on a limestone crag that overlooks the mouth of the Gorges de la Nesque.

Méthamis

ALPES-DE-HAUTE-PROVENCE

In this, the most undiscovered region of Provence, agriculture is still the primary source of income. The Valensole plain is now the most important lavender-producing area of France. Peaches, apples and pears have been planted in orchards only recently irrigated by the Durance, the region's main river, which has been tamed by dams and a hydro-electric power scheme. These advances have created employment and helped bring prosperity to the region. Another modern development is the Cadarache nuclear research centre, situated just outside Manosque. The town's population has grown rapidly to 22,100 inhabitants, overtaking the region's capital, Digne-les-Bains.

The region's history and architecture have also been greatly influenced by the terrain and climate. Strategically positioned citadels crown mountain towns such as Sisteron, which was won over by Napoleon in 1815, and the frontier town of Entrevaux. The design of towns and buildings has remained practical, mindful of the harsh winter and strong Mistral winds. Undoubtedly, the beauty of the region is revealed in the high lakes and mountains, the glacial valleys and the colourful fields of Alpine flowers.

ALPES-DE-HAUTE-PROVENCE

Must See

1 Gorges du Verdon

Experience More

2 Sisteron
3 Barcelonnette
4 Seyne-les-Alpes
5 Mont Pelat
6 Colmars
7 Digne-les-Bains
8 Lurs
9 Les Pénitents des Mées
10 Forcalquier
11 Manosque
12 Gréoux-les-Bains
13 Valensole
14 Riez
15 Moustiers-Ste-Marie
16 Annot
17 Castellane
18 St-André-les-Alpes
19 Entrevaux

Le Dévoluy

Gap

N85

D937

D994

La Roche-des-Arnauds

Veynes

D942

D1085

Durance

A51

D1075

La Motte

D1085

Châteaufort

Laragne-Montéglin

Valavoire

A51

SISTERON 2

Saint-Vincent-sur-Jabron

Bevons

Montbrun-les-Bains

D946

Valbelle

Thoar

Montagne de Lure

Montagne de Lure

A51

Barras

L'Hospitalet

Mallefougasse-Augès

Châteaux Arnoux

N85

Sault

Revest-du-Bion

D951

VAUCLUSE
p154

Banon

St Étienne-les-Orgues

Plateau de
Saint Christal

Montsalier

A51

LES PÉNITENTS
DES MÉES 9

VAUCLUSE

Simiane-la-Rotonde

Revest-des-Brousses

D4096

Le Castellet

Puimichel

Bras-d'A

Vachères

FORCALQUIER
10

LURS
8

Oraison

Gignac

Sainte-Croix-à-Lauze

D4100

Saint-Michel-l'Observatoire

Asse

Brunet

Apt

Reillanne

Puimoisson

MANOSQUE
11

VALENSOLE
13

RIEZ 14

Lourmarin

D4096

A51

Parc Naturel
Régional du Luberon

GRÉOUX-LES-BAINS
12

Lac d'Esparron

D11

Durance

Pertuis

Mirabeau

Vinon-sur-Verdon

Verdon

Quinson

Caderache

Ginasservis

D3

1

GORGES DU VERDON

🅐 E4 ⓘ Parc Naturel Régional du Verdon, Domaine de Valx, Moustiers-Sainte-Marie; www.parcduverdon.fr

France's answer to the Grand Canyon, where the river Verdon slices through deep gorges beneath vertical cliff faces, is a paradise for adventurers and lovers of the great outdoors. Walking, kayaking, river rafting and rock climbing are among the numerous activities on offer in this breathtakingly beautiful ravine.

Castellane

At the east end of the canyon, Castellane is the gateway to the Gorges du Verdon, and bustles in summer with adventurers of all ages setting out on river trips by canoe, kayak and raft. Experiences range from gentle floats for families to hardcore white-water journeys along the full 24-km (15-mile) expanse of runs and rapids to Lac de Ste-Croix, at the western end.

La Palud-sur-Verdon

La Palud is the start-point for a variety of walks in the gorges, from relatively easy-going strolls to much more challenging treks. The most popular and spectacular walk is the Sentier Blanc-Martel, which leads through wooded cliff paths and riverside tunnels.

←

Visitors sailing through the gorgeous Gorges du Verdon

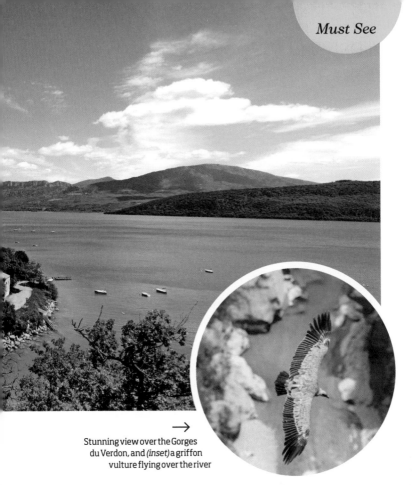

→ Stunning view over the Gorges du Verdon, and *(inset)* a griffon vulture flying over the river

↑ Climber tackling the face of a cliff above the Gorges du Verdon

Pont de l'Artuby

Only the brave dare to plummet 182 m (597 ft) from what is claimed to be the highest bungee jump in Europe, from the Pont de l'Artuby, which spans a southern tributary of the Verdon. Less courageous visitors can enjoy fantastic views of forest-capped limestone cliffs that plummet to the blue trickle of the river far below.

L'Escalès

More than 1,000 hardcore routes attract rock climbers to the Gorges du Verdon. The 400-m (1312-ft) crag of l'Escalès is among the most renowned challenges. Non-climbers can watch in awe as experts tackle it using tiny holds.

Sainte-Croix-du-Verdon

After an adrenaline-powered journey in the Gorges du Verdon, this trendy, purpose-built resort on the shore of the vast, artificial Lac du Sainte-Croix is the perfect place to unwind. For families, there are sandy beaches with lifeguards on duty (in summer) and easy-going activities like paddle-boarding and pedalos.

A DRIVING TOUR
OF THE ROUTE
DES CRÊTES

Length 120 km (75 miles) **Stopping-off points**
La Palud-sur-Verdon has several cafés and Moustiers-
Ste-Marie is a good place to stop for lunch

A driving tour of the Gorges du Verdon takes at least a day, and this
route, made up of two loops, encompasses its most striking features.
At its east and west points are the towns of Castellane and Moustiers-
Ste-Marie. Parts of the tour are very mountainous, so drivers must be
aware of hairpin bends and narrow roads with sheer drops. Weather
conditions can also be hazardous and roads can be icy until late spring.

ALPES-DE-
HAUTE-PROVENCE

*A Driving Tour of the
Route Des Crêtes*

Locator Map
For more detail see p190

Set on craggy heights,
Moustiers-Ste-Marie *is
famed for its faïence (p202).*

0 kilometres 2
0 miles 2

N

*Organized walking trips start
at the village of* **La Palud-
sur-Verdon** *(p192).*

ALPES-DE-
HAUTE-PROVENCE

Le Petit Lac

La Maire

Pont du Galetas

Verdon

Lac de
Ste-Croix

Col de l'Olivier

La Palud-
sur-Verdon

Les Salles-
sur-Verdon

Aiguines

Col d'Illoire

La Graou

Col d' Ayen

Gorge du Galetas

ROUTE DES CRÊTES

VAR

Verdon

*A beautifully restored 17th-century
château crowns the village of*
Aiguines*, with fine views
down to the Lac de Sainte-Croix.*

Car driving through a carved-out cliff face of the Gorges du Verdon

An ancient clock tower and gate remain in the old town of **Castellane**, a popular tourist centre (p202).

Castellane

D4085

D102

D952

Verdon

This is one of the gorge's best viewing points. Signposted walks lead down to the canyon floor, but a torch is required to walk through the long tunnels.

D17

Rougon

D952

Soleils

D955

Le Jabron

D23

Gorge du Verdon

Verdon

Trigance

D90

Le Petit Saint-Maymes

D71

↑ View across the rooftops of Castellane from the Route des Crêtes

Pont de l'Artuby

Artuby

Park at either end of the 110-m (360-ft) **Pont de l'Artuby Bridge**, which spans the Artuby river, and marvel at the superb views (p193).

The stronghold of
Sisteron along the
bank of the Durance ↑

EXPERIENCE MORE

 2

Sisteron

🅰D3 🚉🚌 ℹ️1 place de la
République; www.sisteron-
buech.fr

As you approach Sisteron
from the north or south, it
is easy to appreciate its
strategic importance. The
town calls itself the "gateway
to Provence", sitting in a
narrow valley on the left bank
of the Durance river. It is a
lively town, protected by the
most impressive fortifications
in Provence. However, it has
suffered for its ideal military
position, most recently with
heavy Allied bombardment
during 1944.

La Citadelle, built in the
12th century, dominates the
town and affords superb
views down over the Durance.
These defences, though
incomplete, comprise a keep,
dungeon, chapel, towers and
ramparts. It also offers a fine
setting for the Nuits de la
Citadelle, the summer festival
of music, theatre and dance.

The cathedral in the main
square, Notre-Dame et
St-Thyrse, is an example of
the Provençal Romanesque
school, dating from 1160. At
its east end, the 17th-century
Chapelle des Visitandines
houses the Musée Terre et
Temps, a museum dedicated
to the examination of time. In
the old town, shops, cafés and
bars line the narrow, covered
alleyways called andrones.
Rocher de la Baume on the
opposite bank is a popular
practice spot for mountaineers.

La Citadelle

⊛ 🅰1 allée de Verdun
🕐Late Mar–11 Nov: daily
🌐citadelledesisteron.fr

3

Barcelonnette

🅰E3 🚌 ℹ️Place Frédéric
Mistral 🌐barcelonnette.
com

In the remote Ubaye valley,
surrounded by a demi-halo of
snowy peaks, lies Provence's

northernmost town. It is a
flat, open settlement of
cobbled streets, smart cafés
and restaurants, and quaint
gift shops, selling specialities
such as raspberry and juniper
liqueurs. The town was
named in 1231 by its founder
Raimond-Bérenger V, Count
of Barcelona and Provence,
whose great-grandfather
of the same name married
into the House of Provence
in 1112. The town's Alpine
setting gives it a Swiss flavour,
but it also has a Mexican link:
the Arnaud brothers, whose
business in Barcelonnette was
failing, emigrated to Mexico
and made their fortune.
Others followed, and on their
return in the early 20th century,
they built the grand villas
which encircle the town.

Housed in one of the villas
is the **Musée de la Vallée**,
where the Mexican connection
is explained through illus-
trations and costumes. There
are four other branches of
this museum in the Ubaye
valley, at St-Paul, Jausiers,
St-Ours Bas and Le Lauzet.

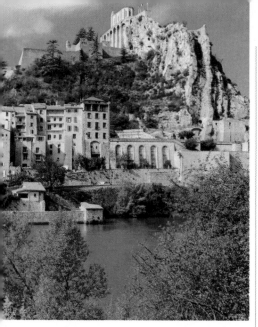

⑤ Mont Pelat

⬛ F3 ⬛ Thorame-Verdon ⬛ Colmars, Allos ⓘ Pl de la Coopérative, Allos ⬛ valdallos.com

This is the loftiest peak in the Provençal Alps, rising to a height of 3,050 m (10,017 ft). All around are mountains and breathtaking passes, some of them closed by snow until June. Among them are the Col de la Cayolle, 2,327 m (7,635 ft) on the D2202 to the east, and the hair-raising Col d'Allos, 2,250 m (7,380 ft) on the D908 to the west.

South of Mont Pelat, in the heart of the Parc National du Mercantour, is the beautiful 50-ha (124-acre) Lac d'Allos. It is the largest natural lake in Europe at this altitude. The setting is idyllic, ringed by snowy mountains, its crystal-clear waters swimming with trout and char.

Another record-breaker is Cime de la Bonette, on the D64 northeast of Mont Pelat. At 2,862 m (9,390 ft) this is the highest pass in Europe. It also has what is perhaps the most magnificent view of this region's extraordinary mountain scenery.

In summer, there is an information point in the town for the Parc National du Mercantour (p80). The park stretches along the Italian border and straddles the Alpes Maritimes region in the south. It is a haven for birds, wildlife and fauna, with two major archaeological sites.

Musée de la Vallée

 ⬛ 10 ave de la Libération ⬛ 04 92 81 27 15 ⬛ Wed-Sat pm (Jul & Aug: Mon-Sat) ⬛ Early Nov–mid-Dec

④ Seyne-les-Alpes

⬛ E3 ⬛ ⓘ Place d'Armes ⬛ blancheserreponcon-tourisme.com

The small mountain village of Seyne dominates the Vallée de la Blanche, sitting 1,260 m (4,134 ft) above sea level. Horses and mules graze in the nearby fields, and there is a celebrated annual horse and mule fair in August.

Beside the main road is Notre-Dame-de-Nazareth, a 13th-century Romanesque church with Gothic portals, a sundial and a large rose window. The path by the church leads up to the citadelle, built by Vauban in 1693, which encloses the still-standing 12th-century watchtower. There are also ramparts visible, part of the original fortifications of this border town.

The village is also a centre for winter sports, with facilities nearby at St-Jean, Le Grand Puy and Chabanon.

NAPOLEON IN PROVENCE

In his bid to regain power after his exile on Elba, Napoleon knew his only chance of success was to win over Sisteron. On 1 March 1815, he secretly sailed from the island of Elba, landing at Golfe-Juan with 1,026 soldiers. With his troops, he scrambled across difficult terrain, and waited for news of the royalist stronghold of Sisteron. The arsenal was empty and he entered the town on 5 March. The people were, at last, beginning to warm to him.

⑥ Colmars

Ⓐ E3 🚌 **𝒊** Ancienne Auberge Fleurie; www. verdontourisme.com

Colmars is a fortified town, nestling between two 17th-century forts with 12-m (40-ft) ramparts, which look across oak-planked roofs. The town is named after the hill on which it is built, *collis Martis*, where the Romans built a temple to the god Mars. Vauban, the military engineer, designed its lasting look. On the north side, an alley leads to the 17th-century **Fort de Savoie**, a fine example of military architecture.

In summer, residents enjoy relaxing on their *soleillades* (wooden sun-trap balconies), or strolling along alpine paths with beautiful views.

Fort de Savoie

🐶🐾 🏠 04370 Colmars
☎ 04 92 83 41 92 🕐 Jun–Sep: Tue pm, Wed am, Fri pm, Sat & Sun am; Jul–Aug: daily; Oct–May: by appt only

⑦ Digne-les-Bains

Ⓐ E3 🚗🚌 **𝒊** Place du Tampinet; www.digneles bains-tourisme.com

A spa town fed by eight hot springs, Digne-les-Bains is well-known for its *Thermes* (thermal baths), which are a short drive southeast of the town. Digne's boulevard Gassendi is named after local mathematician and astronomer Pierre Gassendi (1592–1655). Digne, the *"capitale de la lavande"*, hosts a five-day lavender carnival in August. The town is also a centre for modern sculpture.

The **Musée Gassendi**, in the old town hospice, holds 16th-to 19th-century paintings, contemporary art and 19th-century scientific instruments. Alexandra David-Néel, one of Europe's most intrepid travellers, died in Digne in 1969. Her house, *Samten-Dzong* (fortress of meditation), now the **Maison Alexandra David-Néel**, includes a Tibetan centre and a museum. The grand cathedral of Notre-Dame-du-Bourg, built between 1200–1330, is the largest

Romanesque church in Haute-Provence. Relics in its archaeological crypt date from Roman times.

The **Jardin des Cordeliers**, an enchanting walled garden in a convent, has medicinal plants and a sensory garden.

Musée Gassendi

🐶🐾🏠 🏠 64 blvd Gassendi
🕐 Wed–Mon (Oct–mid-May: Sat & Sun pm only) 🚫 Public hols, 25 Dec–2 Jan 🌐 musee-gassendi.org

Maison Alexandra David-Néel

🐶🐾🏠 🏠 27 ave Maréchal Juin 🕐 Tue–Sun (Dec–Mar: pm only) 🌐 alexandra-david-neel.fr

Jardin des Cordeliers

🐾 🏠 Place des Cordeliers
☎ 04 92 30 81 50 🕐 Mon–Fri 🚫 Public hols

TRAIN DES PIGNES

The Train des Pignes runs four times a day throughout the year from Digne-les-Bains to Nice. It is the remaining part of a network that was designed to link the Côte d'Azur with the Alps, built between 1891 and 1911. It is a popular service, used by locals going about their daily business as much as by tourists. It rattles along the single track at a fair pace, over 16 viaducts, 15 bridges and through 27 tunnels, and is sometimes a little bumpy. The journey takes about three hours each way and can be broken en route. Entrevaux *(p191)* is a good place to stop. Tickets can be booked online *(www.cpzou.fr)*.

⑧ Lurs

Ⓐ D4 🚌 La Brillanne **𝒊** La Mairie, place de la Mairie; 04 92 79 95 24

The Bishops of Sisteron and the Princes of Lurs were given ownership of the town of Lurs in the 9th century by Emperor

↑ Other-worldly rock formations of the Pénitents des Mées

Charlemagne. The town was repopulated after World War II, mainly by printers and artists.

The old town is entered via the Porte de l'Horloge, held in by medieval ramparts. North of the restored Château of the Bishop-Princes is the 300-m (900-ft) Promenade des Evêques (Bishops' walk), lined with 15 oratories leading to the chapel of Notre-Dame-de-Vie, with views over the sea of poppy fields and olive groves of the Durance valley.

The 12th-century **Abbaye de Ganagobie** has beautifully restored mosaics, inspired by oriental and Byzantine design. Offices are held several times a day by the monks – visitors may attend.

Abbaye de Ganagobie

🏛 ⭐ Le Prieuré, 04310 Ganagobie 🕒 Tue–Sun pm 🔒 1 week in mid-Jan 🌐 abbaye-ganagobie.com

---

9
Les Pénitents des Mées

🅰 D3 ✈ Marseille 🚆 St-Auban 🚌 Les Mées
ℹ La Mairie, 18 blvd de la République; 04 92 34 03 31

Les Pénitents des Mées is a row of columnar rocks more than 100 m (300 ft) high and over 2 km (a mile) long. This curious rock formation is said to be a cowled procession of banished monks. In local mythology, monks from the mountain of Lure pursued some Moorish beauties, captured by a lord during the time of the Saracen invasion in the 6th century. They were turned into stone as punishment for their sins.

The small village of Les Mées is tucked away at the north end. The chapel of St-Roch affords a great view of the rocks' strange formation of millions of pebbles and stones.

10
Forcalquier

🅰 D4 🚌 ℹ 13 place du Bourguet 🌐 haute-provence-tourisme.com

Crowned by a ruined castle and domed chapel of the 19th-century Notre-Dame-de-Provence, this town is now a shadow of its former self, though it has a lively weekly market which attracts local artists and artisans.

There are some fine façades in the old town, but only one gate, the Porte des Cordeliers. The **Musée de Salagon** preserves the history of the

EAT

L'Olivier
A delightful family-run restaurant with tasty seafood and meat main courses. There is alfresco dining in good weather.

🅰 X9 ⭐ 1 rue des Monges, 04000 Digne 🕒 Tue–Wed

€€€

people and culture of Haute-Provence. The **Observatoire de Haute-Provence** and the nearby Centre d'Astronomie are a must for star-gazers.

Musée de Salagon

⊕⊕🏛 ⭐ Le Prieuré, Mane 🕒 Wed–Mon 🔒 Mid-Dec–Jan 🌐 musee-de-salagon.com

Observatoire de Haute-Provence

⊕⊕ ⭐ St-Michel-l'Observatoire 🕒 Apr–Sep & All Saints' school holidays: Wed pm only (pre-booking required); Jul–Aug: Tue–Thu pm only 🌐 obs-hp.fr

↑ Medieval gate, Porte du Soubeyran, leading into the town of Manosque

⑪
Manosque

🅐D4 🚩 **ℹ Place de l'Hôtel de Ville; www. tourisme-manosque.fr**

France's national nuclear research centre, Cadarache, has brought prosperity to Manosque, a town which has sprawled beyond its original hill site above the Durance. French skincare company L'Occitane has its headquarters here, which you can visit on a tour. The centre has 13th- and 14th-century gates, Porte du Soubeyran and Porte de la Saunerie. The perfume shop in rue Grande was once the atelier of writer Jean Giono's mother. The second floor belonged to his father. The **Centre Jean Giono** tells the story of his life.

The town's adoptive son is the painter Jean Carzou, who decorated the walls of the **Couvent de la Présentation** with apocalyptic allegories of modern life.

Centre Jean Giono

⊛⊛ 🅐3 blvd Élémir Bourges 📞04 92 70 54 54 🕑Tue-Sun (Oct-Mar: pm only) 🚫Public hols, 25 Dec-2 Jan 🅦centre jeangiono.com

Couvent de la Présentation

⊛⊛ 🅐9 blvd Élémir Bourges 📞04 92 87 40 49 🕑Apr-Oct: 10am-12:30pm & 2-6pm Tue-Sat; Nov-Mar: 2-6pm Wed-Sat 🚫Public hols, 23 Dec-2 Jan

⑫
Gréoux-les-Bains

🅐D4 🚍 **ℹ7 place de l'Hôtel de Ville; www.greoux-les-bains.com**

The thermal waters of this spa town have been enjoyed since antiquity, when baths were built by the Romans in the 1st century AD. Gréoux flourished in the 19th century, and the waters can still be enjoyed at the Chaîne Thermale du Soleil. This spa is on the east side of the village where bubbling, sulphurous water arrives at the rate of 100,000 litres (22,000 gallons) an hour.

The restored castle ruin of the Templars sits on a high spot and an open-air theatre is in the grounds. **Le Petit Monde d'Émilie** is a museum with 148 miniatures from 1832 to the present, including dolls, costumes and toy trains.

LAVENDER HONEY

Busy bees forage the fields, forests and farmland of Provence to contribute sweet and subtle flavours to local honey. For the best lavender honeys, seek the "Miel de Lavande et Lavandin" appellation d'origine contrôlée (AOC) label in stores, where you'll also find honeys tagged with the "Miel de Provence" and "Miel Toutes Fleurs" labels of authenticity. These are tinged with hints of herbs, broom, and wildflowers.

Le Petit Monde d'Émilie

⊛⊛ 🅐16 ave des Alpes 📞06 84 62 71 23 🕑Mid-Apr-Oct: Mon, Wed & Fri pm only 🚫Public hols

---

⑬
Valensole

🅐D4 **ℹ2 rue du Docteur Chaupin; www.valensole.fr**

This is the centre of France's most important lavender-growing area. It sits on the edge of the Valensole plains with a sturdy-towered Gothic church at its height. Admiral Pierre-Charles Villeneuve, the unsuccessful adversary of Admiral Nelson at the Battle of Trafalgar, was born here in 1763. Signs for locally made lavender honey are everywhere, and just outside the town is the **Musée Vivant de l'Abeille**. This fascinating interactive museum explains the intriguing life of the honey bee, with informative demonstrations, photographs and videos. During the

→ Breathtaking view of the rows of lavender fields in Valensole

summer months, you can visit the beehives and see the beekeepers at work.

Musée Vivant de l'Abeille
🕘 ⌂ Rte de Manosque 📞 04 92 74 85 28 🕐 Tue-Sat ⌂ Public hols

Riez

⌂ D4 🚍 🛈 Place Maxime Javelly; www.ville-riez.fr

At the edge of the Valensole plateau is this unspoiled village, filled with small shops selling ceramics and traditional *santons* (hand-painted clay figurines),

Did You Know?

At Musée Vivant de l'Abeille you can see 30,000 bees at work inside a glass hive.

honey and lavender. Its past is reflected in the Renaissance façades of the houses and mansions in the old town. This is entered through the 13th-century Porte Aiguière, which leads on to the tree-lined Grand Rue, with fine examples of Renaissance architecture at numbers 27 and 29.

The most unusual site is the remains of the 1st-century AD Roman temple dedicated to Apollo. It stands in the middle of a field by the river Colostre; the original site of the town where the Roman colony *Reia Apollinaris* lived. On the other side of the river is a rare example of Merovingian architecture, a small baptistry dating from the 5th century.

The village has a number of fountains: Fontaine Benoîte, opposite Porte Sanson, dates to 1819; Fontaine de Blanchon is fed by an underground spring – it was used to wash the clothes of the infirm in the days before antibiotics; and the soft waters of the spring-fed Fontaine de Saint-Maxime were believed to heal the eyes.

15

Moustiers-Ste-Marie

△E4 **ℹ Place de l'Église; www.moustiers.fr**

The setting of the town of Moustiers is stunning, high on the edge of a ravine, beneath craggy rocks. Situated in the town centre is the parish church, with a three-storey Romanesque belfry. Above it, a path meanders up to the 12th-century chapel of Notre-Dame de Beauvoir. The view across the Lac de Ste-Croix is magnificent.

A heavy iron chain, 227 m (745 ft) in length, is suspended above the ravine. Hanging from the centre is a five-pointed, golden star. Although it was renewed in 1957, it is said to date back to the 13th century, when the chevalier Blacas hoisted it up in thanks for his release from captivity during the Seventh Crusade of St Louis.

Moustiers is a popular tourist town. The streets are crowded in summer due to its pretty setting and its ceramics. The original Moustiers ware is housed in the **Musée de la Faïence**, while modern reproductions can be bought in the town. The Musée de Préhistoire in Quinson, 40 km (25 miles) south, is a must.

Musée de la Faïence

🐾🐾🐾 **△ Rue du Seigneur de la Clue** 📞 04 92 74 61 64 🕐 Apr–Oct: Wed–Mon; Feb, Mar, Nov & Dec: Sat & Sun

16

Annot

△E4 🚃 **ℹ Place du Germe; www.tourisme-alpes-haute-provence.com**

The town of Annot, on the Train des Pignes railway line (*p198*), has a distinct Alpine feel. Annot lies in the Vaïre valley, crisscrossed by icy waters streaming down from the mountains. The surrounding scenery, however, is a more unfamiliar pattern of jagged rocks and deep caves.

Vast sandstone boulders, known as the *grès d'Annot*, are strewn around the town, and local builders have constructed houses against these haphazard rocks, using their sheer faces as outside walls. The old town lies behind the main road, where there is also a Romanesque church. The tall buildings that line the narrow streets here have even retained some of their original 15th- to 18th-century carved stone lintels.

Most Sundays (May–Oct) in summer, a 1909 *belle époque* steam train chugs its way from Puget-Théniers up to Annot, providing a pleasant way for visitors to enjoy the unspoiled countryside.

17

Castellane

△E4 🚌 **ℹ Rue Nationale; www.verdontourisme.com**

This is one of the main centres for the Gorges du Verdon, surrounded by campsites and caravans. Tourists squeeze

← The little steam train crossing a viaduct on its way to Annot

↑ The picturesque town and citadel of Entrevaux, built into the rocky hillside

into the town centre in summer and, in the evenings, fill the cafés after a day's hiking, climbing, canoeing and white-water rafting on the rapids of the Verdon. It is a well-sited town, beneath an impressive 180-m (600-ft) slab of grey rock. On top of this, dominating the skyline, is the chapel of Notre-Dame du Roc, built in 1703. A strenuous, 30-minute walk from behind the parish church to the top is rewarded with superb views. Castellane was once a sturdy fortress, and repelled invasion several times. The lifting of the siege by the Huguenots in 1586 is commemorated every year with firecrackers at the Fête des Pétardiers (last Sun in Jan).

The town's fortifications were completely rebuilt in the 14th century after most of the town, dating from Roman times, crumbled and slipped into the Verdon valley. Most social activity takes place in the main square, place Marcel-Sauvaire, which is lined with small

hotels that have catered for generations of visitors.

All that remains of the ramparts is the Tour Pentagonale and a small section of the old wall, which lie just beyond the 12th-century St-Victor church, on the way up to the chapel.

_____

St-André-les-Alpes

E4 🚆🚌 *i* Place Marcel Pastorelli; www.verdon tourisme.com

Lying at the north end of the beautiful Lac de Castillon, where the river Issole meets the river Verdon, is St-André. It is a popular summer holiday and leisure centre, scattered around the sandy flats on the lakeside. The artificial lake is formed by damming the river by the 90-m (295-ft) Barrage de Castillon, and is a haven for rafting, canoeing and kayaking, as well as swimming and fishing.

Inland, lavender fields and orchards make for picturesque walks. Hang-gliding has become so popular here that one of the local producers advertises its wine as "the wine of eagles".

Entrevaux

F4 🚆🚌 *i* Rue de la Porte Royale; www.verdon tourisme.com

It is easy to see why Entrevaux is called a "fairy-tale town" as you cross the drawbridge and enter through the Porte Royale. The dramatic entrance is flanked by twin towers and from here you enter the Ville Forte, inside which the streets are narrow and dark.

Fortified in 1690 by the military engineer Vauban (1633–1707), Entrevaux became one of the strongest military sites on the Franco-Savoy border. Even the 17th-century cathedral, Notre-Dame-de-l'Assomption, was skilfully incorporated into the turreted ramparts.

Unlike most military strongholds, the citadel was not built on top of a hill, but strategically placed on a rocky outcrop. It was last used in World War I as a prison for German officers. A steep track leads to the citadel, 156 m (511 ft) above the village. The 30-minute climb to the top, past basking lizards, should not be made in the midday heat.

NEED TO KNOW

Aerial view of the Gorges du Verdon

BEFORE YOU GO

Things change, so plan ahead to make the most of your trip. Be prepared for all eventualities by considering the following points before you travel.

AT A GLANCE

CURRENCY
Euro

AVERAGE DAILY SPEND

ON A BUDGET	MODERATE SPENDER	SPLASH OUT
€60	€165	€300+

BOTTLED WATER	COFFEE	BEER	DINNER FOR TWO
€1.00	€2.50	€5.00	€60

ESSENTIAL PHRASES

Hello	Bonjour
Thank you	Merci
Please	S'il vous plaît
Goodbye	Au revoir
Do you speak English?	Parlez-vous anglais?
I don't understand...	Je ne comprends pas

ELECTRICITY SUPPLY
Power sockets are type C and E, fitting two-pronged plugs. Standard voltage is 230 volts.

Passports and Visas

For entry requirements, including visas, consult your nearest French embassy or check the **France-Visas** website. EU nationals and citizens of the UK, US, Canada, Australia and New Zealand do not need a visa for a stay of up to three months.
France-Visas
w france-visas.gouv.fr

Government Advice

Now more than ever, it is important to consult both your and the French government's advice before travelling. The **UK Foreign and Commonwealth Office**, the **US Department of State**, the **Australian Department of Foreign Affairs and Trade** and **Gouvernement France** offer the latest information on security, health and local regulations.
Australian Department of Foreign Affairs and Trade
w smartraveller.gov.au
Gouvernement France
w gouvernement.fr
UK Foreign and Commonwealth Office
w gov.uk/foreign-travel-advice
US Department of State
w travel.state.gov

Customs Information

You can find information on the laws relating to goods and currency taken in or out of France on the **Douanes et Droits Indirects** website.
Douanes et Droits Indirects
w douane.gouv.fr

Insurance

We recommend that you take out a comprehensive insurance policy covering theft, loss of belongings, medical care, cancellations and delays, and read the small print carefully. EU and UK citizens are eligible for free emergency medical care provided they have a valid European Health Insurance Card (**EHIC**) or a

UK Global Health Insurance Card (**GHIC**). Visitors from outside the EU must arrange their own private medical insurance.
EHIC
🆆 ec.europa.eu
GHIC
🆆 ghic.org.uk

Vaccinations

No inoculations are needed for France. For information regarding COVID-19 vaccination requirements, consult government advice.

Booking Accommodation

Gîtes de France lists almost 2,500 rural self-catering holiday rental properties, *chambres d'hôtes* (B&Bs) and campsites in Provence. Book well ahead if you plan to visit in summer (June to August) or during events such as the Avignon Festival or Cannes Film Festival.
Gîtes de France
🆆 gites-de-france.com

Money

Most establishments accept major credit, debit and pre-paid currency cards. Contactless payments are accepted in major cities. Most taxi drivers and market traders, as well as many smaller bars and restaurants, accept only cash, so do carry a small amount with you at all times.

Tipping waiters in restaurants is considered polite. If you are pleased with the service, a tip of 5–10 per cent of the total bill is appreciated. Hotel porters and housekeeping generally expect a tip of €1 to €2 per bag or day. For taxi journeys, round up the fare to the nearest euro.

Travellers with Specific Requirements

Most museums are wheelchair-accessible and offer audio tours and induction loops. **Bespoke Holidays** specializes in accommodation for wheelchair users and people with learning disabilities and their carers. Fully supported activity holidays are offered by **Go Beyond**.

To find out about accessible public transport and attractions in Nice, download the handy Nice Accessible PDF from the **Office de Tourisme Nice** website. National train operator SNCF offers **Accès Plus**, which accompanies travellers with specific needs on rail journeys.
Accès Plus
🆆 accessibilite.sncf.com
Bespoke Holidays
🆆 bespokefrance.com
Go Beyond
🆆 gobeyondholidays.com
Office de Tourisme Nice
🆆 nicetourisme.com/nice-accessible

Language

French is the official language spoken in France. English is spoken in large hotels, but not in all smaller establishments, shops, bars and cafés, so mastering a few niceties goes a long way.

Opening Hours

> **COVID-19** Increased rates of infection may result in temporary opening hours and/or closures. Always check ahead before visiting museums, attractions and hospitality venues.

Lunchtime Most shops and businesses close for an hour or two from around noon. Very few restaurants serve lunch after 2pm.
Monday Some museums, smaller shops and many upmarket restaurants close for the day.
Sunday Most shops are closed.
Public holidays Shops, museums and attractions are usually closed.

PUBLIC HOLIDAYS

1 Jan	New Year's Day (Jour de l'An)
Mar/Apr	Good Friday (Vendredi Saint)
Mar/Apr	Easter Sunday (Pâques)
Mar/Apr	Easter Monday (Lundi de Pâques)
1 May	Labour Day (Fête du Travail)
8 May	VE Day (Victoire 1945)
30 May	Ascension
9 June	Pentecôte
14 July	Bastille Day (Fête Nationale)
15 Aug	Assumption
25 Dec	Christmas Day (Noël)

GETTING AROUND

Whether you are visiting for a short city break, a beach holiday or rural country retreat, discover how to get around Provence like a local.

AT A GLANCE

PUBLIC TRANSPORT COSTS

AVIGNON

€1.40
Single bus journey

MARSEILLE

€1.70
Single bus, metro or tram journey

NICE

€1.50
Single bus journey

TOP TIP
Avoid on-the-spot fines by stamping your ticket to validate your journey.

SPEED LIMIT

AUTOROUTE

130 km/h (80mph)

DUAL CARRIAGEWAYS

110 km/h (68mph)

SINGLE CARRIAGEWAYS

90 km/h (56mph)

URBAN AREAS

50 km/h (31mph)

Arriving by Air

Provence has five international airports in Avignon, Marseille, Nice, Nîmes and Toulon-Hyères; all are near their respective cities, with good bus services to the city centres. A shuttle bus (€1.20) connects Marseille airport with Vitrolles TER station for trains to the city and to Arles, Avignon and Nîmes. Monaco has no airport but has a city centre heliport with a helicopter shuttle service to Nice International Airport, taking seven minutes with **Héli Securité**. For information on getting to and from Provence's main airports, see the table opposite.
Héli Securité
🌐 helisecurite.fr

Train Travel

International Train Travel
High-speed TGV trains connect Provence with the UK, Italy, Spain and Switzerland, and most TGV stations are in city centres. Reservations for these services are essential as tickets are booked up quickly. Visit the **RENFE-SNCF** or **Oui SNCF** websites for tickets, depending on your route. You can buy tickets and passes for multiple international journeys via **Eurail** or **Interrail**.

Students and those under 26 and over 60 can benefit from discounted rail travel both to and within France. Visit the Eurail website for details.
Eurail
🌐 eurail.com
Interrail
🌐 interrail.eu
Oui SNCF
🌐 oui.sncf
RENFE-SNCF
🌐 renfe-sncf.com

Regional Train Travel
France's state-owned national railway company SNCF's high-speed TGV trains connect major towns and cities all over France. Regional **TER** trains, operated by SNCF, stop at every station on local and suburban routes.
TER
🌐 ter-sncf.com

GETTING TO AND FROM THE AIRPORT

Airport	Distance to City	Taxi Fare	Public Transport	Journey Time
Avignon	10 km (6 miles)	€25–€30	LER 13 bus	40 mins
Marseille	27 km (17 miles)	€50–€60	L91 Navette Aéroport coach	25 mins
Nice	7 km (4 miles)	€35	Lignes d'Azur tram lines 2 and 3	20 mins
Nîmes	13 km (8 miles)	€25	Navette Aéroport coach	15 mins
Toulon-Hyères to Toulon	24 km (15 miles)	€55	102 Réseau Mistral bus	30 mins
Toulon-Hyères to Hyères	8 km (5 miles)	€22	63 Réseau Mistral bus	20 mins

JOURNEY PLANNER

This map plots the fastest driving routes to help you plan your car journeys between Provence's main towns and cities. Tolls apply on most routes.

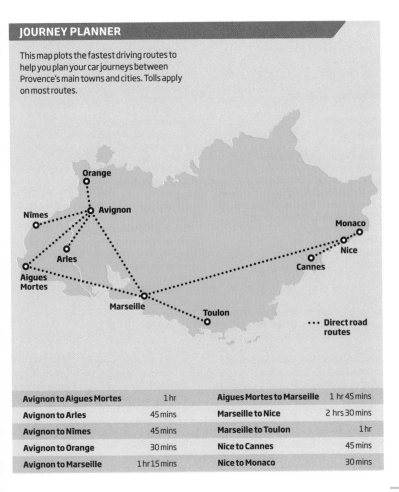

••• Direct road routes

Avignon to Aigues Mortes	1 hr		Aigues Mortes to Marseille	1 hr 45 mins
Avignon to Arles	45 mins		Marseille to Nice	2 hrs 30 mins
Avignon to Nîmes	45 mins		Marseille to Toulon	1 hr
Avignon to Orange	30 mins		Nice to Cannes	45 mins
Avignon to Marseille	1 hr 15 mins		Nice to Monaco	30 mins

Public Transport

Each urban area in Provence has its own public transport system extending from the city centre to the outer suburbs. Safety and hygiene measures, timetables, ticket information and transport maps can be obtained from their respective websites.

City Transport

Orizo is the local transport authority for Avignon and its suburbs, including Villeneuve-lès-Avignon. Hop-on, hop-off electric shuttles (Baladines) trundle around the medieval centre.

In Marseille, **RTM** co-ordinates bus, Métro and tram lines. **CAM** operates buses within Monaco and to Nice and Menton, and seven lifts and escalators connect its waterfront with the upper urban level. **Lignes d'Azur** is the public transport operator for Nice, Cannes and Alpes-Maritimes, including the Nice tramway. **Réseau Mistral** is Toulon's city and suburban bus network.

CAM (Monaco)
w cam.mc
Lignes d'Azur (Nice and Cannes)
w lignesdazur.com
Orizo (Avignon)
w orizo.fr
Réseau Mistral (Toulon)
w reseaumistral.com
RTM (Marseille)
w rtm.fr

Long-Distance Bus Travel

BlaBlaCar coaches connect cities in Provence, including Marseille and Nîmes, with Paris, Lyon, Montpellier, Toulouse and Bordeaux. **Flixbus** connects cities in Provence with Paris, as well as with other French towns and major European destinations.

BlaBlaCar
w blablacar.fr/bus
Flixbus
w flixbus.fr

Tickets

Buying tickets in advance is always cheaper than buying from the driver. *Carnets* (books of up to 10 tickets) and multi-trip passes valid for one or more days are available on all urban transport networks and can be bought at rail and bus stations, designated stores and city tourist information offices.

Remember to always purchase a ticket as ticket inspections are common.

Country Buses

Beyond major towns, local bus routes are served by private companies under regional authority governance. Timetables are geared to the needs of local schools and shoppers, and do not always present the best choice for visitors. **ZOU!** is the one-stop shop for local buses across the region.
ZOU!
w zou.maregionsud.fr

Trams

Trams can be more efficient than buses in Provence's cities. Marseille's tramway operates over three lines, and tickets must be purchased in advance. Nice has a three-route tram system and tickets can be bought from machines at the tramstop. Tickets for Avignon's trams can be bought from machines at tram stations or via the Orizo smartphone app.

Taxis

There are taxi ranks at rail and bus stations, airports and in most main squares in towns and cities. You can also call or text for taxis. **Cab Express Taxi Moto** are motorbike taxis in Nice. A list of key taxi firms is shown below.
Cab Express Taxi Moto
w cab-express.com
Provence Cab (Avignon)
w provencecab-paca.fr
Taxi Cannes
w taxi-cannes.net
Taxi Monaco
w taximonaco.com
Taxi Radio Marseille
w taximarseille.com
Taxi Riviera (Nice)
w taxis-nice.fr
Taxi Toulon
w taxi-toulon.com

Driving

Driving to Provence

It takes 9–10 hours to drive to Avignon from the Channel ferry ports via the A26 and A27 *autoroutes*. Driving from Bilbao in Spain, which is served by ferries from the UK, takes around 8 hours. To take your own car into France, you will need proof of registration, valid insurance documents, a full, valid driving licence and your passport.

Car Rental

To rent a car in France you must be 21 years or over and have held a valid driver's licence for at least a year. You will also need to present a credit card. Driving licences issued by any of the EU member states are valid throughout the EU.

International driving licences are not needed for short-term visitors (up to 90 days) from the UK, North America, Australia and New Zealand. Visitors from other countries should check with their local automobile association.

Driving in Provence

Driving in Provence can be a pleasure, but plan your journey carefully to avoid traffic bottlenecks on rural and coastal roads in summer. For a fast point-to-point journey, the A8 *autoroute* cuts across the Camargue from Menton to Aix-en-Provence, near which it meets the A7 Autoroute du Soleil, so you can drive on *autoroutes* all the way across Provence from the Italian border to Orange in just over 3 hours. The same journey avoiding *autoroutes* takes more than 6 hours but costs less, as the A8 is the most expensive toll road in France.

Routes départementales are the narrowest and slowest roads, but in hinterland regions such as Alpes-de-Hautes-Provence they may be your only option. Bison Futé *(p212)* signs indicate routes avoiding heavy traffic and can be useful during peak French holiday periods.

Driving in the historic centres of Provençal towns is not recommended. Finding your way isn't easy as there are many one-way streets, and parking is difficult and expensive. In summer, traffic on the coast road between Hyères and Nice, and especially the section between Nice and Cannes, is often excruciatingly slow.

Rules of the Road

Always drive on the right. Unless otherwise signposted, vehicles coming from the right have right of way, and cars on a roundabout usually have right of way as well.

At all times, drivers must carry a valid driver's licence and registration and insurance documents. In case of a breakdown, it is compulsory to carry a red warning triangle and a luminous vest. Seat belts must be worn, and it is prohibited to sound your horn in cities. For motorbikes and scooters, the wearing of helmets and protective gloves is compulsory. It is against the law to drive in urban bus lanes. France strictly enforces its drink-drive limit *(p213)*, and random breath testing at mobile checkpoints is common.

Parking

Park only in areas with a large "P" or a *Payant* sign on the pavement or road, and pay at the parking meter with cash or contactless debit or credit card. Avignon, Marseille, Nice and Toulon have numerous underground car parks, signposted by a white "P" on a blue background, and overground car parks are usually located on the edge of historic town centres. Some city hotels have private parking.

Cycling

Most towns (except Nice and Monaco) have few hills and bike rentals are widely available. In the hot summer months, or for less energetic riders, electric-boosted e-bikes take less effort.

Vélopop' in Avignon, **Le Vélo** in Marseille and **Vélobleu** in Nice are bike-sharing schemes with multiple docking stations around each city. **Aixprit Vélo** is a handy bike shop that also rents out bikes in Aix-en-Provence. Bicycles may be taken on most trains, but the service must be booked in advance on TGV trains. To take your bike on a local train, look for the bicycle symbol on the timetable. Wearing a helmet is not compulsory but is strongly advised.

Aixprit Vélo
🆆 aixpritvelo.com
Le Vélo
🆆 levelo-mpm.fr
Vélobleu
🆆 velobleu.org
Vélopop'
🆆 velopop.fr

Boats and Ferries

The free *navette fluviale* (river shuttle), also known as the *bac à traille*, crosses the Rhône between the Quai de la Ligne in central Avignon and Île de la Barthelasse. **Réseau Mistral** runs *bateau-bus* (water taxi) services from Toulon to La Seyne-sur-Mer and Les Sablettes. **Bateliers de la Rade** and **Bateliers de la Côte d'Azur** sail from Toulon to the Îles d'Hyères. Ferries from Marseille's Vieux Port to Pointe-Rouge and l'Estaque are operated by RTM *(p210)*. **TLV** ferries sail from Saint-Pierre Marina in Hyères to the Îles d'Hyères. In Monaco, CAM *(p210)* bus-boats link Quai Kennedy with the cruise ship terminal.

Corsica Linea sails from Marseille to Corsica, Sardinia, Algeria and Tunisia. **Corsica Ferries** sail from Nice and Toulon to Corsica and Sardinia and from Toulon to Majorca and Sicily.

Bateliers de la Côte d'Azur
🆆 bateliersdelacotedazur.com
Bateliers de la Rade
🆆 lesbateliersdelarade.com
Corsica Ferries
🆆 corsica-ferries.fr
Corsica Linea
🆆 corsicalinea.com
Réseau Mistral
🆆 reseaumistral.com
TLV
🆆 tlv-tlv.com

Walking

To the delight of those who like to explore on foot, Provence is blessed with many well-marked long-distance footpaths leading through valleys, mountains, villages, vineyards and along the coastline.

The most rewarding way to take in any city is on foot. In many of the region's cities, sights are only a short distance apart.

PRACTICAL
INFORMATION

A little local knowledge goes a long way in Provence. Here you will find all the essential advice and information you will need during your stay.

AT A GLANCE

EMERGENCY NUMBERS

GENERAL EMERGENCY	FIRE SERVICE AND AMBULANCE
112	**18**

POLICE	MEDICAL EMERGENCY
17	**15**

TIME ZONE
CET/CEST
Central European Summer Time (CEST) last Sun Mar–last Sun Oct.

TAP WATER
Unless stated otherwise, tap water in France is safe to drink.

WEBSITES AND APPS

Bison Futé
Official road journey website and app *(www.bison-fute.gouv.fr)*.

OUI SNCF
Buy and download rail tickets direct to your phone or tablet with this app.

PACA Mobilité
Official app for public transport through the Provence-Alpes-Côte d'Azur area.

ViaMichelin
App for road travel planning, including journey times and traffic information.

Personal Security

Provence is generally a safe region, though petty crime can take place. Beware of pickpockets and bag-snatchers on public transport, especially during rush hour, and in major tourist areas. Use your commonsense and be alert to your surroundings, and you should experience a trouble-free trip.

If you do have anything stolen, report the crime as soon as possible to the nearest police station, and bring ID with you. Get a copy of the crime report in order to claim on your insurance. Contact your embassy or consulate if your passport is stolen, or in the event of a serious crime or accident.

Like the rest of France, Provence is diverse and multicultural. As a rule, Provençals are accepting of all people regardless of their race, gender or sexuality although rural Provence tends to be more conservative than the big cities. Same-sex marriage was legalized in 2013 and France recognized the right to legally change your gender in 2016. Nice, Cannes, Aix-en-Provence and especially Marseille have thriving LGBTQ+ communities. **Gay Map Marseille** lists bars, restaurants, clubs and other attractions in Marseille and Aix-en-Provence.
Gay Map Marseille
🆆 gaymapmarseille.com

Health

France has a world-class healthcare system. Emergency medical care is free for all UK and EU nationals. If you have an EHIC or GHIC *(p207)*, be sure to present this as soon as possible. You may have to pay for treatment and reclaim the money later. For other visitors, payment of medical expenses is the patient's responsibility. It is therefore important to arrange comprehensive medical insurance before travelling.

A green cross indicates a pharmacy. Pharmacists are an excellent source of advice – they can diagnose many health problems and suggest appropriate treatment. Phone 3237 to find the nearest pharmacy.

Smoking, Alcohol and Drugs

Smoking is prohibited in all public places, but is allowed on open-air restaurant, café and bar terraces. The possession of illegal drugs is prohibited and could result in a prison sentence. Unless stated otherwise, alcohol consumption on the streets is permitted. France has a strict limit of 0.05 per cent BAC (blood alcohol content) for drivers.

ID

There is no requirement for visitors to carry ID, but in the event of a routine check you may be asked to show your passport. If you don't have it with you, the police may escort you to wherever your passport is being kept.

Local Customs

Étiquette (la politesse) is important to the French. Upon entering a store or café you are expected to say bonjour and, when leaving, to say au revoir to staff. Be sure to add s'il vous plaît (please) when ordering and pardon (sorry) if you accidentally bump into someone.

The French usually shake hands when meeting someone for the first time. Friends and colleagues who know each other well will greet each other with a kiss on each cheek. If you are unsure about what's expected, wait to see if they offer a hand or a cheek.

Visiting Churches and Cathedrals

There are many notable churches and cathedrals in Provence. When visiting, dress respectfully and keep mobile phones on silent.

Mobile Phones and Wi-Fi

Free Wi-Fi hotspots are available in a number of public spaces, including museums, libraries and parks. Almost all hotels and many cafés and restaurants offer free Wi-Fi for patrons.

Visitors with EU mobile phone contracts can use their devices in Provence without additional data roaming charges. Users will be charged the same rates for data, SMS and voice calls as they would pay at home. Those not on EU tariffs should check roaming rates with their provider. A cheaper option may be to purchase a French SIM card (you will need to show ID).

Mobile phone coverage in most cities, towns and villages is good but mobile and GPS reception in some mountainous areas is patchy.

Post

Stamps (timbres) can be bought at post offices and tabacs (tobacconists) or online via **La Poste**. Most post offices have self-service machines to weigh and frank your mail. Yellow post boxes are ubiquitous.

La Poste
W laposte.fr

Taxes and Refunds

A sales tax (TVA) of 20 per cent is imposed on most goods and services. Non-EU residents can reclaim the TVA they pay on French goods at shops displaying the Global Refund Tax-Free sign as long as they spend more than €175 in the same shop in one day, and take the goods out of France. The retailer will generally supply a form and issue a détaxe receipt at the time of purchase. Make sure that you have your passport with you to prove non-resident status.

Discount Cards

City and regional passes can help you cut the cost of sightseeing and public transport. The **Avignon City Pass**, valid for 24 or 48 hours, offers free access to museums, monuments and gardens in Avignon and Villeneuve-lès-Avignon, as well as official themed guided tours. The **Vaucluse Provence Pass**, valid for two, three or five days, covers the wider Vaucluse region. The **French Riviera Pass** allows free access to many sights, tours and activities, and free travel on public transport throughout the Nice-Côte d'Azur metropolitan area. The **Marseille CityPass** includes free public transport, free admission to museums and galleries and other discounts.

Avignon City Pass and Vaucluse Provence Pass
W vaucluse-provence-pass.com
French Riviera Pass
W en.frenchrivierapass.com
Marseille CityPass
W marseille-tourisme.com

INDEX

Index

Page numbers in **bold** refer to main entries.

PHRASE BOOK

IN AN EMERGENCY

Help!	**Au secours!**	*oh sekoor*
Stop!	**Arrêtez!**	*aret-ay*
Call a	**Appelez un**	*apuh-lay uñ*
doctor!	**médecin!**	*medsañ*
Call an	**Appelez une**	*apuh-lay oon*
ambulance!	**ambulance!**	*oñboo-loñs*
Call the	**Appelez la**	*apuh-lay lah*
police!	**police!**	*poh-lees*
Call the fire	**Appelez les**	*apuh-lay leh*
brigade!	**pompiers!**	*poñ-peeyay*
Where is the	**Où est le téléphone**	*oo ay luh tehlehfon*
nearest telephone?	**le plus proche?**	*luh ploo prosh*
Where is the	**Où est l'hôpital**	*oo ay lopeetal luh*
nearest hospital?	**le plus proche?**	*ploo prosh*

COMMUNICATION ESSENTIALS

Yes	**Oui**	*wee*
No	**Non**	*noñ*
Please	**S'il vous plaît**	*seel voo play*
Thank you	**Merci**	*mer-see*
Excuse me	**Excusez-moi**	*exkoo-zay mwah*
Hello	**Bonjour**	*boñzhoor*
Goodbye	**Au revoir**	*oh ruh-vwar*
Good night	**Bonsoir**	*boñ-swar*
Morning	**Le matin**	*matañ*
Afternoon	**L'après-midi**	*l'apreh-meedee*
Evening	**Le soir**	*swar*
Yesterday	**Hier**	*eeyehr*
Today	**Aujourd'hui**	*oh-zhoor-dwee*
Tomorrow	**Demain**	*duhmañ*
Here	**Ici**	*ee-see*
There	**Là**	*lah*
What?	**Quoi, quel, quelle?**	*kwah, kel, kel*
When?	**Quand?**	*koñ*
Why?	**Pourquoi?**	*poor-kwah*
Where?	**Où?**	*oo*

USEFUL PHRASES

How are you?	**Comment allez-vous?**	*kom-moñ talay voo*
Very well, thank you.	**Très bien, merci.**	*treh byañ, mer-see*
Pleased to meet you.	**Enchanté de faire votre connaissance.**	*oñshoñ-tay duh fehr votr kon-ay-sans*
See you soon.	**A bientôt.**	*byañ-toh*
That's fine.	**C'est bon**	*say bon*
Where is/are...?	**Où est/sont...?**	*ooay/soñ*
How far is it to...?	**Combien de kilometres d'ici à...?**	*kom-byañ duh keelometr d'ee-see ah*
Which way to...?	**Quelle est la direction pour...?**	*kel ay lah deer-ek-syoñ poor*
Do you speak English?	**Parlez-vous anglais?**	*par-lay voo oñg-lay*
I don't understand.	**Je ne comprends pas.**	*zhuh nuh kom-proñ pah*
Could you speak slowly please?	**Pouvez-vous parler moins vite s'il vous plaît?**	*poo-vay voo par-lay mwañ veet seel voo play*
I'm sorry.	**Excusez-moi.**	*exkoo-zay mwah*

USEFUL WORDS

big	**grand**	*groñ*
small	**petit**	*puh-tee*
hot	**chaud**	*show*
cold	**froid**	*frwah*
good	**bon/bien**	*boñ/byañ*
bad	**mauvais**	*moh-veh*
enough	**assez**	*assay*
well	**bien**	*byañ*
open	**ouvert**	*oo-ver*
closed	**fermé**	*fer-meh*
left	**gauche**	*gohsh*
right	**droite**	*drwaht*
straight on	**tout droite**	*too drwaht*
near	**près**	*preh*
far	**loin**	*lwañ*
up	**en haut**	*oñ oh*
down	**en bas**	*oñ bah*
early	**de bonne heure**	*duh bon urr*
late	**en retard**	*oñ ruh-tar*
entrance	**l'entrée**	*l'on-tray*
exit	**la sortie**	*sor-tee*
toilet	**les toilettes, le WC**	*twah-let, vay-see*
free, unoccupied	**libre**	*leebr*
free, no charge	**gratuit**	*grah-twee*

MAKING A TELEPHONE CALL

I'd like to place a long-distance call.	**Je voudrais faire un appel á l'étranger.**	*zhuh voo-dreh fehr uñ apel a laytroñ-zhay*
I'd like to make a reverse charge call.	**Je voudrais faire une communi-cation en PCV.**	*zhuh voo-dreh fehr oon komoonikah-syoñ oñ peh-seh-veh*
I'll try again later.	**Je rappelerai plus tard.**	*zhuh rapeleray ploo tar*
Can I leave a message?	**Est-ce que je peux laisser un message?**	*es-keh zhuh puh leh-say uñ mehsazh*
Hold on.	**Ne quittez pas, s'il vous plaît.**	*nuh kee-tay pah seel voo play*
Could you speak up a little please?	**Pouvez-vous parler un peu plus fort?**	*poo-vay voo parlay uñ puh ploo for*
local call	**la communication locale**	*komoonikahsyoñ low-kal*

SHOPPING

How much does this cost?	**C'est combien s'il vous plaît?**	*say kom-byañ seel voo play*
I would like ...	**Je voudrais...**	*zhuh voo-dray*
Do you have?	**Est-ce que vous avez**	*es-kuh voo zavay*
I'm just looking.	**Je regarde seulement.**	*zhuh ruhgar suhlmoñ*
Do you take credit cards?	**Est-ce que vous acceptez les cartes de crédit?**	*es-kuh voo zaksept-ay leh kart duh kreh-dee*
Do you take travellers' cheques?	**Est-ce que vous acceptez les cheques de voyages?**	*es-kuh voo zaksept-ay leh shek duh vwayazh*
What time do you open?	**A quelle heure vous êtes ouvert?**	*ah kel urr voo zet oo-ver*
What time do you close?	**A quelle heure vous êtes fermé?**	*ah kel urr voo zet fer-may*

This one.	Celui-ci	suhl-wee-see
That one.	Celui-là	suhl-wee-lah
expensive	cher	shehr
cheap	pas cher,	pah shehr,
	bon marché	boñ mar-shay
size, clothes	la taille	tye
size, shoes	la pointure	pwañ-tur
white	blanc	bloñ
black	noir	nwahr
red	rouge	roozh
yellow	jaune	zhohwn
green	vert	vehr
blue	bleu	bluh

TYPES OF SHOPS

antique shop	le magasin d'antiquités	maga-zañ d'oñteekee-tay
bakery	la boulangerie	booloñ-zhuree
bank	la banque	boñk
bookshop	la librairie	lee-brehree
butcher	la boucherie	boo-shehree
cake shop	la pâtisserie	patee-sree
cheese shop	la fromagerie	fromazh-ree
chemist	la pharmacie	farmah-see
dairy	la crémerie	krem-ree
department store	le grand magasin	groñ maga-zañ
delicatessen	la charcuterie	sharkoot-ree
fishmonger	la poissonnerie	pwasson-ree
gift shop	le magasin de cadeaux	maga-zañ duh kadoh
greengrocer	le marchand de légumes	mar-shoñ duh lay-goom
grocery	l'alimentation	alee-moñta-syoñ
hairdresser	le coiffeur	kwafuhr
market	le marché	marsh-ay
newsagent	le magasin de journaux	maga-zañ duh zhoor-no
post office	la poste,	pohst,
	le bureau de poste,	booroh duh pohst,
	le PTT	peh-teh-teh
shoe shop	le magasin de chaussures	maga-zañ duh show-soor
supermarket	le supermarché	soo pehr-marshay
tobacconist	le tabac	tabah
travel agent	l'agence de voyages	l'azhoñs duh vwayazh

SIGHTSEEING

abbey	l'abbaye	l'abay-ee
art gallery	la galerie d'art	galer-ree dart
bus station	la gare routière	gahr roo-tee-yehr
cathedral	la cathédrale	katay-dral
church	l'église	l'aygleez
garden	le jardin	zhar-dañ
library	la bibliothèque	beebleeo-tek
museum	le musée	moo-zay
railway station	la gare (SNCF)	gahr (es-en-say-ef)
tourist information office	les renseignements touristiques, le syndicat d'initiative	roñsayn-moñ tooree-steek, sandee- ka d'eenee-syateev
town hall	l'hôtel de ville	l'ohtel duh veel
closed for public holiday	fermeture jour férié	fehrmeh-tur zhoor fehree-ay

STAYING IN A HOTEL

Do you have a vacant room?	Est-ce que vous avez une chambre?	es-kuh voo-zavay oon shambr
double room, with double bed	la chambre à deux personnes, avec un grand lit	shambr ah duh pehr-son avek un gronñ lee
twin room	la chambre à deux lits	shambr ah duh lee
single room	la chambre à une personne	shambr ah oon pehr-son
room with a bath, shower	la chambre avec salle de bains, une douche	shambr avek sal duh bañ, oon doosh
porter	le garçon	gar-soñ
key	la clef	klay
I have a reservation.	J'ai fait une réservation.	zhay fay oon rayzehrva-syoñ

EATING OUT

Have you got a table?	Avez-vous une table de libre?	avay-voo oon tahbl duh leebr
I want to reserve a table.	Je voudrais réserver une table.	zhuh voo-dray rayzehr-vay oon tahbl
The bill please.	L'addition s'il vous plaît.	l'adee-syoñ seel voo play
I am a vegetarian.	Je suis végétarien.	zhuh swee vezhay-tehryañ
Waitress/ waiter	Madame, Mademoiselle/ Monsieur	mah-dam, mah-demwahzel/ muh-syuh
menu	le menu, la carte	men-oo, kart
fixed-price menu	le menu à prix fixe	men-oo ah pree feeks
cover charge	le couvert	koo-vehr
wine list	la carte des vins	kart-deh vañ
glass	le verre	vehr
bottle	la bouteille	boo-tay
knife	le couteau	koo-toh
fork	la fourchette	for-shet
spoon	la cuillère	kwee-yehr
breakfast	le petit déjeuner	puh-tee deh-zhuh-nay
lunch	le déjeuner	deh-zhuh-nay
dinner	le dîner	dee-nay
main course	le plat principal	plah prañsee-pal
starter, first course	l'entrée, le hors d'oeuvre	l'oñ-tray, or- duhvr
dish of the day	le plat du jour	plah doo zhoor
wine bar	le bar à vin	bar ah vañ
café	le café	ka-fay
rare	saignant	say-noñ
medium	à point	ah pwañ
well done	bien cuit	byañ kwee

MENU DECODER

apple	la pomme	pom
baked	cuit au four	kweet oh foor
banana	la banane	banan
beef	le boeuf	buhf
beer, draught beer	la bière, bière à la pression	bee-yehr, bee-yehr ah lah pres-syoñ
boiled	bouilli	boo-yee

bread	**le pain**	*pan*	vegetables	**les légumes**	*lay-goom*
butter	**le beurre**	*burr*	vinegar	**le vinaigre**	*veenaygr*
cake	**le gâteau**	*gah-toh*	water	**l'eau**	*l'oh*
cheese	**le fromage**	*from-azh*	red wine	**le vin rouge**	*vañ roozh*
chicken	**le poulet**	*poo-lay*	white wine	**le vin blanc**	*vañ bloñ*
chips	**les frites**	*freet*			
chocolate	**le chocolat**	*shoko-lah*			
cocktail	**le cocktail**	*cocktail*			
coffee	**le café**	*kah-fay*			
dessert	**le dessert**	*deh-ser*			
dry	**sec**	*sek*			
duck	**le canard**	*kanar*			
egg	**l'oeuf**	*l'uf*			

NUMBERS

0	**zéro**	*zeh-roh*
1	**un, une**	*uñ, oon*
2	**deux**	*duh*
3	**trois**	*trwah*
4	**quatre**	*katr*
5	**cinq**	*sañk*
6	**six**	*sees*
7	**sept**	*set*
8	**huit**	*weet*
9	**neuf**	*nerf*
10	**dix**	*dees*
11	**onze**	*oñz*
12	**douze**	*dooz*
13	**treize**	*trehz*
14	**quatorze**	*katorz*
15	**quinze**	*kañz*
16	**seize**	*sehz*
17	**dix-sept**	*dees-set*
18	**dix-huit**	*dees-weet*
19	**dix-neuf**	*dees-nerf*
20	**vingt**	*vañ*
30	**trente**	*tront*
40	**quarante**	*karoñt*
50	**cinquante**	*sañkoñt*
60	**soixante**	*swasoñt*
70	**soixante-dix**	*swasoñt-dees*
80	**quatre-vingts**	*katr-vañ*
90	**quatre-vingt-dix**	*katr-vañ-dees*
100	**cent**	*soñ*
1,000	**mille**	*meel*

fish	**le poisson**	*pwah-ssoñ*
fresh fruit	**le fruit frais**	*frwee freh*
garlic	**l'ail**	*l'eye*
grilled	**grillé**	*gree-yay*
ham	**le jambon**	*zhoñ-boñ*
ice, ice cream	**la glace**	*glas*
lamb	**l'agneau**	*l'anyoh*
lemon	**le citron**	*see-troñ*
lobster	**le homard**	*omahr*
meat	**la viande**	*vee-yand*
milk	**le lait**	*leh*
mineral water	**l'eau minérale**	*l'oh meeney-ral*
mustard	**la moutarde**	*moo-tard*
oil	**l'huile**	*l'weel*
olives	**les olives**	*leh zoleev*
onions	**les oignons**	*leh zonyoñ*
orange	**l'orange**	*l'oroñzh*
fresh orange juice	**l'orange pressée**	*l'oroñzh press-eh*
fresh lemon juice	**le citron pressé**	*see-troñ press-eh*
pepper	**le poivre**	*pwavr*
poached	**poché**	*posh-ay*
pork	**le porc**	*por*
potatoes	**les pommes de terre**	*pom-duh tehr*
prawns	**les crevettes**	*kruh-vet*
rice	**le riz**	*ree*
roast	**rôti**	*row-tee*
roll	**le petit pain**	*puh-tee pañ*
salt	**le sel**	*sel*
sauce	**la sauce**	*sohs*
sausage, fresh	**la saucisse**	*sohsees*
seafood	**les fruits de mer**	*frwee duh mer*
shellfish	**les crustaces**	*kroos-tas*
snails	**les escargots**	*leh zes-kar-goh*
soup	**la soupe, le potage**	*soop, poh-tazh*
steak	**le bifteck, le steack**	*beef-tek, stek*
sugar	**le sucre**	*sookr*
tea	**le thé**	*tay*
toast	**pain grillé**	*pan greeyay*

TIME

one minute	**une minute**	*oon mee-noot*
one hour	**une heure**	*oon urr*
half an hour	**une demi-heure**	*oon duh-mee urr*
Monday	**lundi**	*luñ-dee*
Tuesday	**mardi**	*mar-dee*
Wednesday	**mercredi**	*mehrkruh-dee*
Thursday	**jeudi**	*zhuh-dee*
Friday	**vendredi**	*voñdruh-dee*
Saturday	**samedi**	*sam-dee*
Sunday	**dimanche**	*dee-moñsh*